History and Film

History and Film:

A Tale of Two Disciplines

Eleftheria Thanouli

BLOOMSBURY ACADEMIC
NEW YORK • LONDON • OXFORD • NEW DELHI • SYDNEY

BLOOMSBURY ACADEMIC
Bloomsbury Publishing Inc
1385 Broadway, New York, NY 10018, USA
50 Bedford Square, London, WC1B 3DP, UK

BLOOMSBURY, BLOOMSBURY ACADEMIC and the Diana logo are trademarks
of Bloomsbury Publishing Plc

First published in the United States of America 2019

A catalog record for this book is available from the Library of Congress.

ISBN: HB: 978-1-5013-4078-9
       PB: 978-1-5013-4077-2
     ePDF: 978-1-5013-4080-2
    eBook: 978-1-5013-4079-6

Typeset by RefineCatch Limited, Bungay, Suffolk
Printed and bound in the United States of America

To find out more about our authors and books visit www.bloomsbury.com
and sign up for our newsletters.

To Thomas Elsaesser

Contents

Acknowledgments

I dedicate this book to Thomas Elsaesser because his writings enabled me to engage with the topic of representation, a topic that I had deliberately avoided for years, being a formalist, and all. History is an interest I owe to my husband Achilleas. He has a Contextualist philosophy in the way he practices medicine and a Reconstructionist appetite in the way he devours history books, both of which helped me develop an approach that could address complexity without sliding into relativism. "Creative contradictions," is what Elsaesser once said that define me, and I have learned to live and be inspired by them.

This book was written over the course of two incredibly busy years during which I had to rely on the encouragement and support of many friends and colleagues. Betty Kaklamanidou and Yannis Tzioumakis fall into both categories, so their intellectual input, their patience and their faith in this project were life-saving. I would also like to thank Dudley Andrew who was one of the first people who read my book proposal and enthusiastically supported it. The same goes for Vrasidas Karalis, who is always there to offer brilliant advice. Many thanks go to Panagiotis Thanassas, Warren Buckland, Paris Mouratidis, and Stamatis Valasiadis who contributed to my writing at various phases. Antonis Daglidis, my talented colleague from the scenography division, stepped in to help with the cover at a moment's notice. Katie Gallof, of course, was a gracious and generous editor, as always. My special thanks goes to my talented student George Dimoglou who assisted me with many technicalities.

I would like to make a particular mention of Robert Rosentone's review of a part of the manuscript during the final stages. Those two pages instantly bring tears to my eyes every time I read them. They gave me great strength to see the whole thing through in a way that leaves me satisfied.

Finally, I have to thank my mom and our friend Manoussaki for standing by me all the time in every way possible. Of course, I am forever grateful to my two kids, Anastasia and George, for being so gifted and mature. They and the book benefitted immensely from, what Elsaesser would call, their "antagonistic mutuality."

Preface

Historical books and historical films are two forms of historical thinking that have a lot more in common than people tend to think. As objects of study, the former are analyzed by historians and theorists of historiography, while the latter are mostly examined by film theorists with a particular interest in the representation of history on the screen. The gap that divides these two branches of scholarship is abysmal. For the vast majority of practicing historians, a historical film is a work of art, a figment of someone's imagination. To argue that *Schindler's List* has fundamental formal and conceptual similarities with any written account of the Holocaust would be considered ludicrous, if not blasphemous. Film scholars, on the other hand, appreciate historical films for their cultural contribution to our society and for familiarizing a wide audience with important and often neglected moments in history but they would equally hesitate to base the value of cinematic history on its similarities with written history.

In this book, I attempt to renegotiate the dividing lines between written and filmic historical accounts by launching an extensive investigation into the historical, philosophical, formal, and institutional parameters that regulate them as generators of historical knowledge. I strive to illustrate that the dominant views on cinema's inability to match the accuracy and objectivity of academic history are derivative of a very specific epistemic context that was born in the nineteenth century and continues to cast its shadow to this day. I believe it is time to look back and carefully trace all those conventions that have convincingly passed for objective truth for so long. In fact, the more we historicize the concept of history the more we are likely to welcome historical films as meaningful representations of the past that form a symbiotic relation with written histories. In this light, historical films should not be valued for their supposedly unique ways of resurrecting the past but for the fascinating similarities they share with their written counterparts.

The tale of history and film that I begin in the following pages is not going to be one of fierce antagonism and hostility but one of intricate interactions, unexpected exchanges and ironic mirrorings between two different forms of history. Ultimately, I argue that what is more ironic is how history on film positions us in an exceptional vantage point for observing all the ways in which representing the past whether in spoken words, written elements or moving images is tied to very specific mechanisms for handling knowledge and power in a given society.

Introduction: History and Film in Parallel Orbits

For most historians films are first and foremost artifacts, human-made objects for particular human use much like the many other objects with which man fills his environment.

Susman (1985, 26)

The term "artifact" regularly featured in the first scholarly attempts to study the relation between film and history. In his seminal piece "Film and History: Artifact and Experience," Warren Susman takes his cue from Giambattista Vico and his *New Science* to argue for the multifold significance of filmic artifacts in the study of history (Susman 1985). It is an interesting choice of word that etymologically condenses several of the key concerns of this book, namely how art, man-made objects, and facts can relate to each other and how the significance of this relation evolves in time.[1] Susman does not delve into the heart of these concerns but he does offer a blueprint of the debates that would follow for more than thirty years, while, at the same time, prefiguring several points of conflict and lengthy consideration. For Susman, the relation between film and history should be investigated along four different programmatic axes: first, film can be studied as a "product" of history, comprising all the technological, economic, ideological, and even moral conditions that made its creation possible. Secondly, film could be approached as a "reflection" of history, i.e., as an image that records and embalms, in a Bazinian sense, specific historical elements, such as human speech, movement, and behavior, which could then be further studied for historical and sociological purposes. Thirdly, film works as an "interpreter" of history, providing "an explanation of historical development, and an analysis of the process of history itself" (31). Finally, films also become "agents" of history, as they exert a powerful impact on people's minds and imagination and they shape their wider cultural experience.[2] Of these four diverse areas of research, this book will mostly address the third, i.e., the cinema as an interpreter of history, while often expanding on how this particular area interconnects with the others. Susman is, thus, a useful starting point for demarcating the territory of my investigation because terms, such as cinematic history, film history, history as film etc. can, in fact, refer to very different objects of study. He is also a valuable source for the insight he gives us on the role of the film as an interpreter. As he writes:

> [...] the filmmaker, simply because he operates directly in terms of the actual manipulation of time and space, because in his editing he makes arrangements of time and space that shatter simple chronology, the traditional unities of time and space act as an historian faced with the same problem of finding the proper arrangement of materials to provide a view of the process that is his history.
>
>   Ibid.

In this passage, Susman compares the filmmaker to the historian and traces significant similarities in the way they both handle and manipulate time and space in order to "properly arrange" their material and construct "their stories." Yet, this point of convergence, or this "structural similarity" in Jennifer E. Smyth's words, between filmed and written history was not picked up by the researchers who followed in Susman's lead (Smyth 2006, 18). Neither was the oblique argument that every historian merely offers *his own* version of history. Instead, the focus switched to the material differences between cinematic images and written texts, taking for granted what written history is and exploring what visual history is not but might be. In his collection *Image as Artifact: The Historical Analysis of Film and Television* (1990), John O'Connor resonates with Susman's work not only in the title but also in the quadruple division that he suggests for the study of history on the screen, big or small. O'Connor's schema includes the following four frameworks: first, the moving image as representation of history; second, the moving image as evidence for social and cultural history; third, actuality footage as evidence for historical fact, and fourth, the history of the moving image as industry and art form. Evidently, the role of representation is amplified here, whether it involves historical themes or not, while a more institutional approach to cinema and television as industries and art forms seems to combine what Susman had earlier described as a "product" and "agent" of history. Most importantly, what Susman and O'Connor share is their appreciation of the visual media and their effort to protect them from the criticism and the intellectual disdain of the majority of the professional historians. By carving out a legitimate scholarly area of research and by lining up key questions and concerns, they laid the foundations for the serious consideration of film and television's contribution to historical knowledge.

The most influential thinker who followed in their path was Robert Rosenstone, whose work has been a major influence on this current project. His invaluable contribution is best approached in chronological order, from the mid-1990s and mid-2000s to his latest ones around the mid-2010s, which allows us to glimpse his evolving views on history. In his first major publication, *Visions of the Past* (1995), Rosenstone is fully engaged with the study of cinema as historical representation, which he considers as the only "radical" tendency outside the practices of traditional history (3). Acknowledging that film can be a medium for reconstructing the past, he seeks to understand the various ways in which films have tried to "do history" using their inherent expressive means. Based on his strong conviction that "a film is not a book," he sets out to chart the intrinsic standards of visual history, which he calls "history as vision" (15). This new type of history comes in three major forms: the dramatic feature, the documentary, and the postmodern film.[3] Rosenstone describes the general characteristics of each category, using broad terms, such as invention, anachronism, condensation, and omission, without taking advantage of the conceptual wealth of film theory. As a result, his mapping remains open and tentative, a weakness he seems to acknowledge when he repeatedly pleads for the need to understand further and deeper the workings of cinematic history. As a traditional historian entering a new territory, Rosenstone finds himself in a bind; he wants to explore what he feels is new and different but he considers it wrong to do so with the help of the same old tools of academic history. Thus, he dreams of speaking a language he does not fully comprehend, while he shies away from speaking loud and clear in his own native tongue. To the extent that he does relate his study of cinematic history to that of written history, he puts forward an interesting argument regarding postmodern history. After presenting a very dense summary of what constitutes the postmodern trend in academic historiography, he argues that this type of history can fully materialize only in the form of filmic history. As he writes:

> If you long for new kinds of history, if you think we need new ways of relating to the past, don't despair. Postmodern history has been born and is currently alive and well. It exists not on the page but on the screen, and is the creation of filmmakers and videographers.
>
> Rosenstone 1995, 206

This celebratory attitude toward the historical potential of postmodern films is coupled with a severe judgment toward mainstream Hollywood dramas, which are deemed less satisfactory, compromised, and often shallow, mostly because they remain enslaved to classical linear narrativity (228). The skepticism toward classical fiction films is toned down in his later work, *History on Film/Film on History* (2006), and so is the discussion about postmodernism. In the years that intervened, postmodernism had lost part of its explanatory clout, so Rosenstone renames the third category as "innovative drama" and approaches all the films in a more equal and balanced manner, seeking to appreciate each for its merits. For instance, he draws on Frank Ankermit's work to defend the "metaphorical" power of fictional dramas, while he advises scholars to avoid prescriptive arguments (36). Instead of wasting their efforts in telling what films should do, according to expectations formed by professional history, they should scrutinize films for the numerous ways, in which they have brought history onto the screen for over a century. Insisting on his thesis that "a film is not a book," he notes the following:

> It is time, in short, to stop expecting films to do what (we imagine) books do. [...] Dramatic films are not and will never be "accurate" in the same way as books (claim to be) [...] Like written histories, films are not mirrors that show some vanished reality, but constructions, works whose rules of engagement with the traces of the past are necessarily different from those of written history.
>
> Rosenstone 2006, 37

This compilation of statements presents a paradox: the dichotomy between image and word that Rosenstone strives to build is simultaneously undermined by his profound knowledge of the historian's métier and his tacit allegiance to the deconstructionist theory. The parenthetical comments running parallel to the main text undercut his key rationale and hint at the fact that written history is not really what we have been led to believe; a fact, however, that would bridge the gap to its visual counterpart rather than open it.

The nature of the relation between visual and written history and the purpose of a prescriptive attitude towards cinema is what makes the dialogue between Rosenstone and Natalie Zemon Davis quite noteworthy. Davis' work *Slaves on Screen* (2000) has exerted enormous influence on most writing on cinematic history since its publication and Rosenstone engages in a lengthy discussion of her main arguments in order to criticize her strict adherence to the principles of empiricism (Rosenstone 2006, 24–31). Davis appreciates the potential of the filmic language in our understanding of the past and she is willing to withhold her reservations to give this new medium some time to mature. As she writes, "film is only beginning to find its way as a medium for history" (2000, 5). To Davis, films on a historical subject can work as "thought experiments" and as sources of "valuable and even innovative vision" that probe questions parallel to those of historical books (14–15). Yet, for cinema to develop its role as a medium for history in due time, filmmakers should commit to "telling the truth." The starting point should always be a respect for the evidence and whatever invention they need to resort to "should be in the spirit of the evidence and plausible, not misleading" (130). Her position on this matter is consistent with her proper historical work, which clearly adheres to empiricist principles and maintains a solid faith in fact-oriented research, even if she is categorized within the more nuanced approach of Constructionism[4] (Munslow 2001, 23). At the same time, she expresses a rather evolutionary take toward the history of cinema, hoping that eventually conditions will mature and films will be able to stand up to the historian's task.[5] On both counts, namely the evidence-based methodology and the call for cinema's maturity, she makes little effort to understand the specific workings of film language and the long bifurcating paths of cinematic history.

A corrective move was made recently by two other traditional historians, William Guynn and Marnie Hughes-Warrington, who put their effort into taking the discipline of history closer into the field of film studies. Unlike Davis' remarkable impact on the debates, Guynn's work remains significantly less influential to this date, partly because he plunges into demanding issues in the philosophy of history, striving to unearth the "essential" differences and similarities between written and cinematic accounts (Guynn 2006). In his thorough and meticulous presentation of the arguments against cinematic history raised on both sides of the Atlantic, Guynn underlines how unwilling historians have been to raise "the question of their own discursive practice" as well as to acknowledge how tremendously recent their own profession really is (16–18). This is a point I will discuss in greater detail later on, together with Guynn's other argument presented as follows:

> Reconstructing the past is a broad cultural enterprise that cannot be confined to the closed circle of an academic discourse. Cinema, as I argue, has a legitimate role to play in that enterprise.
>
> Guynn 2006, 19–20

The role of cinema in the enterprise of "doing history" and its legitimacy as a generator of historical knowledge are prominent issues to be addressed in this book and Guynn's work will be a considerable ally in my own attempt to defend them. What I do take issue with, however, is the fact that he fails to take into consideration the key narrative theories of film that have been widespread since the mid-1980s. Instead, he relies heavily on Gerard Genette's theories of literary narratives and when confronted with the need to address the visual elements, he turns to semiology and Christian Metz (68). This might seem like a minor misstep to an outsider, but to a film narratologist, it is as if he were bringing a gun to a knife fight. Over the past three decades, prominent theorists like David Bordwell and Edward Branigan have developed sophisticated, comprehensive, and applicable narrative theories, having fully reworked and adapted earlier literary and semiotic concepts like those employed by Guynn.[6] The choice of a less fitting methodological toolkit for the analysis of cinematic narratives, inevitably leads Guynn to equally less precise observations regarding the process of constructing history for the screen, leaving several questions unanswered. Apart from this notable weakness, nonetheless, it is crucial to stress that Guynn's exploration of filmic history in relation to the philosophy of history, literary theory, semiology, and rhetoric is carried out with significant theoretical rigor that enriches the ongoing research on the topic and sets a high standard for other scholars.

In a similar vein, Hughes-Warrington, a trained historian herself, takes a step further into the film studies vocabulary, engaging with concepts such as genre, identity, and propaganda, while maintaining a clear and systematic comparison between "images and words," as each closing subchapter indicates (Hughes-Warrington 2007). Underlying this back and forth between the theory of history and the various aspects of screened history is her conviction that cinema cannot stand alone in the debates about History with a capital H. And it cannot stand alone for three major reasons. First, because academic history, despite the limitations of its own historicity and the blows of the deconstructionist critique, is still the safest path to an objective approach to the historical past. Secondly, as a result, filmic versions of historical events should be welcome as complements or, in her words, as entry points "to prompt discussion on the features and functions of history" (7). Finally, historical films do not merely function as texts but as cultural sites where meaning is negotiated. As she points out:

> To begin to understand historical films, we must see them rather as sites of relation, agreement and even contestation among film producers, critics and scholars, promoters and viewers. In this relationship, no single group consistently emerges with the controlling hand.
>
> Hughes-Warrington 2007, 6

These three interconnected premises that I extracted from Hughes-Warrington's study sometimes seem to work but most of the time they generate inescapable contradictions. In her chapter on realism, for instance, her professional principles become explicit; she aligns herself with R.G. Collingwood and E.H. Carr's constructionist approach to historical facts and defends a certain type of "objectivism" that allows for "objective principles of judgement, standards and concepts that are not decided solely by personal preference or the whim of individuals" (117). Yet, the problem of objectivism is not related to issues of representation in the cinema, as one would expect in a discussion on realism. Nor is there any in-depth consideration of matters that involve indexicality, verisimilitude, and referentiality. Instead, she talks about hyperreality and "reality effects" referring to Jean Baudrillard and Roland Barthes, only to debunk them a few pages later based not on their theories of representation but on their broader theory of the ideology of consumerism and masculinity. A similar problem regards her deployment of Michel Foucault's concepts. The latter appear regularly in the text in support of her argument that history is not a "single path" and that historical films are "sites" of multiple temporalities but she neglects to confront the fact that these views are on almost complete opposite sides of any notion of objectivism, however loosely defined (76). Such theoretical inconsistencies derive partly from the fact that academic historians are very little versed in film theory and the problematics of cinematic representation. Like Davis and Guynn, Hughes-Warrington lacks the relevant tools for examining how cinema fits into her objectivist framework and she eventually bypasses the problem by merely saying that "film is not enough, we need to look for context too." Although hardly anyone would disagree that context matters for the production of historical meaning, I would like to argue that we are far from done with the study of historical films as texts. In fact, we are only just at the beginning.

If we look at the literature on screened history over the last two decades, we witness an impressive surge in publications that no longer come from academic historians but from "native" film theorists. The discipline of film studies has increasingly met the challenge of exploring how history on film works and has sought to defend the medium's right to represent "things of the past," despite the ongoing reservations and criticism.[7] On their part, film scholars have focused on the difficulty of defining the "historical film," particularly as a distinct genre. The concept of genre in the theory of cinema plays an essential role, not only because it was institutionally significant for the Hollywood industry, but also because it works as a category that helps us classify textual features, industrial practices and audience expectations.[8] At the same time, however, defining a genre at a textual level has proven more difficult than one would imagine. Even when we deal with more straightforward cases, such as the musical or the western, definitions risk being tautological or creating more questions than answers (Altman 1999a). How inclusive is a genre? How stable is it? How does it change through time? How pure is it or how does it relate to other genres? These are questions still open to discussion among film scholars and their tentative answers become exponentially more problematic when dealing with historical films.

One prominent attempt to define the historical film as a genre is found in Robert Burgoyne's book *The Hollywood Historical Film* (2008). In his introduction, Burgoyne classifies most historical films into five variant groups (the war film, the biographical film, the epic, the metahistorical film, and the topical film) and he clarifies the theoretical principles of his argumentation. First, he addresses the key historians who offer him "an effective place to begin," which are none other than Davis and Rosenstone (3). The former provides a working definition of the historical film,[9] while the latter emphasizes the need to understand how films have dealt with history in more intrinsic terms. By briefly anchoring his study on these two distinguished representatives from the discipline of history, he is ready to proceed to the field of film theory—his own turf—in order to build a new taxonomy of the Hollywood historical film. The best theoretical tool for the task, according to Burgoyne, is Rick Altman's semantic/syntactic/pragmatic approach. Already its name indicates the complexity and the multi-leveled tactic to capture the slippery nature of the cinematic genres. According to Altman, each genre is built on three levels; first, the semantic, which involves the iconography, the characters, the settings, and other building blocks; second, the syntactic, which regards the organization and the structuring of the semantic elements; and third, the pragmatic, which regards the ways in which films generate different meaning for different audiences (6–7). Burgoyne mostly focuses on the semantic/syntactic traits,[10] arguing that the key "semantic register" of the historical genre is the principle of "reenactment" (7). What brings together so many diverse film narratives into the same framework is "the act of imaginative re-creation that allows the spectator to imagine they are 'witnessing again' the events of the past" (ibid.). Given that the semantic register of the "reenactment" can take on a wide array of shapes, Burgoyne seeks to handle the diversity of the historical genre with the following argument:

> The reimagining of the past takes shape through particular stylistic and narrative devices in film, generating a range of historical styles, from the realism of Roberto Rossellini to the cinematic écriture of Sergei Eisenstein. The array of styles, subjects, and approaches in the Hollywood historical film can be understood as the syntactic register of the historical film, a syntax that is expressed in the form of the war film, the epic, or the biographical film.
>
> Burgoyne 2008, 8–9

Therefore, it seems that the semantic/syntactic rules of other well-established genres become elements in a second-order syntax, which together with re-enactment form the core of the historical film and explain several of their formal characteristics. Even though Burgoyne does not develop the idea of a second order system and he does not account for the transformation of style into structure, I would prefer to address another more striking problem that immediately succeeds this supposed settlement of the generic identity of the Hollywood historical films. Burgoyne feels compelled to pose the heated question pertaining to the relation between fiction and history. He asks,

> Why should dramatic fiction films be considered a medium of historical reflection in the first place? What is gained by analyzing films such as *Spartacus* or *Schindler's List* as examples of "historical thinking"?
>
> Burgoyne 2008, 9

With these questions, he enters the maelstrom of history's contested identity. He probes us to decide whether cinematic history is proper history or whether it merely contributes to "historical thinking," "historical imagination," "historical vision," or other activities where "history" is only present in the form of a qualifier but not as a noun. Yet, just as he puts his finger on the most difficult spot, he thinks he attends to the problem by turning our attention to the "presentist thesis." As he observes, "it is this uneasiness with the fictional aspect of dramatic historical films that has led many theorists and historians to argue from a 'presentist' position" (10). Arguing from a "presentist" position actually means claiming that fiction films address present concerns rather than past affairs and, therefore, are not adequate means for "doing history." Burgoyne disagrees with the rejection of cinematic history on these grounds and responds with a more moderate position, underlining cinema's dual focus "by reenacting the past in the present, the historical film brings the past into dialogue with the present" (11).

This statement would appear sufficiently convincing to most film scholars, including myself; at least, it did, until the point when I started acquainting myself with the theory and history of historiography. When I entered this other world, I was surprised to realize that the problem of "presentism" addressed by Burgoyne as a predicament of the historical film was, in fact, not new at all. Historians have ceaselessly pondered upon the role of the present in the approach of the past and a wide variety of views have been put forward in the course not of decades but of centuries. For instance, Donald R. Kelley's overview of the versions of history from the Antiquity to the Enlightenment notes that the tradition of "presentist" historians dates back to Thucydides and Polybius (Kelley 1991, 6). If we limit our scope to the twentieth century, R.G. Collingwood's work stands out as a milestone for the presentist position summed up by the following words; "All history is an attempt to understand the present by reconstructing its determining conditions" (Collingwood, 1994, 420).[11] Finally, as we move closer to deconstructionist historians, such as Foucault or Keith Jenkins, the presentist quality of all history becomes merely another standard aspect of its relativistic nature (Munslow 2006, 120). In view of these long-standing debates in the realm of historiography, the concerns about cinema's reflection on current states of affairs rather than past ones are recast in a different light. It seems that filmed history has not been doing anything new or anything exclusive to the cinematic medium. And yet, the lack of this historical and theoretical perspective in most writings on historical films perpetuates the impression that audiovisual history is something entirely different and separate from written history.

Burgoyne's work is representative of a group of film scholars working on the topic of historical cinema who often provide detailed and thought-provoking analyses of film examples but resist touching upon theoretical and philosophical matters of history.[12] Jonathan Stubbs does a wonderful job presenting an overview of these contributions, while also underlining their weaknesses (Stubbs 2013). His own take is still cut off from the wider concerns of the historical studies but he explicitly considers history on screen as a legitimate form of history, siding with Alun Munslow's compact statement: "Just like written history, film history is a fictive, genre-based, heavily authored, factually selective, ideologically driven, condensed, emplotted, targeted and theorized representation" (cited in Stubbs, 17). As a result, he seeks to understand how the forms of cinematic history work, suggesting an open definition of the historical film, which is characterized by textual and extratextual engagements with the past. The former includes prologues and epilogues using words to connect the film to its historical framework, while the latter contain all the discourses generated in the context of the film in the form of promotional material, public debate, or academic criticism (20–35). It is interesting that Stubbs presents an entire subchapter named "Robert Rosenstone," an indication of Rosentone's decisive contribution to the field. As a point of criticism, however, he notes that Rosenstone, for all his warm support of historical cinema, still remains skeptical towards the vast majority of historical films produced, especially in Hollywood.

Stubbs is in line with my own critique of Rosenstone's writings mentioned above, but I think there is a new direction in the latter's thought expressed only recently, which marks a turning point in his career and potentially in the entire study of history on screen. In his chapter entitled "The History Film as a Mode of Historical Thought," Rosenstone performs a very daring act of self-criticism and compares his reading of *Reds* (1981) to that of Leger Grindon's in order to bring to the surface the complete opposite assumptions held by academic historians and film scholars when approaching a film with a historical subject (Rosenstone 2013). The former tend to examine whether the narrative conforms to their notion of factual accuracy and the interpretations of existing written accounts, while the latter focus on the visual and aural elements of the film, judging whether its ideological implications adhere to specific concerns of the present. The chasm between such polar extremes is unbridgeable, unless both sides reconsider what written history is and what we expect from its cinematic version. The new Rosenstone is willing to make the first step, arguing that *Reds* is "a piece of historying[13]—a mode of thinking that uses traces of the past and turns them into a coherent and meaningful narrative" (83). In this light, the "film is not a book" dogma is recanted as follows:

> What I am saying is this: in order to understand the historying done by the history film, we need to analyze it as a visual, aural, and dramatic presentation that engages—as any work of history does—with past, present, and future moments, events, people, beliefs, and ideologies. The history film cannot be judged through the current canons either of written history or of the genre analysis of film studies, but by combining the two.
>
> Rosenstone 2013, 84

In this reconciliatory passage, written and audiovisual history need not continue their parallel orbits. Their mechanisms share enough common ground, so that one can convincingly explore them with a combination of tools and concepts from both disciplines. Rosenstone still calls for the need to develop a "new vocabulary" for understanding how screened history works, but he no longer considers it as something essentially different. In fact, this avowed affinity between diverse types of historying helps him take his conceptualization to a higher level and hint, however tentatively, at a wider paradigm change when it comes to our societies' attitude toward the process of "dealing with their past." He notes that if we ignore the type of history produced and disseminated into society by the historical film, we risk appearing to future generations as naïve and shortsighted as those who thought that Herodotus and Thucydides were "despoilers of the truths and wisdom conveyed in the oral tradition" (86).

This book starts at the exact point where Rosenstone leaves off. I will attempt to implement several of his suggestions and, particularly, those that imply the ways in which history in a book and history on film relate to each other. So far, as I have demonstrated here, the dialogue between the two disciplines has been carried out with a blatantly uneven distribution of power. The stature of the historical profession left very little room for cinema to stand up and defend its own potential for creating and distributing historical knowledge. Scholars of either side would hardly consider bringing historical books and films to a face-off. As a result, the discussion of historical cinema would be restricted to a limited repertoire of terms and concepts, such as reenactment, genre or just plain accuracy, which would perpetuate the long-standing power divisions in the privilege to historical truth. Here, in *History and Film: A Tale of Two Disciplines*, history in words and history in moving images will be placed under a microscope to reveal the minute details of their symbiotic relation. This research will have to delve simultaneously deeper into the theory of history and the theory of film, addressing and conceptualizing a series of continuities and discontinuities both at the formal and the institutional level.

The treatment of continuities and discontinuities, or more simply similarities and differences, has profound philosophical implications, as I will be able to explain along the way. For now, I would like to introduce the two central hypotheses that will be investigated and developed in the course of several chapters. First, I will argue that a historical film is a magnified miniature of a historical book. This means that a historical account in the cinematic form magnifies, intensifies and, at the same time, multiplies all the characteristics of written history. Thanks to these magnified distortions, however, the historical cinema gives us a rare opportunity to observe up-close the workings of historical imagination at all three levels: the modal, the formal, and the institutional. On all three counts, history on screen flaunts a degree of knowingness and sophistication that does not hesitate to acknowledge the fundamental premise of all historical knowledge, namely that a representation of the historical past will always be a failed representation. Secondly, I will argue that historical cinema, or more broadly "historiophoty" as Hayden White calls the representation of history in visual images,[14] should be regarded as the dominant form of history in the twentieth and twenty-first centuries, because it produces historical knowledge according to a distinct set of epistemic principles characteristic of our contemporary age. Whereas academic history developed in the nineteenth century as an embodiment of the spirit of the Modern Age, cinematic history developed in the twentieth and carries on into the twenty-first, stronger than ever, as the manifestation of larger ongoing epistemological conditions.

To support these two, admittedly, difficult and complex hypotheses, my study will have to combine a macro level that pertains to key issues in historiography with a micro level that reaches all the way down to specific narrative devices. Writing at the beginning of a new millennium and having a century's worth of cinematic representations of history makes this project not exactly easy but, at least, imaginable. It will require an often complicated transition from the particular to the general and from the written to the cinematic, which I will try to signpost as clearly as possible so that the reader is not lost en route. The investigation into the intricate relation of historical writing and historical filmmaking will be organized into the following chapters.

Part One of this book will address a long series of conceptual and theoretical issues that pertain both to historiography and historiophoty. In chapter 1, I will dig into the archaeology of written history's relations to other media practices and, particularly, cinema and literature, by looking closely at the works of Siegfried Kracauer, Roland Barthes, and Jean-Luc Godard. The sense that historians, novelists, and cinematographers have common problems to solve, similar questions to address, and shared difficulties to face in their treatment of historical reality is dominant in the thinking of these three figures. All three of them challenge in very different ways history's exceptionality whether in terms of its form or methodology, and they pave the way for breaking its unique privilege over the historical past. Their observations highlight a shared enterprise between history and other media, while at the same time they bring to the foreground one of the thorniest aspects of historical representation, which is none other than the problem of medium specificity.

Therefore, chapter 2 tackles the issue head-on, explaining what medium specificity is and how it determines most of the approaches to historical cinema, even the most favorable ones. If, however, we decide to take a distance from the essentialist definitions of mediality and allow the common forms and practices of the diverse media to come to the fore, then the gap between historiography and historiophoty begins to close.[15] As a useful tool for highlighting the continuities between history in words and history in images, I suggest that we continue the analogical thinking that was inaugurated by Kracauer, Barthes, and Godard; only this time, the analogy between cinema and history will be expanded to include analog and digital cinema. As I explain, the problem of medium specificity was painstakingly explored within film theory when it came to differentiating between analog and digital cinema. All that historical and theoretical wealth can be additionally illuminating if we apply it to the binary historical book/historical film. By placing written history and analog cinema on one axis and historical cinema and digital cinema on the other, we will be able to discuss a series of terms, such as materiality, form, reality, simulation, and realism, all of which will allow us to grasp the point of the "magnified miniature" that I presented above. At the same time, all these terms will indicate the limitations of any research that focuses only on the textual or visual elements and discounts the context in which these elements are generated and disseminated.

As a result, in chapter 3 I seek to expand on Rosenstone's indication of a paradigm change that shifts the boundaries of what is now considered as "legitimate historying." To this end, I need to address the historical and institutional contexts in which historical knowledge is produced. I delve into the history of historiography to illustrate how academic history is an invention of the nineteenth century based on a set of beliefs about what constitutes facts, science, and truth. To emphasize the historicity and the contingent nature of all these concepts, I discuss an interesting intra-historical "dialogue" between two famous historians, E.H. Carr and Isaiah Berlin that exemplifies a tremendous lack of consensus within the community on what constitutes science and what its relation to history should be. And in parallel to the historical profession, a new medium like cinema and a growing film industry like Hollywood begin to carve their own points of access to the historical past. In fact, as I explain, their universe, from the start, is never really quite parallel to academic history; the institutional parameters of historical filmmaking in Hollywood consistently nurtured the osmosis between filmmakers and historians in ways that tend to go unnoticed. By the end of the twentieth century, however, the roles of academic and cinematic history in the public consumption of historical knowledge are significantly altered; the devolution of the historical profession in education and the evolution of historical appetite in new media forms probe us to reconsider once again the very definition of history.[16] My response to this predicament is to look into the philosophy of history once more and sift the tools and concepts with which we can make sense of these developments. For that purpose, I single out Michel Foucault and his idiosyncratic intellectual work that aspires to occupy a place outside traditional notions of history and philosophy. By introducing a series of his concepts, such as archaeology, genealogy, and episteme, I aim to reconfigure the key parameters of the discussion about historical cinema and to lay the foundations of my second thesis, i.e., the role of historiophoty as the dominant mode of historying in the contemporary Age.

Yet, to sustain such a wide-ranging argument about the role of cinematic history, we need to be able to take into consideration a large number of films. One cannot base such a claim on a few examples nor on evaluative distinctions between good and bad historical films. Therefore, in Part Two, I will move to the middle ground where I will develop the poetics of the historical film. In chapter 4, I examine the poetics of written history, as they were formulated in White's monumental work entitled *Metahistory: The Historical Imagination in Nineteenth-Century Europe,* first published in 1973. Unlike his term "historiophoty," which has had significant import in the discussion of cinema, the wealth of knowledge contained in *Metahistory* remains largely unexplored. Therein, White crafts the most comprehensive study of history as narrative, where detailed categorizations of formal, argumentative, and ideological mechanisms explain how historical accounts come together as poetic acts. My goal is to examine how his poetics of history can help us formulate the poetics of the historical film with a number of necessary adjustments. Of course, I need to clarify at this point that my use of the term "historical film" is purposefully inclusive.[17] It contains all the fiction films and all the documentaries that represent the historical past. Notice, however, that being set in the past is a necessary but not a sufficient condition. And here, Davis' definition is of considerable help. As she writes, "by history films I mean those having as their central plot documentable events, such as a person's life or a war or revolution, and those with a fictional plot but with a historical setting intrinsic to the action" (Davis 1987, 459). The phrase "a historical setting intrinsic to the action" is the key, I believe, for differentiating between historical films and those that are vaguely set in the past.[18] Similarly, we can extend the description by analogy to historical documentaries that deal with history whether in the foreground or the background of their stories.

Thus, chapters 5 and 6 focus on the category of the historical fiction film and the historical documentary, respectively, in an effort to build this "new vocabulary" for historical cinema that Rosenstone has been calling for all this time. Ironically, its foundations will be laid by the old vocabulary of written historiography; not because we have run out of inspiration but because the magnifying effects of the filmic narration allow us to observe all those formal, argumentative, and ideological mechanisms that historical films share with their written counterparts. In chapter 5, the new terms will be drawn primarily from David Bordwell's historical poetics and the narrative models he constructed in *Narration in the Fiction Film* (1985). I will investigate how each mode of narration provides the historical film with a distinct set of formal, argumentative and ideological explanations. I will refer to various film examples along the way, but my main case studies will include films representing the Second World War and the Holocaust. Specifically, I will offer analyses of *Saving Private Ryan* (Spielberg 1998), *The Thin Red Line* (Malick 1998), *Dunkirk* (Nolan 2017), *Life is Beautiful* (Benigni 1997), *The Son of Saul* (Nemes, 2015), and *Inglourious Basterds* (Tarantino 2009). Along the same lines, in chapter 6, I will rely on Bill Nichols' typology of the modes of representation in the nonfiction film to identify the possible combinations of form, argument, and ideology in a historical documentary (Nichols 1991; 1994). My case studies here will comprise documentaries that deal with the Vietnam War and the biography of prominent figures. These are: *The Fog of War* (Morris 2004), *Regret to Inform* (Sonneborn 1998), *Sir! No Sir!* (Zeiger 2005), *Going Upriver: The Long War of John Kerry* (Butler 2004), *The Last Bolshevik* (Marker 1992), and *Thirty-Two Short Films About Glenn Gould* (Girard 1993). The samples in both chapters are deliberately limited to American or European films, as the historical, philosophical, and institutional context within which I have situated the concept of history is exclusively of the Western tradition. Given that a significant part of my argument is the emphasis on the historicity and the conceptual positionality of historical knowledge, I would hesitate to apply all this vocabulary, old and new, to films from other cultural contexts.[19] In fact, doing so would defeat the purpose of the entire project.

Finally, my concluding chapter will bring this long tale of history and film into a close by recapitulating its main arguments and extending on the two central theses, which I laid out above. Most importantly, it will address the core problem of historical representation through the ages, namely the impossibility of any type of historying to show us the past as it really was. In fact, historical cinema both as form and as institutional practice that produces historical knowledge offers a unique vantage point for revisiting and reconsidering the workings of historical imagination from the nineteenth century to our present day. Through their intricate interaction with written history and their blatantly ironic play with fiction, historical films pose as successful performances of failure, as instances of what Rosenstone once called "Samuel Becket history;"[20] attempts, that is, at understanding and making meaning out of the historical past, despite knowing that they are destined to fail by objectivist standards. Failed representations, however, are not meant to be hopeless or pessimistic; the measure of their success as failures depends on forces other than objective reality or even rational thought. In Beckett's paradoxical quote "You must go on. I can't go on. I'll go on,"[21] the power lies in one's ability to know their predicament and, yet, carry on. I have to admit that it was the same three phrases that often sustained me during this impossibly vast exploration of history and film in this book. I hope the failures of my tale are successful enough to encourage further attempts to fathom the power of historical images on the screen and the meaningful relations they build with our past.

Notes

1 According to the OED, artifact derives from Latin arte (by or using art) + factum (something made), while the significance of factum, from "something made" to "a thing that is known or proved to be true," developed only after the sixteenth century.

2 A similar, if less structured, argument was put forward around the same time by another influential theorist on the topic, Marc Ferro. As he notes, "Grasping film in its relation to history requires more than just better chronicles of the works or a description of how the various genres evolved. It must look at the historical function of film, at its relationship with the societies that produce and consume it, at the social processes involved in the making of the works, at cinema as a source of history. As agents and products of history, films and the world of films stand in a complex relationship with the audience, with money and with the state, and this relationship is one of the axes of its history" (Ferro 1983, 358).

3 Even though the term "postmodern film" is not constructed as an explicit third category, it constitutes a separate kind of historical film that includes both fiction films and documentaries and is more in line with the principles of postmodern history.

4 For the three main trends in professional history (Reconstructionist, Constructionist, and Deconstructionist) see chapter 2 and the conclusion.

5   The evolutionary model in cinematic historiography is generally outmoded, while
    research into historical films in Hollywood in the 1930s indicates that such linear
    progress is unsubstantiated (Bordwell 1997; Smyth 2006).

6   Indicatively, see Bordwell (1985) and Branigan (1992).

7   Robert Brent Toplin's book title *Reel History: In defense of Hollywood* (2002) is
    indicative of the situation. Hollywood films have been in the center of the polemic
    against history on film, but Toplin and Rosenstone's defense is equally persevering.

8   Even though the majority of the writings on genre focus on the textual formulas that
    ensure the formal consistency of the films within each genre, it is now widely
    expected that these formulas will be positioned within a larger framework that
    contains institutional discourses and audience reception practices as well (Neale
    1995).

9   Davis' definition of the historical film will also provide the basis for my own use of
    the term "historical cinema" explicated further on.

10 This is not necessarily a weakness on Burgoyne's part. Altman's theory of the
    pragmatic approach to genre is, in fact, an addendum to his previous
    semantic/syntactic approach and it is briefly presented in the concluding pages
    of his book *Film/Genre* (Altman 1999b).

11 Notice how John Dewey relates the process of selection with the presentist thesis:
    "All historical construction is necessarily selective. Since the past cannot be
    reproduced in toto and lived over again, this principle might seem too obvious to be
    worthy of being called important. But it is of importance because its
    acknowledgement compels attention to the fact that everything in the writing of
    history depends upon the principle used to control selection. This principle decides
    the weight which shall be assigned to past events, what shall be admitted and what
    omitted; it also decides how the facts selected shall be arranged and ordered.
    Furthermore, if the fact of selection is acknowledged to be primary and basic, we are
    committed to the conclusion that all history is necessarily written from the
    standpoint of the present, and is, in an inescapable sense, the history not only of the
    present, but that of what is contemporaneously judged to be important in the
    present" (Dewey 1938, 235).

12 Philip Rosen is a notable exception and his work will be discussed in some detail in
    chapter three and again in the conclusion.

13 The term "historying" signifies the act of narrating the historical past according to
    certain epistemological principles. It was popularized by Alun Munslow in his effort
    to unveil the diverse epistemological assumptions of practicing historians and to
    break the unity and opacity of the term "history." See Munslow (2010; 2015).

14 The complete definition is "the representation of history and our thought about it in
    visual images and filmic discourse" (White 1988, 1193). Historiophoty is a term that
    will be used throughout the book.

15 As I will argue, this was White's intention all along, when he coined the term "historiophoty."

16 The definition of history is a perennial problem in historiography through the millennia, as I will explain in chapter 3.

17 As a result of this inclusive definition of the historical film, I take the liberty of referring to my object of study with a variety of names, such as "historiophoty," "cinematic history," "filmic history," "history in (moving) images," "history on film," and even "audiovisual history" at times. Moreover, given that I deliberately avoid a very strict division between media, I recognize the relevance of television in the entire debate. However, when it comes to my terminology, I draw terms and concepts exclusively from film theory, limiting thus the possibility of including television series and other TV productions in this research. This will have to be the focus of a different project.

18 I understand that "what is intrinsic" and "what not" can also be subject to debate, generating a gray area of films set in the past whose ties to "history" may or may not be substantial. Given that "what constitutes history" and "what not" is also subject to change in the course of time, we realize that the place of a film within the category of the historical cinema is not as stable as we would hope it could be.

19 For the complex theoretical and political agenda of a "world historiography," see Fuchs and Stuchtey (2002).

20 As Rosenstone wrote back in 1995: "Even if I know that we historians constitute our objects of study on the basis of ideological and political agendas, and create narratives (or even analytic articles) shaped not by data but by linguistic rules and prefigured tropes, I still believe we have something important to learn from studying long-gone people, beliefs, moments, movements, and events (yes, we need these, too). So if my faith in the truth of what we can know about the past has diminished, my need for such knowledge remains firm. From Dragnet history I have moved on to Samuel Beckett history—I can't go on, I'll go on" (Rosenstone 1995, 200).

21 These are the last three lines in Beckett's novel *The Unnamable* (Beckett 2010).

Part I

Historical and Theoretical Questions

1

The Archaeology of the Debate: Cinema and Literature as Analogies for History

It may come as a surprise that a number of key thinkers and practitioners in cinema, visual media, or art in general, should take an interest in the theory and philosophy of history. Yet, it is hardly a coincidence. The study of cultural phenomena, and particularly film, photography, and literature often raised questions regarding the epistemological nature of historical writing. As newer and older media were theorized for the ways they can or cannot communicate the world to us, it was inevitable that similar issues would surface regarding the ways that traditional historical writing could or could not communicate the world of the past. In this chapter, I would like to begin my long exploration into the disciplines of history and cinema by tracking a line of arguments, which surfaced from the 1960s onwards and began investigating the porous boundaries between the two fields. These arguments come from three very diverse, but equally influential, figures: Siegfried Kracauer, Roland Barthes, and Jean-Luc Godard. All three of them were fascinated by history and the idea of mediality, even though they specialized in different areas: Kracauer in film theory, Godard in film practice, and Barthes in literature. What binds them together and what renders them essential for this book is their attempt to develop the notion of analogy between historical writing, on the one hand, and cinema and literature, on the other. The value of analogical thinking, i.e., the attempt to identify correspondences and partial similarities between two distinct practices, was instrumental in their understanding of history. Cinema and literature provided for them a series of concepts and formal devices that seemed to permeate similar processes in written history. This chapter will offer a kaleidoscopic view of their theoretical explorations, as they struggled to address key historiographical problems across diverse media. The dots that connect the ideas of these three intellectuals will be noted along the way, even though the purpose is not to understate their different origins. By walking through the history of the dialogue between cinema, literature, and historical writing, my goal is, first, to formulate a context for debating the multiple ways in which film theory and historiography can intersect and, then, to isolate the questions that will enable me to reconfigure the relation between history and cinema on a fundamentally new basis.

I would like to start the discussion with Kracauer, the German critic and theorist, who is famous for his study on German cinema in *From Caligari to Hitler* (1947) and, of course, for his *Theory of Film* (1960). Kracauer was one of the first scholars to formulate a comprehensive theory of film and who, ironically enough, found absolutely no common ground between cinema and the representation of history. As he definitively put it, "as matters stand, the historian's quest and history on the screen are at cross-purposes" (Kracauer 1960, 80). In his examination of the historical film, Kracauer is consistently dismissive, noting how filmic attempts to portray historical themes go against all the essential features of the cinematic medium, namely its affinities towards unstaged reality, the fortuitous, the endless, and the indeterminate (18–20). Kracauer sees no potential in the historical film whatsoever. The use of décor, costumes and props create such an air of artificiality that it contradicts the real purpose of the camera, which is none other than to reveal and redeem physical reality. Quoting Cavalcanti, Kracauer claims that the camera is so "literal-minded" that when it shows us actors dressed up, we go to great pains to suspend our disbelief and see them as characters (77). Moreover, historical films present a closed diegetic world, which is "radically shut off from the space-time continuum of the living, a closed cosmos which does not admit of extensions" (78). According to the rigorous principles of his cinematic theory, historical fiction films rely on conventions that are "hardly compatible with a medium which gravitates toward the veracious representation of the external world" (79).

Despite the wholesale dismissal of historical fiction expressed in the *Theory of Film*, Kracauer would go on to write a book on historiography inspired by the very workings of cinema and photography. In *History: The Last Things before the Last* (1969), a monograph published posthumously, Kracauer explains that he entered the domain of historiography guided by the same drive that had previously led him to the theory of film, notably the need to serve the following purpose: "the rehabilitation of objectives and modes of being which still lack a name and hence are overlooked or misjudged" (Kracauer 1969, 4). He acknowledges that working with the photographic media was significantly easier, but he appears confident enough to make an equally original contribution to the field of historiography.[1] Even though people have been writing about history for centuries, Kracauer argues that it is still a "terra incognita" (ibid.). Thus, he knowingly signs up for this overwhelming task with his film theory as a compass; it is the tool that will guide him to discover new areas of inquiry, while it will also hand him the equipment to shed new light on charted territories. In *History*, Kracauer consistently develops the analogy between history and photographic media in ways that can benefit both areas. His strategy is explicated by openly posing the question: "But what is the good of indulging in analogies? Why dote on a subject only to jilt it for a similar subject?" (59). His response offers two reasons. Firstly, analogical thinking is fruitful because history and cinema produce works that depend on "identical conditions," i.e., they both strive to capture "worlds of comparable structure" and in that process they entail similar creative possibilities. Secondly, the photographic media can breath some fresh air in our thinking about history. They can help "defamiliarize habitual aspects in the historical field," setting it free from the long-standing discourses of science and philosophy, which have burdened it for so long (60).

Kracauer's analogy between cinema and history is based on the idea that both constitute modes or operations for generating knowledge about the world we live in. While cinema strives to reveal and record physical reality, history strives to reveal and record historical reality. Their parallel quest is characterized by a series of similarities that should not go unnoticed, for they allow us to get to grips with complexities that traditional historians are not willing to face. First and foremost, the realistic and formative tendencies that were identified in the practice of photographic media are equally present in the historical profession.[2] The historian, like the photographer, is both a recorder and a creator of history; he is required to discover raw data and then figure out a way to present and explain it (47). The goal in both cases, according to Kracauer, is to find the "right balance," which is achieved with the help of the following "simple, quasi-mathematical formula: Realistic Tendency $\geq$ Formative Tendency" (56). The prescriptive tone that dominated his *Theory of Film* remains intact when Kracauer describes what historians should do to attain their craft's higher aspirations.[3] His firm conviction regarding the parallel destinies of history and photographic media stems from his approach to the nature of historical and external reality respectively. As he notes:

> Small wonder that camera-reality parallels historical reality in terms of its structure, its general constitution. Exactly as historical reality, it is partly patterned, partly amorphous—a consequence, in both cases, of the half-cooked

state of our everyday world. And it shows features which are of a piece with the characteristics of the historian's universe.

Kracauer 1960, 58

The historical reality and the "*Lebenswelt*," a term borrowed from Husserl to signify our everyday world, are endless, open-ended, and susceptible to contingencies; what historians and cinematographers are expected to do is respect these qualities and record them in ways that do not falsify or distort their true nature. To that end, they both need to handle the switch from the micro to macro level using "close-ups" and "long shots." Kracauer explains that in historical writing the large bulk of micro events risk being damaged when transported to a higher level of generality, as they inevitably lose some of their peculiarities and meanings (126). This is called "the law of levels," a principle that controls the "traffic" between the micro and macro dimensions. To explicate how a historian should control this traffic, Kracauer refers to D.W. Griffith's close-up of Mae Marsh's clasped hands in the trial scene of *Intolerance* (1916); a close-up that does not merely serve the narrative purposes but reveals a new aspect of physical reality. In the same vein, he argues, the historian's close-up is apt to suggest possibilities and vistas not conveyed by the identical event in high-magnitude history (ibid.). With this analogy, Kracauer highlights procedural similarities between written history and cinematic language, despite their modal differences.

The comparison is further pursued in the chapter entitled "General History and the Aesthetic Approach," where he discusses a number of problematic premises in the genre of "general history." The general historian studies a very broad spectrum of events within a given period, constructing a unity and consistency that is mostly fictional. By striving for wholeness, general history begins to resemble the works of art and thwarts the historical universe's penchant for openness and indeterminacy. The same "deviation" is illustrated in what Kracauer names "the theatrical film." Even though truly cinematic works remain porous to the complexities and contingencies of the flow of life, theatrical films sacrifice "porosity to dense composition" (181). They structure their stories upon invented patterns, which close off the possibility of camera-reality to freely unfold. In his words, "The general narrative resembles the theatrical film. In both media compositional exigencies set the tune" (182).

In fact, the similarities between history and cinema run far deeper than Kracauer realizes. The search for unity and cohesion, the construction of temporality, and the tendency to establish clear cause-and-effect chains of events are narrational devices that characterize the large majority of films made in

Hollywood as well as worldwide. As later studies argued, the so-called "classical film" is a complex formal system that follows a specific range of causal, temporal and spatial rules of construction, while trying, at the same time, to appear natural and transparent (Ray 1985; Bordwell 1985). At the other end, historical books have also been found to comply with various constructional patterns. According to White's famous *Metahistory*, first published in 1973, all written historical accounts, and not just general histories, describe and explain historical events using different emplotments (White 2014). For us in this book, both White and Bordwell will provide the foundations for the new relation between history and cinema that I will attempt to ascertain. Here, it is important to realize how traces of this relation can be found in Kracauer's work, which, at the time, sought to establish a parallel between history and cinema as two modalities of the real. It is also intriguing to notice the very brief encounter between Kracauer and White in the footnote section before they go their separate ways again. In the chapter on general history, Kracauer quotes from White's article entitled "The Burden of History," first published in 1966, in order to argue that traditional historical writing imitates the structure of the nineteenth-century art, and particularly the novel (Kracauer 1969, 245). Yet, instead of investigating further the implications of the narrative similarities between historical books, novels, and films, he chooses to move higher again toward the philosophical level of these affiliations.

The result of this gesture is his final chapter called "The Anteroom," which attempts to locate the common enterprise between history and cinema in an area located right before the realm of art and philosophy. It is thus worth quoting him at length:

> One may define the area of historical reality, like that of photographic reality, as an anteroom area. Both realities are of a kind which does not lend itself to being dealt with in a definite way. The peculiar material in these areas eludes the grasp of systematic thought; nor can it be shaped in the form of a work of art. Like the statements we make about physical reality with the aid of the camera, those which result from our preoccupation with historical reality may certainly attain to a level above mere opinion; but they do not convey, or reach out for, ultimate truths, as do philosophy and art proper. They share their inherently provisional character with the material they record, explore, and penetrate.
>
> Kracauer 1969, 191

Kracauer establishes this intermediary area, the place of the last things before the last, in order to stress how historical and photographical realities are all at once material, ambiguous, and provisional. Neither history nor photography can sustain absolute truths; they cannot enter the exclusive realm of philosophy and art, where the truly last things reside. Instead, as Dagmar Barnouw observes, "Kracauer's historian travels in the realm of the nonabsolute, noncomplete, nontotal, nonradical—the anteroom of the relational with its risks and surprises" (Barnouw 1994, 165). Throughout the book, Kracauer supports and justifies his moderate views on history's potentiality, emphasizing why it is useful to "take the middle road" following Erasmus' example (Kracauer 1969, 14), or to talk in degrees rather than absolutes (100). When writing history, just as when filming reality, one is not expected to reveal the ultimate truth of things but to bring out elements of the historical reality or the *Lebenswelt*, which will enhance our knowledge of the world.

At that point, Kracauer inadvertently crosses paths with Michel Foucault, another influential thinker of philosophy and history, who will feature prominently in the following chapters. The connection with Foucault was pointed out by David Rodowick. In his lengthy review of *History*, Rodowick begins by juxtaposing two quotes from Kracauer's introduction and Foucault's *The Order of Things* (1973). Their views are not only contemporaneous[4] but also eerily similar when it comes to the problem of historical knowledge. Despite feeling awkward about the comparison, Rodowick explains how both intellectuals understand history as "an intermediate, yet privileged epistemological space," which challenges philosophy's "pretensions to universal understanding" by questioning its temporality and its inability to address the "minutiae of everyday life" (Rodowick 1987, 110). Realizing Kracauer's affinities with other deconstructionist thinkers was equally troubling for Gertrude Koch. Despite identifying a common ground, Koch emphatically notes:

> However, it would be wrong therefore to conclude that Kracauer was a precursor of the postmodern critique of the link between a history of philosophy and historiography. Kracauer welcomes the loss and collapse of the major systems of religion and of promised salvation, but he by no means greets it with some new heathen fiery joy. Instead he regards the fact that they have lost their core with mixed feelings.
>
> Koch 2000, 118

I am not convinced that having "mixed feelings" can disqualify anyone from belonging to a postmodernist school of thought, but I do understand how uncomfortable one might feel when faced with the challenge to change one's categorizations and move Kracauer, for instance, further away from the Frankfurt

School and closer to Foucault and White. But the value of Kracauer's writings lies in their fascinating density and their deep insight into cultural phenomena from a wide range of perspectives without any fixed ideological commitments. It should not come as a surprise that his views on cinema have been subject to reinterpretation many times over (Elsaesser 2014). Indicatively, I would like to mention how Miriam Hansen refutes the dominant belief that Kracauer was a proponent of realism in a fashion akin to André Bazin. As she argues:

> It is remarkable how little Kracauer's theorization of the salient features of the film experience depends on the logic of the trace and the indexical temporality of photographic exposure that has been taken to be the centerpiece of classical theories of cinematic realism.
>
> Hansen 2012, 279

In fact, what interested Kracauer the most in photographic media was their ability to fulfill a certain way of knowing and experiencing the world around us. It was the same purpose that drew him to historical writing and helped him approach cinema and history as epistemological conditions with shared practices rather than ontological differences. His relaxed take on medium specificity is also attested by the fact that he regularly resorts to examples from modernist literature. Even more frequent than the analogies between films and historical books is Kracauer's mention of Marcel Proust. *Remembrance of Things Past* is a recurring example of complex temporality and subjectivity, while *Tristram Shandy* and *Don Quixote* feature as inspirations for his own digressions and impossible quests.

His knowingness about the inability to reach the "last things" was simultaneously his greatest strength and weakness. The parallel between history and photographic media enabled him to detect a series of epistemological issues that plague both fields, but his own response to the problem remained tentative. As Barnow aptly puts it, "the analogy between photography and historiography, a composite of fragmented, tentative, illustrative, suggestive relations rather than a sustained, coherent argument, does show in a different light some of the most entrenched conundrums of historical representation" (Barnow 1994, 206). In other words, Kracauer's analogical thinking did achieve what analogies are supposed to achieve, i.e., enlarge and clarify specific areas of interest. What they do not provide is solutions, especially when one cares so much to prescribe. At any rate, Kracauer's *History* is an astonishingly insightful and knowledgeable work, which constitutes the very first attempt to consider history and cinema as two similar modes and forms of knowledge. Despite his rejection of the historical representation in the cinema and the criticism of the concept of fiction in general, his observations in *History* did break new ground and did shed light on the terra incognita of historiography, in the way he had hoped. Perhaps, in the future this last posthumous publication will attract the attention that it deserves.

In contrast to the limited visibility of Kracauer's *History*, however, Roland Barthes, the second scholar that I would like to discuss, has had an enormous influence on the discipline of history.[5] Despite the fact that his observations on historical writing were fragmentary and scattered in various books and collected essays,[6] Barthes' contribution to the theory of historiography remains noteworthy to this date (White 1988; Jenkins and Munslow 2004; Munslow 2010; Rosen 2001). He shares with Kracauer not only the interest in the mechanics of history but also his love for Proust and photography. Unlike Kracauer, however, Barthes chose the nineteenth-century novel as an analogy for exploring the profound formal similarities between literature and historical writing. In his famous piece "The Discourse of History" he formulates the following question: "Does this form of narration really differ, in some specific trait, in some indubitably distinctive feature, from imaginary narration, as we find it in the epic, the novel, and the drama?" (Barthes 1981b, 7). Instead of examining the analogy at the philosophical level, arguing about history's status as art, Barthes plunges the inquiry into the very process of narration. He draws on Roman Jakobson's narrative concepts and breaks down the historical discourse into the "act of uttering," the "utterance," and the process of "signification." When classic historians assume the task of writing a historical account, they employ various types of "shifters,"[7] common to literature and other types of speech. For instance, the shifters of listening (phrases like "from what I heard," "to my knowledge") allow the historians to transfer information as testimony and present it in their own words. In addition, they organize their material using temporal and locational expressions that accelerate time or allow movement between different moments in time or help the writer inaugurate his utterance. As a general rule, the signs of the "act of uttering" do not seek prominence; on the one hand, they almost eliminate the position of the receiver, while, on the other, the utterer seeks an objective role that will allow the story to tell itself. As Barthes notes, "this type of illusion is not exclusive to historical discourse. It would be hard to count the novelists who imagined—in the epoch of Realism—that they were 'objective' because they suppressed the signs of the 'I' in their discourse!" (11).

The troubles with historical writing do not end with the historian's imaginary objectivity but carry on with the contents of his account, particularly the process of naming historical objects. Barthes distinguishes between "existents" (agents) and "occurrents" (actions), and explains that designating those elements is not a natural and unproblematic procedure. Depending on one's theme, the historian chooses the type of subjects who will be given agency and the type of events that will punctuate the overall story. For instance, Herodotus reduces existents to dynasties, princes, generals, and soldiers, and the occurrents to actions such as laying waste, putting into slavery, making alliances, organizing expeditions, reigning etc. (12). Apart from these central narrative "units," the historian, just as the novelist, must contain several others, which can take the form of "indexical signs," "enthymemes," or "functions."[8] Depending on which type of unit becomes dominant, the historical account takes on a different shape; Jules Michelet, for instance, relies heavily on indexical signs veering towards metaphor and lyricism, while Augustin Thierry opts for functional units, which create metonymic relations that resemble the structure of the epic (15).

Finally, in the third section on "signification" Barthes touches upon the core problem of historical discourse, which is none other than its relation to external reality. Apart from the historian's intervention at the level of the collection of facts and their interpretation, there is a fundamental linguistic trap that prevents historical writing from ever reaching the "real" events. It is worth quoting at length his description of this conceptual slide:

> Historical discourse takes for granted, so to speak, a double operation, which is very crafty. At one point (this break-down is of course only metaphorical) the referent is detached from the discourse, becomes external to it, its founding and governing principle: this is the point of the *res gestae*, when the discourse offers itself quite simply as *historia rerum gestarum*. But at a second point, it is the signified itself which is forced out and becomes confused with the referent; the referent enters into a direct relation with the signifier, and the discourse, solely charged with *expressing* the real, believes itself authorized to dispense with the fundamental term in imaginary structures, which is the signified.
>
> Barthes 1981b, 17

Through this process of latently replacing the signified with the referent, the historical discourse simply misleads the reader. It creates the illusion of having a direct access to the referent, whereas, in fact, it is an auto-referential construction, which can only refer back to the text and nothing else.[9] In the triangle signifier–signified–referent, the referent becomes all-powerful, eliminating the role of the signified, producing what Barthes describes as the "reality effect." By emphasizing their connection to the referent and the real, historical signs take on the mask of objectivity, emulating their ties to *res gestae*, without any means of actual corroboration. Our society's preference for realism has led to the development of specific genres not only in historical writing but also in literature, news reporting, and museum exhibition in a wider cultural effort to save the relics of the past and claim access to an illusionary reality long gone (18).

The notion of the "reality effect," which appears towards the end of "The Discourse of History," becomes the central theme in his homonymous article that came out a year later. There, Barthes compares passages from Gustave Flaubert and Michelet to bring to the surface the mechanism that generates the impression of realism. He traces details in their descriptions that do not serve any structural functions of the texts, but appear as insignificant notations that, little by little, build a relation between the text and the concrete reality surrounding it. Again, by replacing the signified with the illusion of the referent and by multiplying those referents in a superfluous manner, novelists and historians alike appear to objectively record the world around them (Barthes 1986). This craving for objectivity in the parallel lives of the novel and history has been noted in several of Barthes' writings, starting from *Writing Degree Zero* (1970) and reaching all the way to *Camera Lucida* (1981a). Even before detecting specific textual mechanisms, as in "The Discourse of History" and "The Reality Effect," Barthes was convinced of their significant affinities viewed in the background of the nineteenth century sensibility. As he notes:

> The Novel and History have been closely related in the very century, which witnessed their greatest development. Their link in depth, that which should allow us to understand at once Balzac and Michelet, is that in both we find the construction of an autarkic world which elaborates its own dimensions and limits, and organizes within these its own Time, its own Space, its population, its own set of objects and its myths.
>
> Barthes 1970, 29

Barthes did not shy away from history's fictional nature throughout his writings, but his views became even more definitive when he compared written discourse to photography. In *Camera Lucida*, Barthes is fascinated by photography's "unique" ability to show "what has been," thanks not to the painters, who had "invented" framing and perspective, but to the chemists (Barthes 1981a, 80). It is the chemical transformation of light into an image that entirely alters the composition of the photographic sign, causing it to "emanate" from the referent. In contrast to other systems of representation, photography's referent is present in the act of recording and its very existence is undeniable. In light of this revolutionary development, the representation of history in written discourse appears even more arbitrary and illusionary. Whereas photography is a "certificate of authenticity," written language is considered, by nature, as fictional and can appear natural and realistic only with great effort and difficulty (87). And there lies a paradox, according to Barthes, namely that it was the same century that invented history and photography, two opposing signifying tendencies. In his words, these two compare as follows: "History is a memory fabricated according to positive formulas, a pure intellectual discourse which abolishes mythic Time; and the Photograph is a certain but fugitive testimony" (93). His unshakeable belief in photography's natural attachment to the "profilmic" element compared to history's unquestionably fabricated nature is, in fact, another paradox on its own. Barthes manages to remain unequivocally deconstructionist in his approach to history and, yet, romantically realist in his take on photography. As David Bolter and Jay Grusin observe, writing *Camera Lucida* in 1980,[10] the time when the first desktop computers were being developed and marketed, was "almost the last moment when any sophisticated writer could still claim that an analog photograph was not a representation but an emanation of its subject" (Bolter and Grusin 1999, 112).

For Barthes, the emergence of photography revealed the problem of representation in history and literature, as it was the one that could finally claim unique ties to an external world; in written discourse these ties could only be forged. By pointing out the materiality of language and the impact of its form in the shaping of history's fundamental ingredients (agents, actions, causality, time, and space), Barthes paved the way for White's poetics of history and the systematic research into how the form shapes the content of history. In some respects, *Metahistory* is a painstaking attempt to map the formal, argumentative, and ideological means with which a historical text produces its reality effects. As White confesses about Barthes' influence, "It was under his inspiration that I turned not so much to linguistics as to discourse theory, and began to see history as discourse rather than as discipline" (Rogne and White 2009, 67). The distinction between discourse and discipline is indeed the key for understanding the forms and functions of historical representation in any medium, as I will be pointing out several times in the course of this book.[11] It is also the key for reconceptualizing the relation between history on paper and history on screen, once the institutional parameters of the academic discipline are set aside.

What is also intriguing about Barthes is his emphatic distinction between photography and cinema. Whereas Kracauer considered photography and cinema as interchangeable, Barthes placed cinema on the side of history and the novel and left photography at the other end, as the sole medium with intrinsic ties to reality. For Barthes, it was the presence of movement that never left any doubt about the fictitious nature of the cinematic image. While in a photograph something has posed in front of the camera and stayed there, in the cinema something has merely passed and has been transformed into something else. Thus, cinema is an illusion, just like language. They both depend on fiction in order to represent reality (Barthes 1981a). Where Kracauer and Barthes come closer though is when they discuss fictional representation. The following passage eerily echoes Kracauer's reservation towards the fictional side of cinema:

> Here again, from a phenomenological viewpoint, the cinema begins to differ from the Photograph; for the (fictional) cinema combines two poses: the actor's "this-has-been" and the role's, so that (something I would not experience before a painting) I can never see or see again in a film certain actors whom I know to be dead without a kind of melancholy: the melancholy of Photography itself (I experience this same emotion listening to the recorded voices of dead singers).
>
> Barthes 1981a, 79

In this brief mention of cinema, Barthes indicates the difficulty of transforming a profilmic element (the actor) into a diegetic one (the role) from a phenomenological point of view, meeting Kracauer half-way in his position that cinema is at its best when redeeming physical reality rather than staging it. Thus, the topic of representing historical reality in the cinema largely remains off-limits. For all their meticulous interest in historiography and their analogical thinking, Barthes and Kracauer do not see how cinema can provide its own form of historical representation. The power of the written tradition is not challenged as the only legitimate form of historical discourse, despite its flawed (Kracauer) or inherently fictional (Barthes) nature. In Godard's case, however, this monopoly begins to crumble.

Jean-Luc Godard, the third figure in this showcase, is a filmmaker who has worked, thought, and spoken extensively on the nature of the cinematic medium, a preoccupation that, as in the other cases, inescapably led him to questions about historicity, memory, and epochal shifts. Godard is one of the most idiosyncratic filmmakers in the history of cinema, partly because he combines his cinematic activity with so many others. As Michael Witt notes, Godard "was, and remains, less a conventional feature-film director than a multimedia poet, philosopher, critic, and essayist" (Witt 2013, 7). Through an inexhaustible experimentation with diverse media in the course of his career, Godard has explored a vast array of themes and issues, including twentieth-century history, film history, and historiography, all of which converged in *Histoire(s) du Cinéma* (1998). In this multi-media project, Godard combined a four-and-a-half-hour video series in eight parts together with a four-volume set of art books and a box set of five audio CDs and multilingual books released in 1999.[12] Through all these different media platforms, he seeks to put forward one central idea, notably that cinema, an offspring of the nineteenth century, is ideally suitable for telling its own history, reflecting simultaneously the history of the twentieth century. It is a complex "theorem," as Witt calls it, which is further complicated by Godard's multi-layered aesthetics and semantics. Already the choice of "Histoire(s)" for the title indicates Godard's explicit language game with the notion of "history," "story," and "stories." As he explains, the goal was "to play on the different meanings, the way histories can mean tall stories or hassles. It was to point out that it's both History with a big H and histoires with a small one, French has these different usages for the word but other languages don't" (cited in Godard and Ishaghpour 2005, 59). Underlying this deliberate use of "histoire" is his awareness of the conceptual and ideological stakes in historical writing as well as his uneasiness with the established ideas of history. Godard expresses his skepticism toward history on multiple levels, ranging from visual and textual references in the actual film and the accompanying volumes to real-life conversations with eminent professional historians. *Histoire(s) du Cinéma* was created as an audiovisual piece of history, which would primarily tell the history of cinema, while featuring the history of the twentieth century and posing questions, at the same time, on the very act of historicizing. This incredibly dense rationale, however, would be overlooked by the commentators; instead, they opted for a more banal categorization of the work as an audiovisual poem, stripping Godard of his aspired role as a historian. Godard regretted such treatment (Witt 2013, 70). With *Histoire(s) du Cinéma* he had hoped to sit alongside Eric Hobsbawm, for instance, on an equal-to-equal basis, discussing each his own version of history of the twentieth century. Yet, when the moment came, in an encounter staged by Marc Ferro in 2000, Hobsbawm could not see the point. To him, Godard was not a colleague but rather a "poetic visionary" (Witt, 76).

The discrepancy in their perspectives should not have come as a surprise. Traditional historians, to this day cling to standard notions of objectivity and fact-oriented research in an effort to tell "what really happened," without worrying at all if and how their goal is attainable. Godard, on the other hand, like most philosophers of history, seeks to understand the methods at one's disposal for approaching the past and the forms that such an approach may take. In *Histoire(s) du Cinéma*, he puts forward the idea that the emergence of cinema at the end of the nineteenth century has furnished a new mode of historiography, not through words and texts but through images and sounds. As he notes, "Now, there's a new cinema, a different art form, whose history will be made in fifty or one hundred years time. Now there's a new chapter of humanity, and perhaps even the very idea of History will change" (cited in Temple and Williams 2000, 21).

As we go though Godard's various statements contained either in filmic segments in *Histoire(s) du Cinéma* or expressed in extra-filmic outlets, such as interviews and public discussions, we come across a broad range of ideas regarding the nature of history and cinema. These ideas are often contradictory and incoherent, expressed in figural speech or piecemeal remarks that strive to maintain a sense of mystique, refusing to give away a full-fledged exposition of what really goes on in his mind.[13] In contrast to Kracauer and Barthes, Godard's theory of history and cinema does not come in an analytical form but in an artistic mode that emulates the very intellectual processes that he wishes to explore and expose. From this ocean of signifiers, I would like to single out a number of statements that are relevant to issues discussed previously by Kracauer and Barthes but also to highlight others that have a direct bearing on my own research in this book. For instance, it is noteworthy that Godard oscillates between the realist and the constructionist approach to cinema, aligning himself both with a Bazinian take on recording reality and an Eisensteinian faith in montage. On the one hand, he claims that cinema is made from the same "raw material" as history and functions as a "registrar," particularly because it records the actions of men and women and, given the proper scientific research, it works as a testament to social conditions (Godard and Ishaghpour 2005, 87–8). Similarly, he argues that the real purpose of cinema was to function as "an instrument of knowledge, like a microscope or telescope, but very quickly it was prevented from playing its role and was turned into a toy" (cited in Temple and Williams 2000, 19). On the other hand, Godard's own cinema tirelessly explored the power of montage and its infinite creative potential. As Witt underlines in his brilliant analysis of Godard's oeuvre:

By recording the relations between disparate phenomena and between people and the world, and then revealing those relations to audiences at the moment of projection, cinema, for Godard, operated as a vast montage machine, which automatically and mechanically enacted the work of the historian as a monteur. Thus the age of cinema, he can claim, is "the only time in the past four hundred million years that a certain way of telling stories was 'history.'"

Witt 2013, 28

The notion of the historian as a "monteur" is reminiscent of Warren Susman's position, with which I opened my introduction. It is indicative of a line of thought that seeks structural similarities between history and cinema but that would never become prevalent in either discipline. Godard was fairly lonely when mapping the theory and practice of audiovisual historiography but his maps were modeled upon the works of several French historians, philosophers, and art critics, such as Élie Faure, Charles Péguy, André Malraux, Fernand Braudel, Emil Cioran, and, above all, Michelet.[14] Michelet provided a poetic, subjective, and anti-positivist stance toward history, which enabled Godard to explore a method for thinking about the past by cinematic means. As he confessed, "it seemed to me that history could be a work of art, something not generally accepted, except by Michelet" (cited in Godard and Ishaghpour 2005, 28). Thus, it does not come as a surprise that both Godard and Barthes would be drawn to the fictional and artistic nature of Michelet's historical narratives. Commentators have traced a number of similarities between Michelet's historical writing and the history put forward in *Histoire(s) du Cinéma*, particularly the foregrounding of the historian's persona and the personal commitment and inspiration fuelled into the work.[15] Jacques Aumont offers an eloquent description of what could have been Godard's mission statement:

This is not just a confession, it is also a personification: I, the cinema, am speaking; or more exactly: I, Jean-Luc Godard, who for the moment and for the needs of the cause incorporate the cinema, am speaking. So I express myself in the language of cinema, through moving images and sounds, and my phrasing is that of cinema, i.e. configurations of time, successions, encounters, and concomitances. In order to remind itself of itself, the cinema must utilize its own modes of memory, and therefore above all its invention, the only one perhaps at the end of the century it has ever proposed, montage.

Aumont 1999, 13

Montage was celebrated by Godard as cinema's unique feature, which separated it from painting and the novel, and yet, it was with video that he felt more at ease. Witt minutely chronicles Godard's creative trajectory from film to video, noting that his video works outnumber his films by far, especially from the 1970s onwards. What is more intriguing, though, is how Godard's excitement about video technology was related to the artistic freedom and the formal malleability that aligned video-makers with writers and painters (Witt 2013, 52). So we are back to the paradoxes of medium specificity that we encountered previously with Kracauer and Barthes; on the one hand, all three of them are fascinated by the newness and singularity of each emergent medium, while, on the other, they end up, explicitly or not, tracing affinities and shared practices with the older ones. What they also share is an amalgam of pessimism and fascination with the myth of Orpheus.[16] Compare how Kracauer and Godard relate history, cinema and the historian's task via the Orphic myth; the former notes:

> Like Orpheus, the historian must descend into the nether world to bring the dead back to life. How far will they follow his allurements and evocations? They are lost to him when, re-emerging in the sunlight of the present, he turns for fear of losing them. But does he not for the first time take possession of them at this very moment—the moment when they forever depart, vanishing in a history of his own making?
>
> Kracauer 1969, 79

In fewer words, Godard says; "Cinema authorizes Orpheus to look back without causing Eurydice's death" (cited in Witt 2013, 24). In both cases, history is about looking back, trying to reconnect the dead and the living, but in Godard's version, the myth is transformed. For him, cinema is actually capable of accomplishing the mission without killing Eurydice. Yet, we should not confound this purportedly unique—this troublesome word again—cinematic trait with neither a naïve realism nor the Bazinian notion of "mummification." According to Godard, the past is never entirely dead because it always awaits remembrance. Cinema resuscitates the past by transfiguring it; first, it kills it off, then it mourns it, and finally it attempts to resurrect it during projection. In the words of his voice-over in *Histoire(s) du Cinéma*, part 1B:

> because / here is what happened / in the early hours of the twentieth century / technologies decided / to reproduce life / so photography was invented / and cinema / but as morality / was still strong / and they were getting ready / to extract from life / even its identity / they mourned / this putting to death/ and it was in the colors of mourning / in black / and white / that the cinematograph came into existence.
>
> Cited in Witt, 26

Thus, Eyridice's actual return is always already doomed to fail. Cinema does not contradict the myth but, rather, performs it in a way that foregrounds Orpheus' and its own failure. For that matter, Godard equally plays with the notion of error and distortion, acknowledging that each "attempt at resurrection"[17] of past reality is filled with mistakes, omissions, and fictional elements. Hence, the double meaning of "histoire"—meaning "story" as much as "history"—and the use of plural in the title of this work.

The possibility of error and distortion, which is inherent in the cinematic/ historical enterprise, however, is separate from Godard's disappointment about the ways in which cinema failed to perform its mission. In contrast to his nuanced and theoretically informed contribution to cinematic historiography, his thesis on the demise of cinema around the time of the Second World War is too absolute and overstated. As he puts it, "Cinema 'stammered' history, and then at a given moment it no longer did it. The concentration camps weren't filmed; people didn't want to show them or see them. And that was the end: cinema stopped there" (cited in Witt, 127). The concentration camps were filmed, of course, both by the Nazis during their power[18] and by the Allies after their victory, even if, indeed, their public screenings were received with mixed feelings.[19] Godard's definitive rejection of the ways in which cinema handled the Holocaust, mirrors the lengthy debates on the limits of representation after Auschwitz, especially from the part of those who criticized any attempt to portray the horrors of the concentration camps.[20] For instance, it is interesting how he hatefully rejects Spielberg's *Schindler's List* (1994) for its factual inaccuracies, calling it a "falsified document" (cited in Witt, 128). But why is not this inaccuracy part of the "package" called cinema, in exactly the same way, as his own inaccuracies, which were so often so playfully orchestrated? What is it that differentiates one distortion from another and who is authorized to interpret an inaccuracy as legitimate and meaningful or not? Difficult questions.

And this brings us to the problem of fictional representation and history, which is touched by all three figures, albeit from different angles and with different points of emphasis. Kracauer senses the affinities between cinema and history as epistemological tools but he is critical of the fictional aspects of general history and even more so of fictional historical films. To be precise, he does not even consider categorizing historical films as forms of history, while general history works are regarded as a genre of history, even if a problematic one. Thus, when it comes to the narrativization process and the ensuing distortions at work both in writing and in filmmaking, the standards are double. In Barthes' case, the rationale is rather reverse; both history and the novel share narrative practices, which render their discourse fictional and autonomous from external reality. Even though he does not develop a theory of cinema, his passing references indicate that cinema falls largely within the same category as literature and history, given the fictional status of their discursive practices in contrast to photography's unique bonds to external referents. In this light, Barthes remains at least consistent with his deconstructive method whether he refers to historical writing, novels, or films. Godard, on the other hand, is not. On the one hand, he is conscious of written history's limitations and considers the cinema as the most apt medium for "doing history" in the twentieth century. He forcefully believes in the possibility of an audiovisual historiography and he presents his own attempt at that not only in *Histoire(s) du Cinéma*, but also in several other works.[21] Yet, when it comes to delineating the forms and shapes of this new mode of history, his approach is far from coherent. Sometimes, he celebrates cinematic images as records, sometimes as metaphors and others as conceptual collages. And the problem expands exponentially when he has to connect his theorem on history with specific films, other than his own. How many films like *Histoire(s) du Cinéma* have there been or can there be out there? Admittedly, not many. But, then, how can one elevate the entire cinematic medium to the key historiographical mode of an entire century when the films that can actually perform this role, according to Godard, are nothing but a handful? Conceptually, Godard's theorem is not only fascinating but it also feels right. But when we try to connect the theory to the specifics that it supposedly designates, we face an enormous discrepancy that we need address.

One of the goals of this book is to develop Godard's argument about audiovisual historiography in a way that not only encompasses a large part of the cinematic output but that it also positions cinema's historiographical strength at the very heart of historical representation. Kracauer, Barthes, and Godard's thoughts are invaluable for understanding the historical trajectory of aligning history with cinema and literature and for appreciating the power of analogical thinking. Their observations, as I presented them here, illustrate how the theory and practice of history was placed under scrutiny due to the pressure of other media. It was the skepticism raised by the formal and material parameters of the cinema and the novel that identified a series of ruptures in history's purported direct access to the historical past. What is still a blind spot in their accounts, however, is the role of historical representation on film. To bring this into the picture, we need first to reconsider a series of assumptions related to medium specificity, historical theory and practice as well as the function of the narration in describing and explaining the past. This will be the task of the subsequent chapters.

Notes

1   The impact of Kracauer's *History* has been minimal, despite the ongoing debates on the fallacies of objectivism, as Dagmar Barnouw observes in her book-length study (1994). Even among film scholars who specialize in Kracauer's writings, the attention falls largely on his *Theory of Film* or on other texts on mass culture, rather than his work on historiography. See Hansen (2012) and Koch (2000). The few notable commentators of *History*, apart from Barnow, include Rodowick (1987) and Jay (1986).

2   For the description of the realistic and formative tendencies in the cinema, see Kracauer (1960, 30–7).

3   Dagmar Barnouw notes that it was Kracauer's prescriptiveness in the *Theory of Film* that got him into trouble with critics supporting a less-controlled development of the cinematic medium (1994).

4   The French edition of *The Order of Things,* entitled *Les Mots et les Choses*, was first published in 1966. Kracauer's *History* was for the most part complete with several chapters already in print at the time of his death on November 26, 1966.

5   Roland Barthes even has his own entry in *The Routledge Companion to Historical Studies* (Munslow, 2006).

6   The chronology of Barthes' writing can be slightly difficult to establish since there are publications in French and in English, while several of his shorter pieces were first published in journals and then appeared in compilations. I always refer to editions in English, taking into consideration, however, the original dates of each publication as I discuss the progression of his arguments.

7   A shifter is a particular class of grammatical unit whose general meaning cannot be defined without reference to the message. See Jakobson (1971, 131–3).

8   For the origins of the terms "index," "enthymeme," and "function," in Peirce, Aristotle, and Propp's works respectively, see Peirce (1991); Furley and Nehamas (2015); and Propp (2010).

9   Compare Barthes' description of the process of representation with a more elaborate version formulated by Frank Ankersmit discussed in the conclusion.

10 The French original version came out in 1980.

11 See particularly chapters three and the conclusion.

12 Michael Witt provides the most detailed and comprehensive exploration of Godard's *Histoire(s) Du Cinéma*. See Witt (2013).

13 In the interview with Youssef Ishaghpour, Godard's responses are always brief and suggestive, whereas Ishaghpour's questions are long and analytical trying to interpret and develop his interviewee's ideas. See Godard and Ishaghpour (2005).

14 Michael Witt dedicates an entire chapter on the close scrutiny of Godard's influences from the fields of history, art history, cinema history, and other relevant domains. See Witt (2013).

15 See Witt (2013, 82) and Temple and Williams (2000, 83–5).

16 Barthes' references to the Orphic myth are also numerous in his writings on literature. See Barthes (1970).

17 The notion of "resurrection" was prominent in Jules Michelet's approach to history and it is lengthily discussed by Barthes as well in his monograph on Michelet. As he explains, "In the Micheletist resurrection of the past, death is heavy. It is neither paradise nor grave, it is the very existence of the dead person, but dreamed, reconciling in itself the familiar (touching) features of life and the solemn knowledge of death. In this fashion, every flaw is corrected, every misstep conquered between life and death, between the timorous solitude of the living historian and the communion of all the dead who are no longer afraid. It is for this that Michelet so readily shifted his own organism to the countless people of the dead; constantly touching death, like Antaeus his mother earth, he attached himself to History as to the apprenticeship of his own death." See Barthes (1987).

18 A compilation of rare German footage is found in *The Nazi Plan* (1945), a film that was produced and presented as evidence at the Nuremberg Trials. See Delage (2013).

19 For details about the first documentaries shot by the Allied Forces, see Kerner (2011, 177–93).

20 The debate on the limits of representation with respect to the Holocaust will be discussed in chapter 5.

21 Witt presents a thorough account of Godard's works that relate to historical representation (2013).

2

Media Specificity and the Analogy of the Digital

Every time a new medium appears, an alarm goes off. It triggers a certain anxiety as well as eagerness among people to fathom the qualities and functions of the newcomer before determining its place in their lives. The effort to understand the role of the new medium always entails a renegotiation with those that they have had before. The comparison between old and new media exemplifies a paradox; on the one hand, it draws together media that instinctively look or feel similar, while, on the other, it urges their conscious and deliberate separation. Notice, for instance, how cinema was immediately compared a lot more to the theater and painting than to the novel, so that it could then be differentiated on various technological or physiological grounds. For similar reasons, the advent of photography did not leave historians apathetic. While they sensed the affinities of their instruments with those of the camera, the impulse was to focus on the differences. Considering it as an instrument of mechanical reproduction, they were compelled to distinguish photography from history and their own role from that of the cameraman. In *Historik*, Johann Droysen notes the following: "The narrative presentation does not want to give a picture, a photography of that which once was [...] but our apperception of important events from that standpoint, from that point of view" (cited in Kracauer 1969, 226). Almost a century later, Lewis Namier would reiterate: "The function of the historian is akin to that of the painter and not of the photographic camera: to discover and set forth, to single out and stress that which is of the nature of the thing, and not to reproduce indiscriminately all that meets the eye" (Namier 1952, 8). There are two noteworthy observations to be made about these views. One is found in Kracauer's following passage:

> Such references to the photographic medium would be entirely uncalled for were not the historians making them alert to the possibility that history and photography have something to do with each other after all. On the other hand,

they hint at this possibility only to deny it categorically. Why do they reject the very comparisons they themselves care to suggest?

Kracauer 1969, 51

Indeed, the comparisons between history and photography would be meaningful only if various affinities were sensed between them. Nobody would be inclined to compare two entirely dissimilar practices, since their differences would be self-evident. In all likelihood, insightful historians, ranging from Droysen to Namier, felt that their profession and their methods had possibly something to do with photography, but they could not jeopardize their academic prestige by bringing them too close. This new technological development and its future potential could challenge their established privilege for providing knowledge about the historical past, and therefore, it should be contained. On the other hand, it is even more striking that Namier opts for painting as a medium that resembles history the most. And thus, he inadvertently raises the questions: Is history so subjective and so contingent on the talent and inspiration of its creator? What happens to the search for objectivity and truth in historical writings when they, in fact, are nothing but personal renderings of objects and actions in the same way as paintings? The responses vary depending on a historian's place in the history and theory of their profession, which is a crucial subject to be addressed in the subsequent chapter. For now, I am interested in highlighting how the discussion about a medium's "nature" is almost invariably pervaded by medium-specific views that seek to raise walls between diverse media rather than examine their common ground.

The so-called "medium-specificity" thesis is best articulated and explored by Noël Carroll in the first four chapters of *Theorizing the Moving Image* (1996). As he explains, "the idea [. . .] that each art form, in virtue of its medium, has its own exclusive domain of development was born in the eighteenth century, almost at the same time that the distinctions between the aesthetic and the nonaesthetic and between the fine arts and the practical arts crystallized" (1996b, 25). It is important to bear in mind this historical positioning of the medium-specific approach, as we often tend to neglect the historicity of such terms, endowing them with a certain universality that can be misleading. Cinema and photography, thus appeared in a century characterized by intense innovation, technological revolutions, and a proliferation of media that called for an awareness of the limits between technology and art. Although Carroll discusses the concept of medium-specificity in film theory in relation to cinema's process of acquiring the status of art, most of his arguments are widely applicable to the broader concern of detecting and defining the "true nature" or "essence" of any medium. His examples are drawn from the writings of Kracauer, André Bazin, and Stanley Cavell—all members of the realist tradition—who clearly believed in cinema's unique properties as well as its fated destination to capitalize on its privileged relation to external reality.[1] It is important to note that the medium-specificity thesis, according to Carroll, has two components, an internal and an external one (1996a, 8). The former specifies the best qualities of the medium and prescribes their exploration, so that its full potential can be reached. For instance, Kracauer considers staged historical films as cinema's weak spot, and he suggests that films should focus on their realistic tendencies, instead, and their yearning for openness, infinity, and contingency. This is a medium-specific position with an internal logic that prioritizes certain formal options over others within the repertoire of the medium. The external component, on the other hand, is that which predicates the areas at which each medium excels. In other words, it designates the advantage of each medium over the others. For example, according to this line of thought, history is best served in written speech rather than cinematic images. This means that there is something in the nature or the essence of writing that allows historians to fulfill their purposes more effectively in their effort to understand the past. And there, precisely, lies the heart of the problem of cinematic history and the debate of whether the practice of history is amenable to diverse media, including cinema. Carroll can help us formulate a tentative explanation regarding the monopoly of written language over historying with his description of the "division of labor" argument. He explains that people tend to compare diverse media and evaluate their capacities in order to establish a certain division of labor, which allocates roles and practices. As Carroll observes:

> In order to maximize the efficient use of scarce resources, to avoid waste in terms of unnecessary duplication, and to meet a set quota of needs, society and business parcel out tasks, ideally to those best suited for them. Similarly, medium specificity theorists seem to rely implicitly on a value placed on the type of efficiency afforded by the division of labor.
>
> Carroll 1996a, 16

However, unlike industrial and other professional areas, art and history do not have scarce resources nor do they suffer from inflation. One could hardly argue that too many art works or too many histories in diverse media can be endangering in any way, other than those related to institutional power and professional privilege. The fact that historical discourse is considered as such only when it is in writing and only when it conforms to specific academic requirements is more indicative of societal power relations than actual formal capacities. Yet, the power play is disguised beneath the façade not only of the division of labor argument but also of the so-called "tool analogy" (1996b, 32). As Carroll explains, medium-specific positions embrace the analogy of the tools to argue that each medium is tailor-made for certain uses just like a tool. If you want to turn a screw, you will choose a screwdriver and not a hammer. Similarly, if you want to do history, you will write a book; you will not make a film or write a poem. The tool analogy seems more plausible than the division of labor but it does not hold water either; art forms and media are neither centrally designed for limited purposes nor can they remain stable and fixed like tools. As contemporary theorists have shown, media are complex entities that emerge as a result of multiple artistic, economic, and political interests, and they perform a plurality of tasks not in a vacuum but always in a dialogue with other media (Thornburn and Jenkins 2003). Thus, at the other end of the medium-specificity thesis, we find scholars, such as André Gaudreault and Philippe Marion, who refuse to describe a medium as an autonomous entity. Instead, they define it as a "kind of evolving patchwork of 'federated' cultural series reflected through a prismatic identity whose existence is only temporary"[2] (Gaudreault and Marion 2012, 32). Over the past couple of decades, media theory has advanced our knowledge on the issue of mediality and intermediality, raising a significant awareness both on media historicity and ontology. The clout of earlier medium-specific arguments has been severely challenged, but it has not been eliminated.

In fact, the domain of historiography remains to a large extent immune to contemporary intermedial perspectives. It is remarkable how the majority of theorists, either from the discipline of history or film studies, cling to a strict division between written and audiovisual history based on their different materiality. And when they defend the legitimacy of cinematic history, they do so not by relating it to its written counterpart but by searching for its unique trace. Note, for instance, how Marc Ferro, one of the most pioneering scholars in the field, envisions a *truly* cinematic history in his famous piece entitled "Does a filmic writing of History exist?" He laments the fact that most films merely transcribe the historical vision of others, while he prescribes, as all medium-specific theorists do, a certain path for reaching autonomy. It is worth following his rationale in full:

> First, the filmmakers must have separated themselves from ideological forces and ruling institutions (and this is not the case of directors of propaganda films): if not, their work only furthers, in a new form, dominant (or oppositional)

ideological currents. A second condition is obviously that the writing be cinematic (and not, for example, filmed theater) and that it use specific cinematic means. The contribution of cinema to the intelligibility of historical phenomena varies according to the degree of its autonomy and its esthetic contribution.

Ferro 1987, 84

In his formula, Ferro imagines a world where the filmmakers can work outside ideology and institutional pressure altogether and they can discover those forms that are *essentially* cinematic to create a truly and unequivocally cinematic history. Evidently, Ferro's vision is not only medium-specific but also metaphysical.

Ferro's proposal for a truly filmic writing of history could be justified, however, if we take into consideration the hostile framework of academic history from which it sprang. Early attempts to legitimize history on screen were compelled to carve a separate space on which they would eventually situate the aspired contribution of cinema to historical thinking. Unfortunately, a similar tendency persists even in more recent attempts to delineate cinematic history, such as that found in William Guynn's *Writing History in Film* (2006). As I noted in my introduction, Guynn's work is remarkable for its interdisciplinary perspective but when it comes to ontological issues, his views remain closely tied to the medium specificity thesis, as I will demonstrate. To begin, Guynn poses the problem quite aptly as follows: "We are now raising the crucial question of the vehicle that conveys narrative and discursive information. How do the different mediums of expression—the written language of the historian, the audiovisual language of the filmmaker—shape the representation of historical events? (68). In search for an answer, he delves into the traditional semiotic concepts drawn from Ferdinand de Saussure, Christian Metz, and Louis Hjelmslev.[3] Specifically, he focuses on the signifier/signified distinction in order to identify the differences between written and filmic narratives. The chief differentiating factor is located at the level of the signifier; in plain words, historical books signify via graphic traces that form words, sentences, chapters etc., whereas historical films signify via heterogeneous elements, including moving images and sounds that are edited together in various configurations. While discussing the differences between writing and film in terms of their signifiers, Guynn rehearses the Bazinian and Barthesian views on indexicality and he puts forward a textbook case of a medium-specific argument. The following passage is emblematic:

Differences in the nature of the signifier in literary and cinematic narratives lead to the particular genius of each medium. Cinema gives us a convincing analogue of concrete space, mimics to perfection the flow of time within the single shot,

and reproduces the movement of real phenomena in space. Given the
concreteness of its expression, it is not surprising then that film has difficulty
expressing abstract notions.

Guynn 2006, 72

Mistaking style for essence, Guynn identifies the "genius" of cinema in its
indexical relation to external reality as opposed to its handicap with respect to
abstraction. Thus, almost all the elements of the medium-specific views are in
place: what cinema does best (intrinsically and extrinsically), how labor ought to
be distributed and how tools should be chosen. If you want something concrete,
then opt for the cinematic image and its unique ability to record time and space;
if you want higher abstract meaning, then go for the book. And Guynn goes even
further with his medium-specific case. After presenting a series of examples,
ranging from *Citizen Kane* (1941) to *Battleship Potemkin* (1927), as illustrations
of what is "more cinematic," he reaches a crescendo:

> We come then to the crux of the problem of cinematic representations of history.
> Given the qualities of the cinematic signifier and the kinds of stories film seems
> "destined" to tell, should we conclude that cinema as a signifying practice does
> not show an aptitude for narrating history?

Guynn 2006, 76

For Guynn, as for many other theorists, the crux of the problem is whether
cinema can do history or not, while, in fact, the crux of the problem lies within
the very conception of cinema as a medium with a "certain destination." As soon
as we go down that road, any answer that we may give is inevitably premised on
the wrong ground. Guynn's answer is positive: Yes, cinema can narrate history.
Just like Ferro before him, however, he cannot accept this capacity unconditionally.
In fact, cinema can do history only if it opens up the diegetic world, allowing
various self-reflexive techniques to signal the act of "enunciation." According to
Guynn, "reflexive strategies should aim to restore to historical film the kind of
complexity that written history requires" and, furthermore, to "reveal the process
by which the historian/filmmaker uses historical knowledge to reconstruct
historical events" (80). Clearly, the paradoxes pile up. On the one hand, this list
of self-reflexive devices contradicts his previous presentation of cinema as a
medium "destined" to record space and time as in real life and whose "genius" lay
on its unique indexicality. On the other hand, and most significantly, one is
struck by the suggestion that cinema should reveal its means of historical
reconstruction. Why would that be necessary? Do written histories do so? Hardly

ever, as Barthes demonstrated in "The Discourse of History," discussed in the previous chapter. Why, then, should cinema be any different? Isn't it supposed to strive to be *like* written history?

Once again, we are confronted with the problem of similarity and difference between written and filmic narratives, which, in most cases, is not addressed head-on and remains lingering under the surface. Guynn's contradictions are emblematic of the conceptual deadlocks traced in both sides of the debate, whether they view cinematic history favorably or not. Among those who defend cinema's right to historying, the degree to which they adhere to medium-specific views considerably determines their evaluation of historical films as well as their expectations from the medium's contribution to historical knowledge. Robert Rosenstone's work is emblematic in this respect. As I showed in my introduction, his writings in the mid–1990s were very solidly premised on the "film is not a book" thesis. As a result, his plea toward the community was to understand cinema's unique vocabulary and to identify separate standards according to which film history should be judged. As he explained in *Visions of the Past*, "historians who wish to give the visual media a chance will have to realize that because of the way the camera works and of the kinds of data that it privileges, history on film will of necessity include all sorts of elements unknown to written history" (Rosenstone 1995, 37). Two decades later, the medium specificity would be toned down, while the correlation of filmic narrative devices with those of written history would be deemed essential, especially in light of Hayden White's poetics of history (Rosenstone 2013, 84–5). In fact, White was spot-on all along. In his classical piece "Historiography and Historiophoty," White defined "historiophoty" in a way that parallels historiography, namely as "the representation of history and our thought about it in visual images and filmic discourse" (White 1988, 1193). Even though the larger part of this article examines Rosenstone and Ian Jarvie's debate on the value of historical representation in the cinema, White consistently emphasizes the affinities between historiography and historiophoty, despite their modal difference.[4] As he observes:

> No history, visual or verbal, "mirrors" all or even the greater part of the events or scenes of which it purports to be an account, and this is true even of the most narrowly restricted "micro-history." Every written history is a product of processes of condensation, displacement, symbolization, and qualification exactly like those used in the production of a filmed representation. It is only the medium that differs, not the way in which messages are produced.
>
> White 1988, 1193

Even though White and Rosenstone are explicitly on the same page, quoting and endorsing each other, White's perspective in these debates is slightly, but I believe significantly, different. White maintains his position as a historian without any explicit desire to enter the realm of cinema and the intrinsic properties of its field. From where he stands, history on paper and history on film seem to share a lot more than professional historians are willing to admit. Evidently, this does not come as a surprise, given that White dedicated his entire career, identifying the formal patterns and the narrative mechanisms through which historians produce history.[5] When it comes to cinema, he instinctively identifies the means of construction in cinematic representation in the same way he had traced them in written historical accounts. Rosenstone, on the other hand, does take a leap into film studies in an ambitious effort to designate a new area of research. Mapping historical film for the first time in academic discourse required, indeed, a more medium-specific view that would focus on cinema's intrinsic properties rather than its shared practices. At our current standpoint, however, both Rosenstone and a film theorist, like myself, can and should shift focus on the latter.

To begin to notice the shared practices between written and filmic historical narratives, I would like to propose to take advantage, once more, of the descriptive and explanatory power of an analogy. In the previous chapter, I dealt in detail with the analogical thinking in Kracauer, Barthes, and Godard's work, illustrating how the comparison between diverse media was able to shed new light on elements that had remained impenetrable for centuries. In addition to their analogies, I would like to suggest a more complex comparison that will bring to the surface important facets of the relation between history on paper and history on screen. My contention is that the relation between written professional history and cinematic history is a prolonged version of the relation between analog and digital cinema, as it developed in film theory over the past couple of decades. The advent of digital technology triggered a series of reactions among film scholars, as it seemed to threaten some of the core values of cinematic theory, urging the community to reconsider a number of long-standing assumptions regarding the nature and role of cinema. It was a healthy response that led to a growing self-awareness and a new approach to mediality and intermediality. As media historians Thorburn and Jenkins observe:

> [...] the introduction of a new technology always seems to provoke thoughtfulness, reflection, and self-examination in the culture seeking to absorb it. Sometimes this self-awareness takes the form of a reassessment of established

media forms, whose basic elements may now achieve a new visibility, may become a source of historical research and renewed theoretical speculation.

Thorburn and Jenkins 2003, 4

The impact of digital filmmaking was so direct and swift that traditional notions of cinema had to be reworked and expanded. In the case of the relation between historiography and cinema, however, the impact seemed less straightforward or even irrelevant. When the cinematic medium was invented, historians did not immediately feel threatened or pressured to justify their own practice in relation to the newcomer. Few of them, as I showed in the opening, did address the emergence of photography but, overall, it did not seem as a development that could affect their discipline. This lack of interaction is not unrelated to the fact that historical films in the first few decades of cinema were unlikely to seem comparable to written historical treatises. Not even Kracauer in the 1960s would compare historical films to written accounts of history.[6] My proposal here is that after more than a century of moving images, it is time we ventured a comparison between historiography and cinema on multiple levels, using as a tool for this endeavor the analogy of analog and digital cinema. The comparison between analog and digital cinema foregrounds the issues that should concern us in the relation between historiography on paper and on film, helping us organize the key areas of our discussion. My presentation of the analogy will center on the five following points: first, the material and technical matters; second, the relation of the medium to external reality; third, the representation as a semiotic construction; fourth, the forms of realism and, finally, the process of fabricating reality.

Starting at the technical level, it seems fairly easy to distinguish between diverse media on grounds of materiality. In analog films, a series of profilmic elements emit a light beam, which is captured on a chemically photosensitive surface. With digital cinema, the creation of an image does not require the real existence of an object but the generation of a numerical matrix that will be transformed into pixels.[7] The difference between celluloid and pixels seems just as stark as the difference between historical books and historical films. They appear to be of an entirely different kind. Yet, when we examine the practices and the forms that these media develop through history, the distance between them begins to shrink. For example, Lev Manovich, an eminent media theorist, has argued that digital cinema has done nothing more than bring center stage a number of cinematic practices that were there all along: animation, early cinema, and experimental films (Manovich 2001). In these three cases, the cinematic image did not strive to create a transparent inscription of a real or staged profilmic reality but to accentuate its graphic and painterly spirit. Despite the initial tendency to consider digital cinema as revolutionary and unique, a careful historical and theoretical scrutiny unearthed a significant genealogy of the digital within the analog cinema. In this light, the technical difference between an analog and digital image is less important than its capacity to develop the same forms and fulfill the same narrative or aesthetic purposes. In the same vein, a historical account written on paper or directed for the screen may vary in terms of their actual materiality but their formal patterns, their historical arguments, or their ideological functions might be the same. Note, for instance, how Ferro identified at least two types of historical films that are transcriptions of written historical analyses, whether they adhere to the dominant ideology or constitute an anti-analysis. Even though he personally aspired for a "truly cinematic" history, he did acknowledge that, for the most part, films merely adapt the historical visions already expressed in the historical books (Ferro 1987). Similarly, Kracauer's account of general history indicates remarkable similarities to fictional cinema, which he dismissed, as we saw in chapter 1, as the "theatrical film" (Kracauer 1967, 181). In his words:

> [...] the general historian will therefore automatically try to make any period of his concern appear as a unity. This calls for adjustments of story content, enabling him to blur the discrepancies between coexistent events and turn the spotlight instead on their mutual affinities. It is almost inevitable that, as a matter of expediency, he should neglect intelligible area sequences over cross-influences of his own invention.
>
> Kracauer 1967, 173

The process of creating temporal or causal unity and creatively handling potential discrepancies or irregularities seems well accommodated in the genre of general history, which to this date remains highly influential. As I was reading about Kracauer's disillusionment with the over-simplifications and the inventiveness of the general historians, I could not help thinking of the standard critiques leveled at the average Hollywood historical drama. As I will demonstrate in greater detail in Part Two of this book, written and filmic histories can plot their narratives and form their arguments in ways that are entirely common. Therefore, if we go through the history and the varieties of academic history and filmic history, we will come across several shared formal, argumentative, and ideological characteristics that override any technical differences between history on paper and history on screen.

The material elements of any medium are connected to the real world in various ways and this complicated relationship comes into focus in the next phase of the analogy. The ties of analog and digital cinema to external reality have been theorized from different angles, which in turn could illuminate the relation of written and filmic history to the historical reality in an intriguing fashion. The stake in the analog/digital debate is this: Is cinema's privileged connection to external reality challenged when we employ digital technology? Are filmic images disconnected from the real world as we generate them in a computer? The answers vary; for realists such as Kracauer and Bazin, jeopardizing the inherent indexicality of the filmic material and its unique reproducing capacity would constitute a major blow to the medium's essential identity. The same realist tendency is found in historical studies. Practitioners of the Reconstructionist and Constructionist tradition,[8] who constitute the vast majority of academic historians, cling to the idea of an objective reconstruction of the past via written discourse (Munslow 2015). Just as an analog filmstrip records a part of the external reality, a written account by a trained historian forms an indexical relation to the historical past.[9] This, in a nutshell, was Kracauer's analogy between photographic media and history discussed in the previous chapter. If we add the digital cinema in the comparison, we can expand it to include a second "clause," namely the parallel digital cinema/historical film. In terms of ontology, digital images lack a natural tie to external reality and consist entirely of a numerical code. Even images captured in an analog mode become algorithms as soon as they enter the environment of the computer and, from then on, they can be easily composited, animated and manipulated in infinite ways. This technical "independence" of the digital has been aptly theorized by Friedrich Kittler and Yvonne Spielmann, as one of the unique features of digitality, in contrast to analog media[10] (Kittler 1989; Spielmann 1999). As the digital engulfs the analog (the opposite is not possible), it simulates the latter's affirmative function while it can perform a negative one as well. Instead of showing something that actually existed, the digital simulates its presence, thus "performing" an affirmation, while it can also simulate something that does not exist, thus "performing" a negation. In historical films, everything is a simulation, too. The historical film does not have a natural affirmative power since the past is gone; it is not a possibility for a film of any genre, whether fiction or documentary, to directly record a historical situation.[11] But like digital images, a historical narrative on film can simulate; it can perform both an affirmation and a negation, representing things that may or may not have existed. And there precisely lies the profound skepticism toward both digital images and historical films. Traditional realists of history and analog cinema remain devoted to the romantic idea that only written history and celluloid maintain a privileged access to the external world. Digital images and historical representations on film are not in a position to salvage what is true and authentic about the (historical) reality.

Yet, the analogy is complicated as we move from the realists to the deconstructionists, who switch the discussion from ontology to semiotics. In this line of thought, neither analog cinema nor written accounts have access to reality but they can function as semiotic constructions. This means that analog images are signs whose referents are necessarily absent just as those of written histories, as Barthes plainly demonstrated in his writings on the "reality effect." In both cases, however, the "reality effect" is powerful; it steps in to create the illusion of presence of the referent in the place of the signified. In the cinema, the illusion rests primarily on mechanical reproduction, while in written history on the superfluous multiplication of the signs that generate an impression of reality (Barthes 1986). Neither of them holds an actual relation to *res gestae*, despite claims to the opposite.[12] What appears to be a "re-presentation" of reality is, in fact, nothing but another type of construction analogous to those found in digital images or historical films. As a result, the recasting of representation as an always already simulation, allows us to considerably bridge the gap between the two parts of the analogy, i.e., analog cinema/written history and digital cinema/filmic history. In all four cases, the representation is a code that simulates the presence of an absence. This code may be constructed by different technical means (celluloid, words, pixels) but the performance is actually the same. They all strive to indicate a certain connection with the world by simulating presence. In this light, the concept of indexicality, which is crucial for realist film theorists, still pertains. As Martin Lefebvre and Marc Furstenau's note:

> Like paintings, CGI visuals are less directly connected to the pictured object than traditional photographs. Yet the computer-generated Roman coliseum of *Gladiator*, ship and waves of *Titanic*, storm of *The Perfect Storm*, or tornadoes of *Twister*, are all necessarily indexical of Reality in an unlimited number of ways, *including* in their connections to the existing coliseum, the Titanic, waves and tornadoes.
>
> Lefebvre and Furstenau 2002, 99; emphasis in the original

Defining indexicality simply as "how signs indicate what it is they are about," (97) Lefebvre and Furstenau relieve us of any modal concerns and help us focus on the rich variety of signifying practices that develop within each medium to ascertain its connection to the real world. In terms of our analogy, the continuities between analog and digital indexicality in the cinema can reveal the continuities in the indexical relation that both written and filmic histories attempt to form with the past. Whether on paper or on film, historical discourse is a signifying practice that cannot claim a direct contact or an ontological relation to the things past but it can create meaning through a semiotic system. Since both letters and images simulate a certain connection with external reality, then what should interest us is the ways in which this connection is generated and performed. Thus, our focus begins to switch from the broad concept of reality to that of realism, which is contingent upon specific stylistic and aesthetic choices.

Realism is a set of conventions that determine how and why a sign appears to be truthful and authentic. Like all conventions, too, realism is "infinitely corruptible through repetition" (Elsaesser 1972, 4). The history of cinema is illustrative of how diverse cinematic traditions across time and space developed different realistic approaches, ranging from Hollywood's classical realism to Soviet social realism, Italian neorealism, British kitchen-sink realism and, even what I coined as hypermediated realism in post-classical World cinema (Thanouli 2009a). In all these cases, the purpose was similar—to convey an aspect of real experience—while the means differed. The advent of digital technology did not significantly alter the realistic conventions in filmmaking, as many would have expected. Digital techniques deployed in Hollywood were primarily set at the service of the classical realist conventions that rely on a seamless representation of the story, emulating the classical Bazinian notion of the frame as a "window to the world" (Thanouli 2013a). The passage from analog to digital realism did not bring about any ground-breaking changes in the forms and shapes of the films because the digital immediately simulated the dominant analog practices. Similarly, the majority of historical films did not question the dominant Reconstructionist approach in historical writing. As Robert Berkhofer writes:

> [...] the normal historian's job is to make it appear *as though* the structure of factuality itself had determined the organizational structure of his or her account. The narrative organization, no matter what its mode or message, usually (re)presents its subject matter, in turn, as the natural order of things, which is the illusion of realism.
>
> Berkhofer 1997, 147; emphasis in the original

Just as most Reconstructionist histories purport to tell us about the past "as it really happened," the majority of historical films represent the past, using narrative and stylistic devices that efface the traces of their construction.[13] The dominance and the perseverance of the desire for realism is equally manifest in written and filmic histories, which strive to represent a solid, well-organized, and multiply-motivated historical world, effacing the role of the author and the expressive strategies entailed in the process of narration. In fact, the realist strategies are so similar that contemporary theorists of history, such as Alun Munslow, rely on specialized cinematic terminology to unveil the techniques of the historians. The following passage from *The Future of History* (2010) is quite revealing:

> Conventionally, then, the author-historian adopts what is usually referred to as zero-focalisation in which the past seems to explain itself. [...] In much the same way as filmmakers operate, shifts in focalization can and are readily made, seen and can be understood through their narrative artifice. Often, when viewing films we initially float above the scene seeing it in its entirety. This is contextualization. The same applies to written histories. Sooner or later the perspective shifts (in both the film and the history) as the author-historian focalizes down upon one agent revealing (like a camera) that agent's sense of what is happening to them and about them.
>
> Munslow 2010, 159

Throughout this book, Munslow regularly resorts to terms and concepts from narratology and film theory to explain how traditional history works. What is important to clarify, however—so that we do not slide into medium-specificity again—is that what Munslow describes as "cinema" is nothing more than a very particular case of cinema, namely the classical Hollywood narration. Classical narration, as I will extensively demonstrate in subsequent chapters, is a complex system of narrative and stylistic devices with a very specific historical presence and development. The strategy to maintain zero-focalization and efface the signs of storytelling is not inherent in the cinematic medium; rather, it amounts to a prevalent notion of classical realism that was established for a series of technical, economic, and ideological purposes in a particular moment in space and time. The same holds true for Reconstructionist history. It is a mode of historying that follows certain procedures and complies with a number of professional rules, which became dominant by convention.[14] What the analogy shows us is that the dominant notion of realism following the logic of "immediacy,"[15] i.e., the effacement of the signs of representation, persists both in the cinema and the historical practice, despite the passage from one modality to another.

Finally, even when we acknowledge that an analog image shares several characteristics with its digital counterpart, there still lingers the feeling that we can trust the former more. In other words, the fear that the digital is likely to lie and deceive is very powerful. By analogy, we are more inclined to believe that an average historical film distorts historical reality in more blatant ways than a published historical treatise. Again, technically, such an allocation of trust cannot be easily vindicated. In analog cinema, the creative treatment of reality was available to filmmakers from the start, as matte shots and superimpositions allowed them to manipulate the film shots in much the same ways as a computer manipulates the digital ones. Moreover, the inventive potential of filmmaking was expanded to the staging, framing, and editing techniques where the careful arrangement and the organization of the shots were independent of the filmic material. As Thomas Elsaesser has shown in his article "Louis Lumière—the cinema's first virtualist," Lumière's single shot, single-scene films made with a static camera were the product of extremely meticulous deliberation and planning (Elsaesser 1998a). Similarly, documentary theorists no longer ascribe to nonfiction filmmaking a privileged ontological relation to external reality, as they identified the numerous ways in which analog filmic images lie or distort the truth about their subjects (Nichols 1991; Renov 1993). Despite our growing awareness, however, of fake analog imagery and duplicitous non-fiction films, we are considerably more distrustful toward digital images and their special effects. Correspondingly, the average historical book is unlikely to be met with the same distrust and criticism as a historical film of any kind, whether a Hollywood drama or a documentary. Historical books are presumed innocent whereas historical films are those bearing the burden of proof. Such discrepancy is not justified on material or professional grounds. Cases of historical works containing distortions, which range from statistical misrepresentations to outright lies, have been numerous. Despite the rigorous academic publishing standards in the historical profession, the lining up of expert referees, and the meticulous double-checking, historians have managed to publish false accounts and reap awards and accolades (Hoffer 2004; 2008). The fact that some of these have been uncovered and their prizes have been rescinded has not shaken the wider trust in the historian's profession. This is a deeply ingrained societal attitude that is almost entirely unrelated to the material characteristics or formal capacities of each medium. With respect to the analog/digital division, Elsaesser was insightful to note:

The question of truth arising from the photographic and post-photographic would thus not divide along the lines of the trace and the indexical at all, but rather flow from a complex set of discursive conventions, political changes and institutional claims which safeguard (or suspend) what we might call the 'trust' or 'good faith' we are prepared to invest in a given regime of representation.

                                                              Elsaesser 1998b, 208

This statement shifts our attention toward the importance of the cultural and institutional elements, which determine how we perceive and interpret cinematic signs. It takes the focus away from medium specificity and redirects it to the extra-textual context in which a film or a book communicates its message. Thus, any discussion of history becomes moot, unless it factors in, along with the discursive elements, all those non-discursive conditions that determine its production, dissemination and interpretation. However, before continuing the tale of history and cinema at that level, I would like to recapitulate my discussion of the medium specificity thesis and the analog/digital analogy, presenting my key points in the following schema (Table 2.1).

The table illustrates the continuities between diverse modalities and complicates the long-lasting dichotomies between the two types of cinema and history.

Table 2.1

	Analog cinema	**Digital cinema**	**Written history**	**Filmic history**
Material elements	Celluloid	Pixels	Words	Images
Forms and practices	Photographic and Graphic/ painterly images	Photographic and Graphic/ painterly images	Narrative, Argumentative, and Ideological mechanisms	Narrative, Argumentative, and Ideological mechanisms
Relation to reality (The Realist Approach)	Ontological ties to external Reality	Simulation of Reality	Epistemological ties to historical Reality	Simulation of Reality
Relation to reality (The Deconstructionist Approach)	Representation and simulation of Reality	Representation and simulation of Reality	Representation and simulation of Reality	Representation and simulation of Reality
Realism as dominant trend	Immediacy	Immediacy	Immediacy	Immediacy
Malleability	Yes	Yes	Yes	Yes

Still, the difficult question remains: Should we behave as if they were the same thing? Is analog cinema the same as the digital, since they are both roughly capable of taking the same forms? By analogy, is filmic history the same as written historical accounts, since they are both mere representations of a past long gone? The answer cannot be an unconditional yes or no. The decision to treat two different objects as similar or different hides deeply ingrained philosophical assumptions that I will attempt to unravel in the subsequent chapters. Here, I would like to draw on the digital metaphor once again in order to formulate by central hypothesis. Notice how Maureen Turim handles the relation of the analog and the digital in the following statement: "Digital artmaking has magnified, multiplied, and intensified the codes of analogy" (Turim 1999, 51). In a similar vein, I would like to argue that history on film is a magnified miniature of history on paper. This means that filmic histories magnify, multiply, and intensify all the key traits of academic written history. In a two-hour long historical film, whether fiction or documentary, the filmmaker and his or her collaborators act as historians;[16] they identify, select, and organize the historical facts before they figure out a way to present them using certain narrative formulas. Yet, the process of fact determination and selection as well as the narrative construction becomes more easily discernible in a film. Furthermore, as I will demonstrate in great detail in Part Two, the act of narration in a film applies specific plot patterns onto historical events, producing explanations about the meaning of history, just like any written historical work. Except for the fact that the latter is able to conceal it. The same holds true regarding fabrication. All histories contain distortions but filmic distortions are easier to pinpoint and condemn, just as digital fabrications are easily spotted and criticized.[17] As a result, filmic histories seem to raise our awareness regarding the means of construction of historical discourse and help us realize in retrospect several facets of professional history writing. They act as a magnifying glass that allows us to observe the workings of historical imagination that existed in other modes of historying all along. In this light, filmic history remediates written history and, in that process, it allows certain features of the latter to come forward and acquire a certain visibility that was not possible before.[18]

The magnifying glass of filmic history probes us to consider the problem of similarity and difference not only in relation to the forms and shapes of history but also with regard to the institutional conditions and philosophical assumptions underlying the historical practice. To return to Elsaesser's argument, we should ask why is it that our trust in historical books is safeguarded, while our trust in historical films is suspended? A preliminary answer can be found in Michel Foucault's work and his notion of the "regime of truth" of a given society. As he argues:

> Each society has its regime of truth, its "general politics" of truth: that is, the types of discourse which it accepts and makes function as true; the mechanisms and instances which enable one to distinguish true and false statements, the means by which each is sanctioned; the techniques and procedures accorded value in the acquisition of truth; the status of those who are charged with saying what counts as true.
>
> Foucault 1991a, 73

According to our current regime of truth, the position of written history compared to its audiovisual counterpart is (still) significantly different. We do not take written history more seriously because it is conceptually and materially different from historical films but because, in our society, it is professional historians who are charged with saying what counts as true history and not filmmakers or anyone else. This has not always been the case, however, nor will it surely be in the near future. To begin to understand how our regime of truth determines our divergent attitudes toward history on paper and history on screen, we need to take a longer and closer look into the wider institutional and philosophical matters that relate to the practice of history.

Notes

1   For a different reading of Kracauer's approach to cinema's ties to reality, see chapter one.

2   According to Gaudreault, the concept of the "cultural series" seeks to include forms of signification and cultural practices that are identified by the scholar as belonging together. The role of the scholar is purposefully highlighted in the process of constructing a cultural series, containing thus the danger of media essentialism. See Gaudreault and Marion (2012, 10).

3   Guynn mostly examines the concepts of these linguists through Francis Vanoye's work *Récit écrit, récit filmique* (2005).

4   Note how Guynn interprets White's position incorrectly in the following passage: "Moreover, the image is not just another source of historical information; it can constitute 'a discourse in its own right,' with modes of representation that are fundamentally different from those of written language. White suggests that visual representations of history have their own genius, particularly in the realms of

'landscape, scene, atmosphere, complex events such as wars, battles, crowds, and emotions'. Such representations are not only more verisimilar, he contends, but also more accurate" (2006, 68).

5   Hayden White's poetics of history will come center stage in Part Two.

6   His comparison between historiography and cinema was not related to issues of representation but focused only on the process of recording external reality. See chapter 1.

7   For a more detailed comparison of analog and digital cinema, see Thanouli (2013a).

8   As Munslow notes, despite their differences, "what unites Reconstructionist and Constructionist epistemic genres is a shared belief in practical realism and representationalism" (2015, 162). See more in the conclusion.

9   Philip Rosen explains how professional historians built this myth of indexicality. As he writes, "Documents, remains, survivals, ruins and edifices—in short, indexical traces that attest to a past by emerging into the present from it—achieved a kind of epistemological prestige in an era of intensifying time consciousness. This privilege surely contributed to the credibility of historians, who thought they were formulating a master discipline, and they in turn fortified that privilege" (2001, 115).

10 Kittler and Spielmann identify a third type of image, the electronic, that stands between the analog and the digital. Whereas the electronic is analog in principle, it prefigures several qualities of the digital (Spielmann 1999; Kittler 2010).

11 See the section on observational documentaries and the discussion of Arthur Danto's view of the "Ideal Chronicler" in chapter 6.

12 For a detailed discussion of the realist representation theories of cinema, see Carroll (1996c, 37–48).

13 The majority of historical fiction films and historical documentaries avoid self-reflexive techniques that draw attention to the process of their construction. See chapters 5 and 6.

14 For more on the diverse traditions in professional historiography, see the conclusion.

15 For immediacy and hypermediacy as two representational logics, see Bolter and Grusin (1999).

16 The difficulty of attributing sole agency to the filmmaker in historical cinema and the implications of this difficulty both at the formal and the institutional level are discussed at various points in all the subsequent chapters.

17 Again, the fact that image manipulation is technically faster and easier in digital technology renders it immediately suspicious. The digital needs to prove it is truthful, as if it were presumed guilty to begin with.

18 Notice how Godard used the newer technology of video to re-accommodate his experience with cinema. As he noted, "Video taught me to see cinema and to rethink the working of cinema in another way" (cited in Temple and Williams 2000, 13).

The Theory and Practice of History

For this invention [writing] will produce forgetfulness in the minds of those who learn to use it, because they will not practice their memory. Their trust in writing, produced by external characters which are no part of themselves, will discourage the use of their own memory within them.

Plato 1925, 275a

The trust in the written word as a reliable source of knowledge has not always been so powerful. In Socrates' words above, as they were expressed in Plato's *Phaedrus*, we witness the familiar resistance of people toward innovation and change. Socrates argues that writing offers only "the appearance of wisdom," whereas "true wisdom" requires instruction combined with personal involvement and interaction. Each epoch, as Foucault reminded us in the previous chapter, has had its own regime of truth and it has accorded value to different techniques and procedures for its acquisition, as the case of Socrates seems to indicate. From our current standpoint, such rejection of writing sounds preposterous. The written word bears for us an inherent element of consistency and permanence that renders it an ideal medium for the practice of history. Besides, in spite of its volatile meaning, history goes hand-in-hand with writing. As Donald R. Kelley notes, "history has continued, as it began, as a sort of inquiry and judgment requiring written form" (1991, 497). In this chapter, I would like to present a concise overview of the long and turbulent path of written historiography to help the reader grasp the complexity and the historicity of the term "history."[1] As we go through the discrepancies between the philosophy and practice of history in the course of the last three centuries, we will be able to realize that considering filmic history as a legitimate mode of historying in the twenty-first century is an idea that fits in well with the current regime of knowledge in Western societies.

Kelley's volume *Versions of History: From the Antiquity to the Enlightenment* presents a comprehensive outline of the diverse takes on history over an enormous time span of almost twenty-four centuries, illustrating how the history of history can problematize at least three key issues; first, the definition of history, secondly, the concept of "new history" and, finally, the idea of progress in historiography. According to Kelley, since the time of Herodotus, history has been construed in significantly diverse ways,[2] including the following: as synonymous to the past itself, as a form of literary expression (rhetoric, biography, prose), as a body of data (chronicles), as a method of inquiry, as a process of change or as an interpretation of this process (evolutionary, cyclical, random), and even as a "philosophy of life" (3). This list of incongruous items that have, at various times, qualified as "history" is at odds with the currently dominant notion of academic history that I have been discussing so far in this book and that has guided the entire debate on the distinction between written and audiovisual history. Most historians and film scholars who have argued either for or against history on screen have determined their attitude, having a very specific and narrow definition of history, shaped by the dominant trends in historiography in the nineteenth and twentieth century. The characteristics of this particular definition will be discussed shortly, but what I would like to emphasize at this point is that whatever definition we decide to work with or against, we need to be aware of its particular place and time in the backdrop of an extremely long and bifurcating path of historical thought.

Furthermore, Kelley's account is noteworthy for his emphasis on the continuities of historical writing, identifying a series of recurring questions, problems, and tendencies that render each attempt at a "new history" historically oblivious. The more he delves into the works of writers from diverse epochs the more he realizes the persistence of certain issues that contemporary historians mistakenly consider as new. As he puts it, "the chronic and unseemly claims of historians to an unending series of new histories suggest that not only social scientists but even historians, who presumably should know better, are victims of that scholarly amnesia detected by Pitirim Sorokin, which leads them to pose as 'new Columbuses' [...]" (14). In light of this rich tradition of historical thinking, cinematic history can easily qualify as a different mode of history that, nonetheless, is capable of carrying on the same processes, questions, and concerns as those expressed in written form. As I previously tried to demonstrate through the analogy of the digital, tracing continuities and common practices always requires a good knowledge of history, at least in the sense of a "body of data," as well as an eye for patterns and processes that override any differences at the technical or modal level.

The caution toward claims of "newness" is not unrelated to an underlying suspicion toward the idea of progress itself. When scholars advocate for a new perspective or a "new history" altogether, they implicitly argue for a progressive view on the course of history, one that purportedly solves the problems of previous histories and offers an improved take on the matters in hand. Scholars in historical studies, including practicing historians and philosophers of history, are deeply divided on this idea of progress in historiography as in so many other issues.[3] Kelley's extensive research in historical writing from antiquity to the Enlightenment does not corroborate any clear direction of any kind, much less any substantial progress in the conceptual value of historical thinking. As he writes:

> In many ways, then, the history of history does not exhibit a pattern of growing enlightenment and utility, whether because historians are by nature backward looking or because they are concerned with more fundamental aspects of the human condition. In fact it might be more fairly represented as a series of unending debates on topics of enduring, or at least recurrent, interest.
>
> Kelley 1991, 4

The same lack of linear progress is attested in the historiography from the Enlightenment onwards, as Hayden White points out in his dense overview of the historical consciousness in the nineteenth century presented in *Metahistory*. In this case, however, White attempts to identify a certain pattern that appears to be more cyclical than linear. As he notes, "the history of nineteenth-century historical thinking can be said to describe a full circle, from a rebellion against the Ironic historical vision of the late Enlightenment to the return to prominence of a similar Ironic vision on the eve of the twentieth century" (2014, 432). And from then on, as White notes, the same logic persists; the vast part of historical thought in the twentieth century is concerned to "overcome the condition of Irony into which historical consciousness was plunged at the end of nineteenth century" (434). Despite the dubious regularity, according to which historical consciousness makes a certain circle every 100 years, White's explanations about the recurrently changing streams of historical thought are worth a closer look.

As the quotes suggest, the circles end in irony. But what does irony mean in historical thought? White's elaborate argument is constructed on the basis of four concepts called "tropes" that include the following: metaphor, metonymy, synecdoche and irony.[4] The first three rhetorical figures have been employed in historical writing to express some sort of realism, as their relation to the things depicted is considered more direct, natural, and straightforward. Irony, on the other hand, is their self-conscious counterpart. It is employed to problematize the notion of realism and the possibility of any direct, natural, or straightforward connection between words and things. In White's phrasing, irony is "a model of the linguistic protocol in which skepticism in thought and relativism in ethics are conventionally expressed" (37). In light of these explications, White's historiographical pattern means that historical thought in the nineteenth century reacted to the ironical approach of the Enlighteners (Kant, Hume, Gibbon) who were skeptical of previous types of history, such as the ecclesiastical history, the antiquarian history, and the so-called "*historiographie galante*," which openly mixed facts and fiction. The Enlighteners chose irony to address the shortcomings of earlier historical attempts and combined their faith in rationality with an awareness of its limitations. As a reaction to this critical and somewhat pessimistic perspective, White argues, historians in the nineteenth century sought to delineate and entrench their work in ways that led to the professionalization of historical writing, which we so much take for granted today.

To get an idea of how a certain activity, such as historical writing, leaves the hands of amateurs and becomes a profession in academia, we need to look at the emergence of the institutions that construed it as a discipline.[5] The first step was to inaugurate university chairs and establish societies for the publication of historical documents. Although some form of history was taught at the propaedeutic level at various universities as part of the curriculum of the faculty of theology or law, the first appearance of history as a discipline in the modern sense was at the University of Gottingen in the second half of the eighteenth century (Ziolkowski 2004, 20). Others soon followed. Indicatively, the first Chair of History at the University of Berlin was founded in 1810 and at the Sorbonne two years later (White 2014, 135). In England, things progressed at a slower pace, as Oxford formed the first Professorship of History in 1866 and Cambridge in 1869. In the meantime, academic journals specializing in the advancement of historical studies appeared, such as the *Historische Zeitschrift* (1859), the *Revue Historique* (1876), the *English Historical Review* (1886), and the *American Historical Review* (1895). Through such organizations and practices the study of history was canonized, academic criteria and standards were set, and the familiar processes of inclusion and exclusion in terms of knowledge and power were determined. As White points out:

> The professorate formed a clerisy for the promotion and cultivation of a socially responsible historiography; it trained and licensed apprentices, maintained standards of excellence, ran the organs of intraprofessional communication, and in general enjoyed a privileged place in the humanistic and social scientific sectors of the universities.
>
> White 2014, 136

The disciplinization process and the ensuing power play is one side of White's observation, which I will address later on. The other side, however, is the designated place of history in relation to the humanities and social sciences, which opens up one the most controversial issues in the historical debates. The question is: What kind of discipline should history be? How does it relate to other established areas, such as art, philosophy and science? Again, the demarcations are far from clear and definitive, as history's hybrid nature constitutes one of those enduring and recurrent conundrums across the centuries. The professionalization of historical studies in the nineteenth century did not lead, as one would expect, to a universally accepted research methodology that would allocate historical writing a distinct space outside art, science and philosophy.[6] Part of the difficulty, admittedly, lies on the multiple and shifting definitions of these concepts. Again, a passage from White is illuminating:

> The main line in historiographical work in the nineteenth century stressed the historian's dependence upon principles that were scientific, philosophical, and artistic, all at the same time. But history's claim to the status of an autonomous discipline, with its own aims, methods, and subject matter, depended in large part upon the conviction that the scientific, philosophical and artistic elements within it were not those of the science, philosophy and art of the early nineteenth century, the period in which a "true" historiography was presumed to have first taken shape.
>
> White 2014, 268

The problem of definition is obvious. A true historiography of the nineteenth century could borrow from art, science, and philosophy as long as the artistic elements were not Romantic, the scientific were not Positivist, and the philosophical were not Idealist. Of course, White's own categories are schematic, as not all nineteenth century art was Romantic, nor all science Positivistic, nor all philosophy Idealistic. They serve as yardsticks in an enormously diverse and disorienting terrain of discourse, but the impossibility of coining one stable definition of art, science, and philosophy persists. To the extent that the definition of history and its boundaries remains contingent upon the forms and practices of art, science, and philosophy, the entire discussion is bound to sink in conceptual quicksand.

As a result, the problem would not resolve in the twentieth century; in fact, it would become even graver.[7] Of the long and laborious debates on history in that century, I would like to briefly engage with the writings of two British scholars, Isaiah Berlin and E.H. Carr, from the early 1960s. What I find intriguing in their accounts is the manner in which they handle the concept of science in relation to history in order to reach the exact opposite conclusions. Even though historians have not elevated their disagreement to the status of a "historians' controversy," such as the famous Carr-Elton debate,[8] as a non-historian myself I find it worthwhile to discuss their ostensibly divergent views on the history-science affinities.[9] Berlin's work "History and Theory: The Concept of Scientific History" is of highly symbolic value. It opened, in 1960, the very first volume of *History and Theory*, a journal that signaled a turning point in the theory of historiography. In his thirty-page-long article, Berlin explores the arguments of scientific history, as presented in works by Henry Thomas Buckle, Hippolyte Taine, August Comte, and even Karl Marx, in order to debunk them, one by one, and bring out, instead, the unique and peculiar characteristics of historical studies. First and foremost, according to Berlin, history differs from natural sciences in terms of method. The latter are distinguished by their systematization of knowledge, the formulation of general laws, and abstract models by which future predictions are possible. Moreover, they are theory-bound, as they construct general propositions out of specific causal and functional correlations. Finally, the natural scientist is an external observer who notes "as carefully and dispassionately as he can" the empirical phenomena (Berlin 1960, 22). Which of all these, asks Berlin, holds true for history? Hardly any, he responds. Despite the hard work of thinkers such as those mentioned above, the aspiration to model historical knowledge upon the knowledge of the natural world was doomed to fail. In his words:

> All seemed ready, particularly in the nineteenth century, for the formulation of this new, powerful, and illuminating discipline, which would do away with the chaotic accumulation of facts, conjectures, and rules of thumb that had been treated with such disdain by Descartes and his scientifically-minded successors. The stage was set, but virtually nothing materialized. No general laws were formulated—nor even moderately reliable maxims—from which historians could deduce (together with knowledge of the initial conditions) either what would happen next, or what had happened in the past.
>
> Berlin 1960, 6–7

And yet, Berlin welcomes this failure; he argues that history differs from natural sciences not only in method but also in purpose. The historian has to work with the thick material of life as a whole and his facts, as a result, are "too many, too minute, too fleeting, too blurred at the edges" (14). But that is the beauty and the essence of history, namely to present the diversity of human life and activity on many levels and from many different perspectives. To construe the discipline of history as a natural science is a chimera, Berlin notes, that denotes the "lack of understanding of the nature of natural science, or of history, or of both" (31).

About a year after the publication of Berlin's article, the prominent British historian E.H. Carr delivered a series of lectures at the University of Cambridge, which would be published under the title *What is History?* a publication that has remained highly influential within the historical profession for decades. In one of these lectures, Carr discusses the relation between history and science, arguing for a close affinity between the two, despite the fact that the scientism of the nineteenth century had become démodé in the twentieth. According to Carr, J.B. Bury's famous, if derided by then, quote from 1903 that history is "a science, no more and no less" may actually turn out to be right after all, though for the wrong reasons (Carr 1987, 56). And the key reason that history may continue to pass as science is because science in the twentieth century has lost its crude empiricist character and has adopted a new purpose. Scientific knowledge no longer aims at constructing stringent and comprehensive natural laws but rather at verifying or not certain hypotheses. This change of scope in scientific objectives allows us to carry on the analogies between history and science at least in five areas; first, their capacity to connect the unique and the general; secondly, their ability to "teach lessons;" thirdly, their power of prediction; fourthly, their handling of subjectivity and objectivity issues with regard to the role of the scientist/historian; and, finally, their compatibility with religion and morality. On each of these counts, Carr finds substantial similarities and invites history to become more scientific by meeting higher standards and demands. At the same time, he advocates the bridging of science and history by promoting the history and philosophy of science (86), a branch that would, indeed, flourish in the years to come and would reconfigure the long-standing dichotomy between nature and culture in many intriguing ways.[10]

Despite their temporal and cultural proximity, the distance that separates Berlin and Carr on the topic of history and science is indicative of the impossibility to settle any account on the nature of history, while, at the same time, it illustrates the pressure to keep on trying. This effort to understand the workings of history led, from the 1960s onwards, to a more systematic and reflexive inquiry into the conceptual foundations of historical thought, inaugurating what has been labeled as "the critical philosophy of history." The philosophical questions had already been posed by the Enlighteners and other leading philosophers of the nineteenth century (Vico, Hegel, Dilthey) but the self-conscious and methodical pursuit of answers began in the 1960s, with the launching of *Theory and History* in 1960 acting as a milestone (Dray 2006, 747). This intensive engagement with the tools and concepts of historical studies led to a growing disenchantment with history's capacity to reveal the past and intensified the voices of Irony, in White's sense. In fact, White's own work, *Metahistory*, was written in the ironic mode, too, stirring up enormous criticism for the ways it challenged the realistic approaches to historiography. Around the same time, in France, the writings of Foucault and Barthes, among others, problematized the ways in which language mediates our contact with the external world, contributing to the so-called "linguistic turn."[11] As our discussion of Barthes in chapter one indicated, the concern with language's ability to communicate historical reality brought to the surface the difficulty of proving how objectivity and truth are accomplished in historical descriptions. It also brought to the surface the other perennial topic in historiography, namely the relation of history and art. Even though historians never really excluded the infiltration of artistic elements in historical accounts, their talk of art was always rather loose and commonsensical. With the employment of linguistics, however, the ties between historical and literary accounts were systematically registered rendering it impossible to differentiate fact from fiction at the linguistic level.[12] As the queries accumulated and the capacity of historical narratives to guarantee their unique access to knowledge diminished, the field was ready to consider other types of history as potentially meaningful. In this context, the appearance in the early 1980s of Warren Susman's article on film and history, with which I opened my introduction, and particularly his appeal to Vico's *New Science*, make a whole different sense now. The new effort of academic historians to include films as objects of study rightfully sought for intellectual support in the writings of philosophers who had challenged the Cartesian logic and problematized the notion of truth all along. Even though these preliminary attempts were far from accrediting filmic history with the same status as its written counterpart, as I extensively argued, they are indicative of a gradual, if extremely slow-paced, change in the historian's profession. In fact, throughout the 1990s and the 2000s, historical films increasingly stirred discussions around the problems of representation, causing a number of concepts of film theory, such as focalization, voice and authorship to emigrate to the theory of history.[13] As the dialogue between film theory and the theory of history progresses—and my book certainly aims at contributing to this direction—then the relationship between history and art will need to be redefined, yet again, in the beginning of the twenty-first century.

In view of these historiographical developments, to argue that filmic history can function as a legitimate mode of historying in our society becomes more and more justifiable. The professionalization of history and the sway of academic historical writing may continue to define our standard notion of history but there are also signs of significant philosophical and ideological changes under way. The changes will not only come from the side of history; they also have to come from the side of cinema. Therefore, I would like to take a closer look at the development of historical filmmaking in Hollywood in order to underline a series of institutional parameters that shape the relation between filmmakers and historians. Of course, Hollywood is not the only place where historical films are made; it is, however, the creative environment, which offers the best documentation of its practices, and it is a production system characterized by stability and consistency in its methods. Historical filmmaking in Hollywood has a history almost as long as cinema itself. Looking into the complicated relation of filmmaking practices with traditional history will allow us to understand the fascinating interactions between two media and two practices that began to increasingly feed off each other throughout the twentieth century.

Hollywood and historical filmmaking

Imagine a public library of the near future, for instance. There will be long rows of boxes or pillars, properly classified and indexed, of course. At each box a push button and for each box a seat. Suppose you wish to "read up" on a certain episode in Napoleon's life. Instead of consulting all the authorities, wading laboriously through a host of books, and ending bewildered, without a clear idea of exactly what did happen and confused at every point by conflicting opinions about what did happen, you will merely seat yourself at a properly adjusted window, in a scientifically prepared room, press the button and actually see what happened. There will be no opinions expressed. You will merely be present at the making of history. All the work of writing, revising, collating, and reproducing will have been carefully attended to by a corps of recognized experts, and you will have received a vivid and complete expression.

D.W. Griffith 1915 (cited in Edidin 2005)

D.W. Griffith's often quoted vision of cinematic history expressed in these lines is emblematically scientific. It is rife with all those assumptions that approach history as an ideal form. On the contrary, academic history is rejected as too fragmented, too relativistic, and too confusing. How ironic, no doubt, to argue that cinema will be the one to finally realize Leopold von Ranke's dream of showing the things of the past "*wie es eigentlich gewesen.*"[14] In this fantasy, the filmic images will be projected in a "scientifically prepared environment" and they will provide the viewer with a front-row seat to the spectacle of history. It would not take very long before academic historians would turn to cinema in an effort to tentatively fulfill his prophecy. The Yale project called *The Chronicles of America Photoplays* made in the early 1920s is illustrative in this regard. A team of Yale scholars collaborated with eminent US historians to adapt for the screen a series of best-selling books on American history, starting from Columbus all the way to Woodrow Wilson (Mattheisen 1992). Initially, the plan was to adapt fifty volumes of scholarly work into forty educational films, but then the number was scaled down to thirty-three, of which only fifteen were actually filmed. This radical change in the planning of the photoplays was concomitant with the enormous difficulties awaiting the collaborators as soon as they entered the production phase. Forcing the written pages to transform into filmic images turned out to be a formidable task, which not only led to soaring costs[15] but also to widespread disappointment among all parties involved. Academics saw themselves as "beleaguered champions of historical and educational values in the shoddy and ignorant milieu of commercial filmmaking" (633), while both the regular audience and the educational staff were left unimpressed by the result. The photoplays were not merely an economic flop but, primarily, a historic example of an artistic and pedagogic failure. They demonstrated how a new medium could not be forced to emulate the workings of another in their entirety and neither could it be shaped according to a fixed and predetermined agenda. What it could do, though, is selectively remediate older forms and practices in new and invigorating ways. Indeed, cinema could and would "do history" for the century to come in multiple shapes and forms, reconfiguring several of the principles of academic written history, and particularly the emphasis on primary research and the penchant for referential detail.

The case of historical Hollywood films in the 1930s is another significant point in history for the ways in which an otherwise mainstream entertainment industry embraced the need to express historical thought in filmic images. The groundbreaking study of Jennifer E. Smyth entitled *Reconstructing American Historical Cinema: From Cimarron to Citizen Kane* (2006) makes a compelling argument in favor of a historical filmmaking in Classical Hollywood.[16] After singling out D.W. Griffith as the most prominent and vocal supporter of "historiophoty"[17] during cinema's first steps, Smyth notes that the advent of sound transformed the historical film from an occasional expensive indulgence into "the industry's most innovative, prestigious, and controversial form of feature filmmaking" (Smyth 2006, 6). Typical of Hollywood's professionalism was the inauguration of a systematic and collective effort to address historical matters based on extensive research, meticulous treatment of original and adapted screenplays, collaboration with academic historians, and specific publicity strategies to stir critical attention. Studios would not become academic departments but the research entailed in the preparation of a historical feature clearly resembled the work of traditional historians. As Smyth details:

> When preparing to write a script about American history, screenwriters compiled and consulted a bibliography, not just past film successes. Researchers traveled to national libraries; publicity agents worked with local families and museums. Hollywood's relationship with American historical filmmaking took film production outside the studios.
>
> Smyth 2006, 20

Smyth's meticulous research into the studio libraries and other archival resources demonstrates that historical filmmaking in Hollywood in the 1930s was a tremendously methodical operation. The goal was not to literally transform a history book into an audiovisual account, as in the Yale photoplays, nor to create an irrelevant filmic narration with the historical theme as a veneer. Instead, historical filmmaking sought pathways that would allow academic knowledge and primary source material to metamorphose into a filmic rendition of history. Screenwriters' work developed in close dialogue with traditional and revisionist historiography, "reevaluating accepted interpretations and arguments," while often broadening its thematic scope to include modern or popular subjects ignored by historians (6). Clearly, the latter were not ready to acknowledge filmmakers as peers. The holy grail of historical truth would remain theirs to pursue. But as they remained secluded in the ivory tower of academia, Hollywood writers, directors, and producers delved into the literature and the sources of the historical past in an effort to creatively resurrect it and communicate it to a wide audience. In their own way, they became historians too. According to Smyth, "they not only read, researched, and cited traditional and contemporary historical works but also presented text and documents in the film narratives. While historians attempted to separate the worlds and capabilities of filmmakers and historians, Hollywood was actively breaking those boundaries" (14–15).

Not all historians remained at a distance though. From the very beginning a number of academics became involved in historical filmmaking in various capacities. Some worked as technical advisors; others as critics offering "scholarly evaluations," while others offered their symbolic capital as part of the promotional campaign (Stubbs 2013, 173). Given that the industry was in charge of the filmmaking process, unlike the case of *The Chronicles of America Photoplays* mentioned above, the role of the professional historians was bound to remain secondary. As a result, the experience of working within Hollywood's institutional and creative constraints was not always to the professors' best satisfaction. As Jonathan Stubbs explains, the testimonies of historians who worked on historical features paint a complicated picture. There are those who consider their contribution marginal, consisting mainly of providing referential details for the screenplay or the production set. Others felt their role impacted in more depth the historical arguments put forward by the film and their input was essential for every step of the process (173–9). In all these cases, though, there was a clear trade-off. The industry gained from academic knowledge both in terms of historical accuracy and critical prestige, while academics had the chance to experiment with a new medium and give their work a far more popular outlet. The common ground, on which this long-lasting collaboration was built, other parameters aside, is the shared interest in the importance of the detail. Both Hollywood filmmakers and historians have tended to ascribe to the details of the diegetic world an ontological significance that reveals, on yet another level, the shared indexicality between history on screen and history on paper.

This aspect has been picked up by various scholars, including Stubbs, but I think Philip Rosen's approach in *Change Mummified* (2001) is the most theoretically comprehensive. Rosen addresses the issue as follows:

> Researched detail, with an accounting of sources as grounds for making referential claims, is also an aspect of disciplined historical scholarship. In that sense, Hollywood research departments are, in their own way, another kind of professionalization of historical thinking, one that both assumes and may stand for a certain general cultural penetration of its ideals (if not all of its practices).
>
> Rosen 2001, 154

Indeed, as Hollywood filmmakers relied on the extensive labors of the research departments,[18] they embraced the desire for accuracy and plausibility, as if the detail would guarantee them an access to historical reality. Rosen names this process as "Everett's Game,"[19] explaining how the game to get every tiny detail right became key to the industry ever since the 1910s and worked as proof of its authenticity and prestige.[20] The more emphasis a film placed on historical detail, the more it raised its supposed historical realism. This rationale in filmic historical discourse mirrored the one that Barthes had traced in historical writing and the novel. As we saw in chapter 1, the tendency to rely on detail as a means of attributing authenticity and realism to textuality was shared by the nineteenth-century novel as well as traditional historiography. Just like the Hollywood filmmakers, novelists, and historians alike achieved a "reality-effect" by multiplying concrete details in their texts, creating the illusion that the excess in signifiers could relate directly the words to their historical referents outside the text. The more details a film or a novel or a history book lines up the more one is tempted to think they are authentic.[21] The problem with the historical feature, however, is not that it is, in its essence, more deceitful than ordinary historical writing but that it features two additional characteristics; firstly, a film is a visual medium that carries an enormous information overload, and, secondly, a film is significantly more exposed to critical evaluation than any history book will ever be.[22] A historical film is potentially under scrutiny by millions of viewers and hundreds of experts who can look into every aspect of the filmic discourse and identify mistakes and departures from the written historical records or other sources. Of course, the same thing happens with historical books, as the flaws, the distortions, and the misrepresentations are regularly highlighted among historians.[23] The difference is, though, that the factual discrepancies and the historical controversies become a lot more public in the case of cinema and, as a result, create the impression that these problems are only endemic to Hollywood.[24]

Yet, this public exposure is a mixed blessing. On the one hand, it renders filmic histories more vulnerable to criticism, while, on the other, it raises to an exponential degree their impact on society vis-à-vis the historical books. From its very first steps, and increasingly from the 1930s to date, Hollywood has produced an impressive number of historical features that raised public awareness on numerous historical issues. Despite several changes in production practices and creative procedures in the course of the twentieth century, Hollywood filmmaking carries on into the twenty-first as a powerful source of historying with an extraordinary influence on the discussion of historicity in the public sphere.[25] The gains for Hollywood itself have been, primarily, in prestige and cultural capital, and secondarily, in actual profits. As Stubbs observes:

Historical films, biopics and literary adaptations thus served a dual public relations purpose: they allowed the film industry to broaden its cultural influence and demographic reach by appealing to the professional middle classes and, as Thomas Doherty has suggested, they were promoted as evidence that Hollywood had undergone a moral reformation.

Stubbs 2013, 157

As an extension of this promotional strategy, the industry succeeded in entering the American classrooms and convinced schoolteachers and other educational staff of the importance of filmic images in the teaching of history. It also accompanied the films with supplementary materials, such as study guides and manuals as well as specially edited versions for the classroom, which would assist the teachers in contextualizing the cinematic experience (168). This was, I believe, as close as one could get to Griffith's dream of using cinema in a scientific context to learn about the past.

At the same time, in the other camp, that of professional history, historians began to feel wary. Already in the early 1930s, prominent voices in the historical profession confronted the danger of keeping historical research locked up behind glass doors that rarely open. In his 1931 presidential address to the American Historical Association, Carl Becker posed the importance of Mr. Everyman. It is worth quoting him at length:

Berate him as we will for not reading our books, Mr. Everyman is stronger than we are, and sooner or later we must adapt our knowledge to his necessities. Otherwise he will leave us to our own devices, leave us it may be to cultivate a species of dry professional arrogance growing out of the thin soil of antiquarian research. Such research, valuable not in itself but for some ulterior purpose, will be of little import except in so far as it is transmuted into common knowledge. The history that lies inert in unread books does no work in the world. The history that does work in the world, the history that influences the course of history, is living history, that pattern of remembered events, whether true or false, that enlarges and enriches the collective specious present, the specious present of Mr. Everyman.

Becker 1932, 234

The need to take into account their audience, or perhaps to popularize the fruits of their knowledge, is not new to historians.[26] But the shifting conditions in the twentieth century rendered the issue increasingly pressing again. And yet, historians did not take heed of Becker's warnings. In the years that followed, very little progress was made in that direction as we can conclude from the overview of the field that John Lukacs provides in his forward[27] of the 1985 edition of

Historical Consciousness: the Remembered Past and then twenty-six years later in *The Future of History* (2011). Lukacs' regular monitoring of the institutional parameters of professional historical writing underlines two divergent attitudes, namely the devolution of professional historianship and the evolution of interest in history. On the one hand, historical courses increasingly left the classrooms and remained only in specialized academic departments, while, on the other, the appetite for historical thinking grew stronger and stronger. In this paradoxical situation, as Lukacs observes, academics seem unwilling and, possibly ill-equipped, to feed this appetite, leaving substantial room for other types of historical thinking. The question, thus, that arises is this: How do we approach these new attempts at history, among which filmic history stands out? How do we theorize and historicize them? Do we mourn the loss of professionalism or do we reconfigure the ways in which we evaluate the various modes of history? I believe that the conundrum that arises in the twenty-first century from the growing impact of audiovisual history and the diminishing import of academic history in the public sphere could be properly addressed, if not resolved, with the help of none other than philosophy.

History and philosophy

Philosopher (loud and clear):	Men cannot know the past
Historian (stupidly):	What did you say?
Philosopher (irritably):	I said, "Men cannot really know the past", and you know damn well that's what I said.

Hexter 1971b, 338–9

The key to this imaginary dialogue, devised by J.H. Hexter in *History Primer* (1971b), lies not so much in the philosopher's insistence on the impossibility of knowing the past but, rather, in the evident and conscious separation of the two speaking positions occupied by the two interlocutors. The historian is aware of the limitations of his endeavors as well as the objections raised on the part of philosophy, and yet he is bound to ignore them both. In all likelihood, he would not be able to perform his task, unless, precisely, he dispensed with the theoretical and philosophical hindrances. This brings to the surface the complex relation between history and philosophy, a topic that has preoccupied thinkers as much as that of the history/art/science triangle discussed previously.

Going back to Kracauer and his treatment of philosophy as the "last things" is a good starting point for understanding how the interplay between history and philosophy could help us carve a new epistemological space for the workings of filmic history in the twentieth century. Kracauer, as I showed in chapter 1, places historical reality, as captured in the writings of professional historians, and photographic reality, as captured by the camera, in the location of the "anteroom," an area found right before the realm of philosophy. The statements articulated in the anteroom differ from those of philosophy on four grounds, as Kracauer elaborates. First, philosophical statements are concerned with the ultimate issues that regard humanity, such as the nature of being, of knowledge, of good and evil, to name but a few. Secondly, they reside in the highest level of generality, assuming that their general principles cover the entirety of the particulars that they refer to. Thirdly, philosophers aspire to observations with objective validity and universal applicability. Finally, philosophical truths tend to be rigid, stable, and unsusceptible to the powers of fortuity or indeterminacy that still affect the workings in the anteroom (Kracauer 1969, 193–4). Even though these four main characteristics of philosophy, in general, and philosophy of history, in particular, are receptive of different shades and degrees in various philosophical traditions, the distance that separates the practice of history and the philosophy of the historical work still obtains. In fact, the brief imaginary dialogue above encapsulates ingenuously how the two activities knowingly work at cross-purposes.

By devising the metaphor of the anteroom, Kracauer does not aim to bridge the distance between them. Instead, he opts for the separation of history from philosophy precisely because he does not perceive historical knowledge as stable, linear, or transcendental. As David Rodowick notes, the manifest objective of Kracauer is the "redemption of the power and specificity of historical thought as a particular form of knowledge" that is cut off from philosophy's lofty towers (Rodowick 1987, 110). The same objective is shared, according to Rodowick, by Foucault, when he writes in *The Order of Things* that "all knowledge is rooted in a life, a society, and a language that have a history; and it is in that very history that knowledge finds the element enabling it to communicate with other forms of life, other types of society, other significations [. . .]" (Foucault 1994, 372–3). Locating in this passage a surprising affinity between Kracauer and Foucault is indeed an insightful move that traces continuity in the most unexpected place, problematizing, inadvertently, the notion of "influence," that Foucault dismissed anyway.[28] At the same time, however, there is an important discontinuity that should not go unheeded; Foucault does not advocate the separation of history from philosophy neither here nor anywhere else in his immensely prolific and diverse writings. In fact, Foucault aimed to revolutionize philosophy by embedding it into history and demonstrating their intrinsic ties. When asked if he were a historian or a philosopher, he responded: "If philosophy is memory or a return of the origin, what I am doing cannot, in any way, be regarded as philosophy; and if the history of thought consists in giving life to half-effaced figures, what I am doing is not history either" (Foucault 2002, 227).

Foucault's peculiar position in relation to established disciplines is the object of Allan Megill's study entitled "The Reception of Foucault by Historians" where he trails the impact, or the lack thereof, of Foucault's oeuvre on traditional historical writings and highlights his avowed disdain for academic history encapsulated in the statement: "I'm not a professional historian. Nobody's perfect" (cited in Megill 1987, 117). After considering the properties of the Foucauldian thought in relation to the existing academic fields, Megill is right to observe that considering Foucault as "interdisciplinary" would be misguided. Foucault does not "combine" the disciplines of history and philosophy in some fashion. Instead, he persistently remains outside of all disciplines,[29] while producing work invaluable to all of them. In Megill's words:

> Though Foucault is solitary, he has nonetheless become part of a collective machinery of research, reflection and argument. Though he is not *of* the discipline, he is important *to* it, partly because he has called attention to hitherto neglected field of research, but mostly because he fosters a self-reflection that is needed to counteract the sclerosis, the self-satisfaction, the smugness that constantly threaten.
>
>   Meghill 1987, 134; emphasis in the original

It is precisely for his peculiar positionality that Foucault can prove invaluable for the problems that cinematic history poses in relation to the discipline of history and its wider philosophical implications for the status of knowledge and truth in our current age. As an outsider to both history and philosophy and as a tenacious critic of established categories, Foucault is primarily interested in identifying problems, gaps, and inconsistencies in the ways that people have handled knowledge and, by extension, power in the course of several centuries. Even though cinema as a source of historical thinking never occupied his enormously wide range of thought, his epistemological tools could be directed at this new area in order to unveil innovative angles on the topic in question. For the rest of this section, I would like to engage with Foucault's writings to highlight those aspects that I consider most pertinent to the role of filmic history in the historical imagination of the twentieth century.[30] The goal is not to reach concrete and definitive answers but to reorganize the ways in which our thinking about history on screen should progress.

Foucault's own attempt to resist the connotations of the terms "history" and "philosophy," viewed predominantly as empiricist and transcendental respectively, led him to a new set of epistemological tools and methods that could help us rework the order and the generality imposed on our knowledge about the world. The three key concepts that dominate his entire work are "archaeology," "genealogy," and "practices of the self," each corresponding to a distinct phase in his career.[31] In the archaeological period,[32] Foucault introduced a number of terms that sought to define the discourses of knowledge as "practice," i.e., not merely as linguistic entities but as objects that form certain relations and function according to specific judicative and veridicative norms. Through a complex grid of concepts, such as statement, discursive formation, archive, historical a priori and episteme, Foucault formulates in *The Archaeology of Knowledge* (2002) a method of historical analysis "freed from the anthropological theme" and open to the enormous discontinuities that exist in the ways that knowledge has been pursued, established, and controlled in the course of history (17). Foucault's brand name is "discontinuity," which is often disorienting with regards to his actual intellectual pursuits.[33] What Foucault means by discontinuity and strives to achieve through archaeology is the foregrounding of the disparities, the dissonances, the gaps, and the ruptures that obtain when it comes to the ways that people and societies have handled their relation to knowledge. Thus, he takes the exact opposite direction of the traditional historian; instead of building generalizations and producing unity over diverse historical phenomena, Foucault struggles to identify the breaks and the changes that occur in certain domains, such as madness, the clinic or prison. As he puts it:

> For history in its classical form, the discontinuous was both the given and the unthinkable: the raw material of history, which presented itself in the form of dispersed events—decisions, accidents, initiatives, discoveries; the material, which, through analysis, had to be rearranged, reduced, effaced in order to reveal the continuity of events. Discontinuity was the stigma of temporal dislocation that it was the historian's task to remove from history. It has now become one of the basic elements of historical analysis.
>
> Foucault 2002, 9

Foucault's historical analysis does not aim to demolish everything that professional historians built in the passage of time nor reject as futile or groundless their elaborate continuities and categorizations. He aspires, however, to problematize their certainties, to "disturb their tranquility" and "tear away from them their virtual self-evidence" probing questions and posing problems regarding their foundations (28–9).[34]

This general orientation toward discontinuity carries on into his genealogical phase in the 1970s;[35] only this time, discourse needs to be complemented by the analysis of non-discursive practices in order to elucidate further the relation of knowledge to power and the so-called "regimes of truth" of each epoch. Foucault borrows the term "genealogy" from Nietzsche and his opening statement in *Nietzsche, Genealogy, History* (1991b) is telling of the troubles awaiting every aspiring "genealogist:" "Genealogy is gray, meticulous and patiently documentary. It operates on a field of entangled and confused parchments, on documents that have been scratched over and recopied many times" (76). With the shift of emphasis from discourse to non-discursive practices, Foucault also seeks to emphasize the power struggles entailed in the organization, dissemination, or exclusion of knowledge within certain social conditions. It is a more dynamic approach that builds on archaeology's findings to shed light on the complexity of power/knowledge relations in the constitution of truth and the transformations it undergoes. As Christopher Falzon comments on the passage from the first to the second phase of Foucault's thought:

> The genealogical perspective not only contextualizes discourse in non-discursive power practices but also offers a more thoroughgoing appreciation of difference. In the face of continuous history, genealogy finds difference in multiple practices of power, organizing practices that are themselves engaged in a conflict of interpretations in so far as efforts by one side to order the other are met by resistance and counter-strategies.
>
> Falzon 2013, 291

What remains constant in both phases, however, is the rejection of traditional history's belief that human consciousness is the original subject of historical developments. As Foucault definitively argues:

> One has to dispense with the constituent subject, to get rid of the subject itself, that's to say, to arrive at an analysis which can account for the constitution of the subject within a historical framework, and this is what I call genealogy, that is, a form of history which can account for the constitution of knowledges, discourses,

domains of objects etc., without having to make reference to a subject which is either transcendental in relation to the field of events or runs in its empty sameness throughout the course of history.

Foucault 1991b, 59

Whether analyzing discursive formations or non-discursive practices, Foucault refuses to consider human beings as unified and stable subjects in charge of the discourse or the other practices in which they become embedded.[36] Instead, he strives to illustrate how considering Man as an autonomous subject is a historically situated idea. As he puts it: "In various forms, this theme has played a constant role since the nineteenth century: to preserve, against all decentrings, the sovereignty of the subject, and the twin figures of anthropology and humanism" (Foucault 2002, 14).

Foucault's insistence on the decentering of the subject throughout the archaeological and genealogical phase gave way to a more complex approach to subjectivity in the third, and last, stage, where we witness an attempt to partly rehabilitate a sort of freedom in human action.[37] By "practices of the self" he means the procedures deployed by individuals in their effort to establish, maintain, and develop their knowledge and control of themselves. These procedures, again, are not created by the individuals themselves but they do offer them ways in which they can become free agents within their own "subjectivization."[38] With the addition of this third axis, Foucault's approach to historical analysis becomes an inquiry into the discourses, the power practices, and the practices of the self that have regulated the relation of human beings with the world around them over the course of time. In this light, the three phases in Foucault's oeuvre do not aim to contradict each other. In fact, each new step in his thinking adds new layers, more points of emphasis, and further conceptual stakes that, overall, build a strangely coherent picture. For all his interest in discontinuity, Foucault's arguments present a peculiar internal consistency, without, however, providing closure. The three axes that he worked so hard to designate as a means of researching social phenomena are not definitive; they are merely three sides of a "polyhedron of intelligibility," which can take on an indefinite number of sides without ever accomplishing the "whole picture" (Flynn 2005, 39).

Some of the established sides of this polyhedron, as explicated in Foucault's writings, could render the problem of cinematic history more intelligible to us or, at least, help us locate the questions that need to be addressed, as we try to distance ourselves from the common problems that scholars have discussed so far, namely how filmic history is frivolous and less important than academic history or how words and images are entirely different things, or whether a filmic history should try to be as accurate as a written account, and so on and so forth. Instead, I suggest that we embrace Foucault's arsenal of concepts in order to begin to diagnose the problems that cinematic history poses for the discipline of history and, more widely, for the status of historical knowledge in the twentieth century. Evidently, Foucault's method is not easily applicable, as his concepts form an intricate web that becomes functional as an ensemble and not as single items that can be applied in a piecemeal fashion. Nor is there enough space within the scope of this current project to launch a full-fledged Foucauldian inquiry, along all three axes, into the matter in question. What I would like to suggest, however, is that Foucault's reshuffling of the cards of traditional historical thinking could help us locate new areas of research, new modes of classification and new problems that history on screen gives rise to in relation to knowledge, power, and subjectivity.

Our starting point should be Foucault's section on "Other archaeologies" toward the end of *The Archaeology of Knowledge*. There, Foucault wonders whether his archaeological analysis should be limited to scientific discourses or whether it should aim for a wider applicability. In his own words, "Must archaeology be—exclusively—a certain way of questioning the history of the sciences?" (Foucault 2002, 213). His answer is negative but his suggestions remain highly tentative and they most certainly do not have cinema, let alone cinematic history, in mind. Let us see, however, how his frame of thinking could be adapted to our own object of study. In his brief and sketchy account of other conceivable archaeologies, Foucault refers to the possibility of examining sexuality, painting, and politics in ways akin to the analysis of scientific discourse, proposing various adjustments that foreshadow the introduction of non-discursive practices in his genealogical phase. The case of painting, as a visual medium, is evidently the example closest to cinema.[39] If we substitute "painting" with "film" in his description of the "archaeology of painting," then, an archaeology of cinema

> would not set out to show that *the film* is a certain way of "meaning" or "saying" that is peculiar in that it dispenses with words. It would try to show that, at least in one of its dimensions, it is discursive practice that is embodied in techniques and effects. In this sense, *the film* is not a pure vision that must then be transcribed into the materiality of space *and time*; nor is it a naked gesture whose silent and eternally empty meanings must be freed from subsequent interpretations. It is

shot through—and independently of scientific knowledge (connaissance) and philosophical themes—with the positivity of a knowledge (savoir).

Foucault 2002, 215; my interventions in italics

What stands out in this "modified" passage is Foucault's anti-hermeneutic stance that pleads against the search for deeper meanings by endless interpretations and commentary. In fact, interpretations are fictional constructions that should be studied not for what they supposedly reveal but for what they actually "do" through this process of revelation. The main goal of archaeology would be to study films as "discursive practices" that follow certain rules and produce specific effects. Above all, films are characterized by the positivity of a knowledge that is worth exploring for the ways it connects to a wider web of power relations. As we try to construe this new object for archaeology, however, several problems arise.

First and foremost, we risk jeopardizing the entire Foucauldian rationale if we equate films with discourse, ignoring the discrepancies between visual and written elements. The detailed method that appears in *Archaeology* is tailored for the exigencies of verbal discourse and a direct application to a "non-discursive discourse" is troublesome. So the question is: How do we do historical research into a non-discursive object such as cinema? Again, Foucault's solutions deriving from the analyses of paintings are piecemeal but sufficient for getting us started. Going back to *The Order of Things* and his discussion of Velasquez's *Las Meninas*, we find the following observation: "But the relation of language to painting is an infinite relation. It is not that words are imperfect, or that, when confronted by the visible, they prove insuperably inadequate. Neither can be reduced to the other's terms [...]" (Foucault 1994, 9). As a result, images are autonomous entities that should not be equated with words, yet their functions are not necessarily dissimilar. This was precisely the point of the entire discussion on medium-specificity in the previous chapter. Even though we cannot consider words and images as the same thing, we can trace similar roles and operations that establish a level of commonality. As Joseph Tanke observes, archaeology finds the "unreflective slippage between the visual and the discursive" ill-advised but it still considers the visual thoroughly historical and it scrutinizes the works of art not for "what they mean" but for "what they do" (Tanke 2013, 128).

Secondly, we need to address the peculiarity of our object of study, namely not cinema as a whole but cinematic history, i.e., all the representations of the past in moving images. Historical images on the screen are not easily categorized with respect to the established areas, such as academic history, art, or science. Yet, they do qualify for the category of the "non-discursive formation" as they are constituted according to certain rules and they produce specific knowledge about the world. The question now is whether we will choose to connect this knowledge to epistemological issues or ethical ones instead.[40] When Foucault discusses paintings, the choice is relatively easier, since they are customarily viewed as works of art with aesthetic and moral implications. Filmic images are different though. Approaching them in relation to their art status may legitimately be an option but it is not the option that I espouse here. On the contrary, the entire debate that I have sketched out so far in this book is openly concerned with the epistemological status of the films in question and their repercussions on the function of history and memory in the current age. Therefore, history on film should be analyzed in relation to what Foucault calls the "episteme," i.e., "the total set of relations that unite, at a given period, the discursive practices that give rise to epistemological figures, sciences, and possibly formalized systems" (Foucault 2002, 212). Even though the Greek word "ἐπιστήμη" was introduced for the functions of verbal discourses, visual images can equally participate in the constitution of knowledge and the explication of the phenomena of the world. In fact, images are related to the core of Foucault's problematics, namely the problem of representation and the complex relation of the words to the things of the world.[41] In this light, the intellectual history presented in *The Order of Things* is a history, from the sixteenth to the twentieth century, of the different modes of representing the things with words (Foucault 1994). In the course of these centuries, Foucault identified the following four epistemes: the Renaissance, the Classical Age, the Modern Age and the Contemporary Age.[42] I would like to argue that it is the contemporary episteme that provides the epistemic context in which filmic historical images generate and circulate knowledge. The categorization might seem chronological but it is not. I do not relate filmic history to the contemporary episteme, merely because the films belong to the same time frame. The epistemes are not chronological phases, nor overarching mentalities; rather, they are ways of producing, regulating, and classifying knowledge. In this sense, they are not layers of a palimpsest, each overwriting the other; instead, as Hayden White argues, they resemble the islands in an archipelago: "a chain of epistemic islands, the deepest connections among which are unknown—and unknowable" (White 1973, 28). This means that academic history may continue to exist and produce knowledge in our current age but the principles upon which this knowledge is generated belongs to the Modern Age.

On the other hand, filmic history could be located on the epistemic island of the Contemporary Age for the ways in which it produces "a new order of things," distinct from those prevailing on the other islands. In this light, historiophoty emerges as the quintessential mode of historying in the twentieth and twenty-first century, in contradistinction to the academic historiography of the nineteenth.

This is a significant hypothesis that my book will seek to investigate in the remaining space, acknowledging that the scope of the argument exceeds the limitations of a book-length study. However, I will attempt to address, as I have already in the previous chapters, the questions that one needs to pose in order to do research into historical cinema as a dominant form of historical knowledge. Foucault's ideas and concepts are quintessential for a number of reasons that I would like to briefly summarize here. Firstly, any discussion about history of any kind, whether in written or cinematic form, cannot be conducted without acknowledging the historicity and the philosophical underpinnings of the terms that it entails. In other words, history and philosophy cannot exist without each other. Secondly, Foucault's definition of the episteme and the four ages that he identified provide a very broad epistemological context in which historical knowledge can be situated, comparing and contrasting diverse modes of representing the world and creating knowledge. They can offer a very long-distance view over the battles between historiography and historiophoty. Thirdly, historical films need to be located within specific non-discursive practices that regulate their production, distribution, and exhibition. The knowledge they produce and the power relations that ensue within a given society are tied to mechanisms that determine the relation of the historical works with the other institutional forces at play. Fourthly, every historical film should not be studied for its unique singularity but for the ways it fits or does not fit within a specific historico-visual tapestry. The good knowledge of that tapestry, of course, is a requirement. What is also a requirement is to handle the role of the filmmakers with caution; we cannot treat them as the creators of personal visions but we do not need to eliminate them altogether either; different filmmakers in different contexts are allowed to practice their métier with a range of creative freedom. Finally, when we examine the cinematic forms that perform the representation of history, we need to search for those mechanisms that operate under the surface and produce meaning. This does not mean that we should indulge in symptomatic readings that will reveal hidden interpretations but to identify the standard devices though which interpretations are built.

Thus far, by this final chapter of Part One, several of these goals have already been discussed, even if their discussion was not openly framed within a Foucauldian rationale. The overview of the academic debates in the disciplines of history and film studies in the introduction aimed at historicizing the problem of historiophoty and identifying the key conceptual/philosophical arguments of those who have tackled it over the last few decades. Then, the focus on Kracauer, Barthes, and Godard was an archaeological dig into writings and ideas that provided insights into the complex analogies of historical works with films and novels. Within those analogies I traced discontinuities in the ways the three thinkers handled mediality, historical representation, and the possibility of an audiovisual history. As a result, the issue of medium specificity came center stage in chapter 2 where I argued that the separation of written and cinematic histories should not be premised on essentialist claims. I strived to illustrate that, despite their material differences, historical representation in both media has a complicated relation to the historical past; one that relies on a range of devices in order to simulate the presence of things long gone. Finally, as the differences between history in words and history in images could not be adequately substantiated at the level of medium specificity, I had to turn to the wider historical and institutional environment in which these two forms of historying have been produced in the course of the nineteenth and the twentieth century.

Thus, Foucault came in medias res in this long examination of written and screened history to help us retrace the previous steps and frame the future ones. The following chapters will not be an application of sorts of his theory, as his writings do not build a closed methodological system with necessary and sufficient propositions. His concepts as well as the historical knowledge of the human sciences that he has accumulated in his historical/philosophical works will offer a set of guiding principles for continuing to explore the workings of cinematic history as a powerful form of historical knowledge in the twentieth, and now the twenty-first, centuries. In Part Two of this book, I begin to scale down the level of my investigation in order to examine historical films, both fictions and documentaries. The argument that I will put forward is this: historical films, just like history books, narrate and explain the past through a set of narrative, argumentative and ideological mechanisms. As magnified miniatures, however, the historical films do not pretend to represent, the past as it *really* was. Instead, they construe a relation between the images and the historical past, which problematizes the transparency of representation that written works strive so hard to maintain.

Notes

1   A detailed account of the history of historiography clearly outgrows the scope of this
    volume. I will present a number of key points as well as basic taxonomies that I
    consider pertinent to my own arguments. For a comprehensive volume on the
    theory and history of historiography, see Bentley (2006).

2   Michel Foucault aptly describes a variety of functions of history since ancient times:
    "It is true that History existed long before the constitution of the human sciences;
    from the beginnings of the Ancient Greek civilization, it has performed a certain
    number of major functions in Western culture: memory, myth, transmission of the
    Word and of Example, vehicle of tradition, critical awareness of the present,
    decipherment of humanity's destiny, anticipation of the future, or promise of a
    return" (Foucault 1994, 367).

3   Kracauer offers a comprehensive account of these debates and takes a similar
    position to Kelley: "One might still ask whether historians should not be supposed to
    learn from the errors and misplaced emphases of their predecessors and thus,
    generation after generation, steadily improve on what went before. Improve, a new
    generation of historians may, but the avoidance of past errors hardly protects them
    from committing other ones, and depth of insight is not the privilege of the most
    recent age. It is difficult to imagine that Thucydides will ever be surpassed. The belief
    in the progress of historiography is largely in the nature of an illusion" (Kracauer
    1969, 138).

4   These tropes are part of White's complex system of the poetics of history and they
    will be further discussed in chapter 4.

5   For a brief overview of the academization process of history, see Lukacs (2011). For a
    more detailed account of the development of the historical profession in the United
    States, see Novick (1988).

6   From the standpoint of the twenty-first century, one can easily discern that there has
    not been a universal method for writing history. Writing in 2011, John Lukacs
    re-asserts this lack by quoting Jacob Burckhardt who explained to his students the
    only precondition for writing history: "*Bisogna saper leggere*" (You must know how
    to read) (Lukacs 2011, 10).

7   Kracauer presents a detailed account of the debates on whether history is an art or a
    science, often seeking to compromise the controversies, arguing for "the middle
    ground" or talking of "degrees," especially when he argues that history is in fact both
    a science and an art, "with a difference" (Kracauer 1969).

8   For one of the latest takes on this famous debate and a re-evaluation of Carr's work
    as being positivist, which is also related to my own argument here, see Jenkins
    (1995).

9   Their views are equally divergent on the issue of "causation" as well as "progress" in history, where Carr directly and severely criticizes Berlin's arguments.

10 Indicatively, see the works of Bruno Latour.

11 As the entry on the "Linguistic Turn" in *The Routledge Companion to Historical Studies* notes, "The term 'the linguistic turn', which according to Richard Rorty was coined by the Austrian realist philosopher Gustav Bergmann, has been used by advocates and critics alike to describe the shift in historical explanation toward an emphasis on the role of language in creating historical meaning. The debate over the linguistic turn hinges on the extent to which one believes objectivity and truth are possible in historical descriptions" (Munslow 2006, 164).

12 As Hayden White puts it, "Viewed simply as verbal artifacts histories and novels are indistinguishable from one another. We cannot easily distinguish between them on formal grounds unless we approach them with specific preconceptions about the kinds of truths that each is supposed to deal in" (White 1978, 122).

13 See Alun Munslow's work discussed in chapter 2.

14 This is the most often quoted phrase of Leopold von Ranke, who is one of the most prominent historians of the nineteenth century. His phrase is often mentioned, rightly or not, as an instance of naïve realism. See Rosen (2001, 109–10).

15 As Mattheisen explains, "Thereafter production costs skyrocketed and the enterprise had to 'combat not only vexations and misunderstandings from within but unscrupulous preying harpies from without.' Stories circulated about inane and uninhibited 'professorial' meddling on such a colossal scale that schedules were impossible to maintain. For example, 'a company and production crew [was] held on full salary in an Adirondack location for upwards of eleven weeks while alleged experts debated whether the cabin occupied by the characters should have its logs notched or mortised at the corners'" (1992, 630).

16 A similar study on Hollywood films in the 1950s was conducted by David Eldridge whose scope, however, is significantly more inclusive. See Eldridge (2006).

17 The term belongs to Hayden White and it is discussed in some detail in chapter 2.

18 Eldridge chronicles the development of the research departments in Hollywood and describes in detail the mentality of the research staff, particularly in the ways in which they distinguished themselves from academic researchers (2006, 127–51).

19 This name comes from Charles Everett of Hingham Massachusetts, a film spectator who complained in a letter to Warner Brothers about a detail in the film *The Life of Emile Zola* (1937). He blamed them for mistaking a type of fish called *langouste* in French for lobster, while in fact the word denotes ordinary crawfish (Rosen 2001, 156).

20 Historical films were also promoted as the most prestigious product of the Hollywood output and they were often, although not always, exempted from the

censorship of the Hays code. See Stubbs (2013, 155–72).

21 There is a fascinating line in *Blade Runner 2049* (2017) that touches upon the matter of authenticity. Dr. Ana Stelline, who manufactures fake memories, explains at one point: "They all think it's about more detail. But that's not how memory works. We recall with our feelings. Anything real should be a mess." But there exactly lies the difference between history and memory in terms of our expectations; real memories could be a mess but real history cannot.

22 The same point was made in chapter 2 within the context of the idea of the "magnified miniature."

23 As William H. McNeill writes, "[…] a historian who rejects someone else's conclusions calls them mythical, while claiming that his own views are true. But what seems true to one historian will seem false to another, so one historian's truth becomes another's myth, even at the moment of utterance" (1986, 1).

24 With the advent of new media and, particularly the internet, the rifts between historians also tend to become a lot more public. Note how Niall Ferguson was severely criticized in the media for misrepresenting his primary sources regarding the Obama governance. Indicatively, see O'Brien (2012).

25 Marnie Hughes-Warrington mentions the US-based "Presence of the Past" project, which indicates that 81 percent of the 1,500 people interviewed had watched films or television programs about the past in the previous year. Other projects also indicate the enormous profusion of audiovisual history in audiences across the globe (Hughes-Warrington, 2007).

26 In the eighteenth century, history was a popular form of literature with Voltaire's work as a notable example.

27 Similarly, Fritz Stern introduces the 1973 edition of *The Varieties of History: From Voltaire to the Present* (1956) with a brief note that acknowledges the changes that took place in the seventeen years that intervened. As he writes, "Times have changed since *The Varieties of History* was first published, and so has the place of history in our intellectual world. The study of the past as a uniquely important humanistic inquiry no longer commands the kind of automatic acceptance it once did. […] Historians are aware as well of a growing public indifference to history, born perhaps of a sense that the present is so radically different from the past that the reconstruction of that past seems only of antiquarian interest" (Stern 1973, 9).

28 There are other points of convergence between Kracauer and Foucault, most notably their shared emphasis on the materiality of objects as well as their anti-teleological approach to history. As Kracauer notes, "The idea of progress presents itself differently from different periods whose succession may or may not amount to a progress" (Kracauer 1969, 202).

29 As Alan Sheridan notes, "There was no discipline, with its institutions, journals, internal controversies, conceptual apparatus, methods of work, within which

Foucault could carry the task he had set himself. Indeed, there was a sense in which, like Nietzsche's, his work would have to be carried on outside, even against, the existing academic frameworks" (cited in Megill 1987, 134).

30 It is a tremendous challenge to present a brief but working introduction to Foucault's thought in a few pages without oversimplifying or distorting his arguments. I acknowledge the dangers and suggest that the reader approaches this section as an opening to a whole new terrain of thought that goes well beyond the scope of this book.

31 Thomas Flynn calls the last phase as "problematizations" taking cue from Foucault's use of the term "problematization" in an interview in the later stage of his career (Flynn 2005, 38).

32 The books that belong to this phase are *History of Madness* (1961), *Birth of the Clinic* (1963), *The Order of Things* (1966), and *The Archaeology of Knowledge* (1969). (Note: I am using here the dates of the original publications in order to show their chronological order. When I refer to these works in the text or in my bibliography, I use the publication dates of the volumes that I consulted.) The secondary literature explicating and elaborating on Foucault's terminology is vast. Indicatively, see Gutting (2005) and Falzon et.al. (2013).

33 As Foucault confesses: "This business about discontinuity has always rather bewildered me. In the new edition of the Petit Larousse it says: 'Foucault: a philosopher who founds his theory of history on discontinuity.' That leaves me flabbergasted" (Foucault 1991a, 53–4).

34 Thomas Flynn comments on the relation of archaeology and traditional history arguing, "archaeology is both counter-history and social critique. It is counter-history because it assumes a contrapuntal relationship to traditional history, whose conclusions it more rearranges than denies and whose resources it mines for its own purposes. [. . .] But archaeology is social critique as well. It radicalizes our sense of the contingency of our dearest biases and most accepted necessities, thereby opening up a space for change" (Flynn 2005, 33).

35 In this phase we categorize *Discipline and Punish* (1975) and *History of Sexuality Vol. I* (1976).

36 In *The Archaeology of Knowledge*, Foucault writes, "In the proposed analysis, instead of referring back to the synthesis or the unifying function of a subject, the various enunciative modalities manifest his dispersion. To the various statuses, the various sites, the various positions that he can occupy or be given when making a discourse. To the discontinuity of the planes from which he speaks. And if these planes are linked by a system of relations, this system is not established by the synthetic activity of a consciousness identical with itself, dumb and anterior to all speech, but by the specificity of a discursive practice. I shall abandon any attempt, therefore, to see discourse as a phenomenon of expression—the verbal translation of a previously established synthesis; instead, I shall look for a field of regularity for various

positions of subjectivity. Thus conceived, discourse is not the majestically unfolding manifestation of a thinking, knowing, speaking subject, but, on the contrary, a totality, in which the dispersion of the subject and his discontinuity with himself may be determined. It is a space of exteriority in which a network of distinct sites is deployed" (2002, 60).

37　In this phase we categorize *The History of Sexuality Vol. II* (1984) and *Vol. III* (1984).

38　Foucault defines "subjectivization" as follows: "I will call subjectivization the procedure by which one obtains the constitution of a subject, or more precisely, of a subjectivity which is of course only one of the given possibilities of organization of a self-consciousness" (Foucault 1990, 253).

39　In film studies, Foucault's thought has exerted limited influence and only a few of his concepts entered the vocabulary of film scholars. One of the most noteworthy cases is the reconfiguration of film history as "an archaeology of new media" theorized in Thomas Elsaesser's work (Elsaesser, 2016). Moreover, again under Elsaesser's aegis, the concept of "dispositif" was explored in a volume called *Cine-dispositives: Essays in Epistemology Across Media* edited by Maria Tortajada and François Albera (2015).

40　In his example of the archaeological study of sexuality, Foucault describes another possible direction other than that of the episteme: "Such an archaeology would show, if it succeeded in its task, how the prohibitions, exclusions, limitations, values, freedoms, and transgressions of sexuality, all its manifestations, verbal or otherwise, are linked to a particular discursive practice. It would reveal, not of course as the ultimate truth of sexuality, but as one of the dimensions in accordance with which one can describe it, a certain 'way of speaking'; and one would show how this way of speaking is invested not in scientific discourses, but in a system of prohibitions and values. An analysis that would be carried out not in the direction of the episteme, but in that of what we might call the ethical" (2002, 213).

41　As White explains, "Both *Les Mots et les choses* and the more recent *L'Archeologie du savoir* are attacks upon all of those histories of realistic representation which, from Hegel to Gombrich, purport to explicate the true nature of the relationship between 'words and things'" (1973, 26).

42　Foucault's works primarily focus on the rapture and the discontinuities between the Renaissance, the Classical Age and the Modern Age. He sees that the structures of knowledge of the Modern Age have begun to subside but he does not fully engage with his own age. Part of the difficulty lies in the impossibility of the task, namely to step outside one's own time and analyze the situation with entirely extrinsic criteria. As he writes in *The Order of Things*, "This is because man, in fact, can be revealed only when bound to a previously existing historicity: he is never contemporaneous with that origin which is outlined through the time of things even as it eludes the gaze; when he tries to define himself as a living being, he can uncover his own beginning only against the background of a life which itself began long before him;

when he attempts to re-apprehend himself as a labouring being, he cannot bring even the most rudimentary forms of such a being to light except within a human time and space which have been previously institutionalized, and previously subjugated by society; and when he attempts to define his essence as a speaking subject, prior to any effectively constituted language, all he ever finds is the previously unfolded possibility of language, and not the stumbling sound, the first word upon the basis of which all languages and even language itself became possible" (1994, 330).

Part II

History on Film: Narrating and Explaining the Past

4

The Poetics of History and the Poetics of the Historical Film

[...] an awareness that written history is itself only a representation—and not a definitive truth—was also fostered as filmmakers came into contact with historians, advisors and self-appointed "custodians" of historical memories.

Eldridge 2006, 197

The osmosis between historians and filmmakers in Hollywood has been pivotal for the shapes and forms that historical films have taken throughout the twentieth century to the present day. Films were called upon to fill the void left by academic historians in public consciousness and to feed the increasing appetite of the audience for the remembrance of the things past. This new form of historying provided by cinema did not develop in a vacuum; instead, as I have repeatedly argued so far, it was bound to remediate the forms and practices of earlier modes of history, including both the scientific type found in academic history books as well as the popular versions that have survived through the ages. The question now is how to approach this sort of remediation and how to conceptualize the perennial issue of sameness and difference at play in this process. Foucault's work, introduced in the previous chapter, is invaluable if we want to start from the highest level of generality. Each of the epistemic conditions that he identifies from the Renaissance to the current age puts a different emphasis on how to organize things and how to constitute our knowledge of the world. In our case, should we classify history books and films in the same category based on their sameness, according to the principles of the Renaissance? Should we completely separate them once and for all, according to the Classical episteme? Should we view them as a linear succession and examine them in terms of their analogies, as one would probably do in the Modern Age? Or should we attempt to figure out how sameness, difference, and analogy are reworked and problematized in our current situation? Foucault's assistance at this point becomes limited, given that his outline of the contemporary episteme is only tentative. He senses that we have moved away from the nineteenth century epistemological choices and he argues for the demise of Man as the dominant figure of thought in the Modern Age; and, yet, the new, so far, is nothing but "a thin line of light low on the horizon" (Foucault 1994, 383). His references to Nietzsche and Freud point to the extensive problematization of history and subjectivity through linguistics in the twentieth century, underlining the growing awareness of the problematic relation of representation and reality. The opacity of language and its ontological debasement into the world of the things leads us to question all previous attempts at creating an order of some sort without, however, establishing a new type of order in their place. Or at least, we are not yet in a position to discern one at this point.

Foucault's complex epistemic typology was introduced to the American public via Hayden White's piece "Foucault Decoded" (1973), while it was further elaborated on in *The Content of the Form* (1987). White is highly appreciative of Foucault's thought as he defends him against his critics and strives to elucidate several of his obscure points. Above all, White explicates the concept of the episteme with the help of his own favorite tools, i.e., the concepts of metaphor, metonymy, synecdoche, and irony, while he attempts to "complete" Foucault's last episteme through this system of linguistic tropes. Specifically, by correlating irony to the Contemporary Age, he is able to bring to the fore a number of elements that characterize our epoch, such as skepticism toward the role of human agency and the correspondence of representation with external reality. Irony does not replace other tropes with something new, and therefore it does not introduce a new order of things; instead, it plays on its similarities and differences with its predecessors, while it introduces the very notion of order and representation as a problem in itself. Despite the difficulty of working with a typology "under construction,"[1] I believe it is worthwhile to diagnose the problems posed by filmic history as part of a larger epistemological condition, which is critical of established categories and foregrounds the road to knowledge as a problem in its own right.

In this light, I suggest that we take a step further from discussing analogies and similarities, as we did in chapters 2 and 3, and bring into focus the play of differences and similarities at work in every filmic account that attempts to reconstruct the past. My general thesis, as I have argued so far, is that cinematic history is a magnified miniature of written history. This means that watching a two-hour historical film may not be the same as reading a ten-volume historical book, but the former condenses and amplifies several features of the latter. As the miniature of the book, the film contains all the key qualities of historical thinking, but its size and form produce an exaggerated and distorting effect that can be interpreted in two ways. One is to claim, as most theorists and critics have done for decades now, that the exaggeration and distortion is such that any correlation between these two types of historying is preposterous. The other, which my work here suggests, is that the exaggeration and distortion should be considered as an invaluable form of irony that will allow us, if we look closely, to observe an intricate play of similarity and difference and will enable us to better understand not just cinema but written history as well. Specifically, the three main aspects of historical thought that should catch our attention in the passage from the written to the audiovisual form are the functions of discursivity, authorship and narration. Firstly, an audiovisual history is always already non-discursive, forming a complex relation to discursive elements, on the one hand, while highlighting, on the other, the importance of the non-discursive realm in our understanding of the world. It combines and condenses, in a way, the problematics of archaeology and genealogy, as I explained them in the previous chapter, and it urges us to reconsider the limits of discourse analysis. Moreover, authorship in historical cinema becomes a puzzle. A historical film is not attributed to a single "author" in the way that a history book is regarded as the product of a sole writer. Even though some filmmakers have been foregrounded as "historians," such as Oliver Stone or Roberto Rossellini, the characterization remains extremely loose, and for a good reason. The collective effort in filmmaking practices and the mechanisms involved in the production of a film prevent us from a single-handed attribution of historical authorship. In historical films, authorship is problematized as the agencies controlling the final outcome are multiple, diverse, and often invisible. The quest for those visible and invisible forces at work openly point to the workings of non-discursive elements and bring to the surface the structures of power and knowledge in any mode of historying.[2] Finally, what distinguishes history on screen is the dominant role of the narration. Historical books surely contain narration, too, but the process itself is downplayed by the historians who seek to keep it as unobtrusive as possible, as Barthes has plainly demonstrated.[3] In cinematic history, on the other hand, visual narration is bound to stand out to a greater or lesser extent. As a result, the audiovisual work that reconstructs a moment of the past *appears* to rely significantly more on narration and, therefore, construction than its written counterpart. It is precisely this point that led Kracauer to dismiss historical fiction in cinema altogether. He did acknowledge that written history contains fabrication as well, but filmic narration was a step too far for him, or "a body too much" in Jean-Louis Comolli's famous words (Comolli 1978).[4] The role of narration in historical films may come in many shapes but, compared to a written account, it always comes across as openly fabricated and, by extension, potentially false.[5] On all three counts—discursivity, authorship, and narration—the exploration of filmic history can provide invaluable insights on concepts and processes that obtain in academic written history but have been treated as givens, as black boxes that are never to be opened.

Here, my primary focus will fall on the role of narration in historical cinema. In this second part of the book, I will move to a middle ground where the wider historico-philosophical issues posed in the previous section become related to precise functional and formal tools that help us understand what historical films do and how they do it.[6] To detect the complex play of similarity and difference between the written and the filmic historical work, I will develop a method of analysis that combines the poetics of history in academia with the historical poetics of film. For the former, I will rely on Hayden White's theoretical concepts presented in great detail in his first legendary book *Metahistory*, which sought to flesh out the intricate bonds between form and content in historical writing. For the latter, I will deploy theories of narration developed within film studies that identify the particularities of the cinematic discourse and provide specific categories and models of filmic narration, whether in fiction or nonfiction filmmaking (Bordwell 1985; Nichols 1991, 1994). Favoring one side over the other, i.e., history or film studies, has had a limiting effect on other research on this topic so far. For instance, historians like William Gyunn and Natalie Zemon Davis were unable to identify the intrinsic particularities of the cinematic form, whereas film scholars like Robert Burgoyne downplayed theoretical issues of history in favor of cinema specificity. Yet, the object of our study, that of history on film throughout the twentieth century to this date, cannot be adequately examined unless we bring these two disciplines together. To fathom the forms, the contents, and the role of historical cinema in the production of historical knowledge for over a century, we need to develop a method that contains terms and concepts from both fields. Not because we want to prove that they are the same, neither because we want to show how different they are. We need to meticulously craft an approach to filmic history that can do justice to its own intrinsic properties, while it also captures its complex relation to earlier modes of historical thought. The combination of the poetics of history from the academic domain and the historical poetics of film will enable me to construct a complex set of tools for detecting and diagnosing the kind of historical knowledge that films produce through their narration.[7] This theoretical and methodological merger is not an easy task and it may require more than a few disclaimers in the process. I am confident, however, that it is a task worth undertaking, if we want to understand how the shapes of historical imagination evolve through time.

Thus, let us begin with the key concepts that I will draw from White's work in order to compose this new approach to filmic history. White has had an impact on film scholars with his short piece on "historiophoty," discussed in chapter 2, but it is *Metahistory* that presents a series of detailed theoretical arguments and conceptualizations for the study of history. There, he begins by defining the historical work as "a verbal structure in the form of narrative prose discourse that purports to be a model, or icon, of past structures and processes in the interest of *explaining what they were by representing them*" (White 2014, 2; emphasis in the original). Through the analysis of four major historians (Ranke, Michelet, Tocqueville, Burckhardt) and four philosophers of history (Hegel, Marx, Nietzsche, and Croce), White aims to reveal a range of processes and formal strategies that are at work in the writings of all of the above, regardless of their "raw materials" or other extrinsic factors. He delves into their monumental writings to extract a series of "possible models of historical representation or conceptualization" (3). As a starting point, he distinguishes between five concepts that belong to different levels of generalization: the chronicle, the story, the mode of emplotment, the mode of argument, and the mode of ideological implication (5). Every historical account transforms a chronicle of events into a story by organizing them into a certain temporal and causal order. By means of its narrative act, the historical work not only presents certain events (what happened, when, and why) but also suggests an additional meaning of the story that responds to questions such as "What is the point of it all?" or "Where does it all lead to?" (7). This second layer of answers results from the following three types of explanation: first, explanation by emplotment, secondly, explanation by argument, and thirdly, explanation by ideological implication. Each of these explanations provides historians with a distinct set of options that require further elaboration.

Starting with the mode of emplotment, White borrows from literary theory four different types, such as Romance, Tragedy, Comedy, and Satire, which amount to different kinds of narrative structures, each with its own explanatory implications. These genres guide the narrative trajectory of a historical work, whether the historian realizes it or not. The key question is to notice how these modes shape the meaning of history that comes out of them. If, for instance, a historian plots the historical events as Romance, they implicitly present "a drama of self-identification symbolized by the hero's transcendence of the world of experience, his victory over it, and his final liberation from it" (8). On the contrary, the emplotment of Satire views all the hopes and possibilities of human existence ironically and it rejects the possibility of redemption. In the middle stand the modes of Comedy and Tragedy, each with an optimistic or pessimistic overtone respectively, which suggests that humans are at least partially capable of liberating themselves and mastering, even if provisionally, the world around them. Each emplotment, i.e., each story type, sets a different framework for human action and telos.

The second level of explanation, according to White, is the formal or discursive argument put forward by historical narratives, which adheres to "some putatively universal law of causal relationships" (11). If the emplotments build explanations through "artistic" functions, the arguments in this second category pertain to the "scientific" aspirations of a historian's work. Every historical account not only lines up a number of historical facts but also attempts to explain why they happened as they did. In most cases, such explanations do not reveal the implicit philosophical assumptions of their author, and yet, they do spring from specific "world-hypotheses" in Stephen C. Pepper's terms. White relies on Pepper's typology of world-views to identify four types of argument presented by historians as explanation: first, the Formist; secondly, the Organicist; thirdly, the Mechanistic and fourthly, the Contextualist. A historian who explains the events in the Formist mode seeks to identify the objects in the historical field as unique and self-contained historical occurrences that do not necessarily build up to specific generalizations about the historical process. An Organicist historian, on the other hand, will approach each individual occurrence merely as a part of a whole, which is greater in importance. As a result, such a historical account is more abstract in nature and it puts emphasis on synthetic processes or the crystallization of dispersed events into integrated entities (15). The Mechanistic historian takes this rationale a step further by reducing historical events to specific governing laws. Like an Organicist, they, too, are interested more in classes of phenomena than in individual events but the ultimate goal is to prove that these phenomena are nothing but the result of their universal rules akin to those found in science. Finally, the Contextualist historian opts for a certain balance between the particular and the general; each historical event needs to be placed within the context of its occurrence, so that the "functional interrelationships" among diverse agents and agencies can come to the fore (17). Any of these four arguments can technically govern the narrative in a historical work, but academic practices have regularly and openly opted for the Formist and Contextualist type as "the main candidates for orthodoxy" mostly due to ideological reasons, according to White (19–21).

The dominance of the Formist and Contextualist paradigm in academia led White to add another kind of historical explanation that consists of extra-epistemological considerations, namely the explanation by ideological implication. He defines "ideology" as "a set of prescriptions for taking a position in the present world of social praxis and acting upon it" and he adopts Karl Mannheim's four-part division that identifies the following ideologies: Anarchism, Conservatism, Radicalism, and Liberalism (21). Each of these general ideological preferences contains a value system that regulates the meaning of terms, such as reason, realism, science, and social change. Every historian carries a certain ideological load, which determines not only his stance toward the events he is supposed to study but also the implications that stem from his narrative prose. White stresses the need to differentiate ideology from politics and to look for ideological traces even when there appear to be none. As he puts it:

> I am interested only in indicating how ideological considerations enter into the historian's attempts to explain the historical field and to construct a verbal model of its processes in a narrative. But I will attempt to show that even the works of those historians and philosophers of history whose interests were manifestly nonpolitical, such as Burckhardt and Nietzsche, have specific ideological implications.
>
> White 2014, 26

The hidden assumptions of each historical work and the moral lessons that underlie each account of the past can largely be classified under Mannheim's four categories, despite the numerous varieties and the fine nuances found on the ideological spectrum. What is important, finally, is how White correlates this type of explanation with the preceding two, namely the emplotment and the argument. As White explains, even though the historian may appear to simply describe and analyze historical phenomena, what, in fact, happens is this: the historical events are emplotted in a certain way (aesthetic operation) putting forward a certain argument (cognitive operation) to generate prescriptive statements about how the world should go about (ideological/moral judgment) (ibid.). In this scheme, the raw data in the hands of each historian undergo a triple conditioning, first, by the type of plot structure in which they are accommodated, then by the type of discursive argument in which they are assembled and, finally, by the ideological filter that determines their direction and meaning.

White's intriguing conceptual scaffolding for approaching historical works can be particularly illuminating for the workings of historical filmmaking, provided we implement two key modifications. The first regards the explanation of emplotment that consists of the plot structures of Romance, Tragedy, Comedy, and Satire. Even though we may trace some relevance of these terms in a number of historical films, their descriptive value for cinematic narrative structures is extremely limited. If we want to understand how history on screen works, we need to adopt the vocabulary furnished by film narrative theories in greater detail. For the same reason, I suggest that the poetics of cinematic history does not have much to profit from White's theory of tropes (Metaphor, Metonymy, Synecdoche, Irony), which has been prominent in his thinking not only in *Metahistory* but also in most of his writings from then on. For all their explanatory value, the tropes remain linguistic protocols that cannot easily adapt to the parameters of audiovisual work. Their usage in the description of filmic material has always been carried out with enormous effort and with partial, if not outright problematic, results.[8] As Bordwell aptly argued, right before presenting his narrative theory back in 1985, "we need a theory of narration that is not bound to vague or atomistic analogies among representational systems, that does not privilege certain techniques, and that is broad enough to cover many cases but supple enough to discriminate among types, levels, and historical manifestations of narration" (1985, 26).

Thus, this is where Bordwell's pioneering work in the poetics of cinema needs to come into the picture. After a long, and yet indispensable, journey into the theory and history of written historiography, my project will continue its course by relating all this knowledge to the specifics of the cinematic medium. Unlike the academic historian who is committed *a priori* to a truthful and accurate representation of the historical past, a filmmaker who wants to "do history with film" is initially confronted with a significant generic choice, namely the choice between fiction and nonfiction filmmaking.[9] Each generic category presents them with a different set of creative options, different extra-textual commitments as well as different audience expectations. Even though the dichotomy between fiction and nonfiction is far from definitive,[10] the narrative strategies and the constructional principles of fiction films, on the one hand, and documentaries, on the other, have been mapped separately in film theory in a way that facilitates the treatment of the enormous variety of historical cinematic works. Thus, the division between fiction and nonfiction films[11] will be maintained throughout this book. The former have been thoroughly researched and theorized by Bordwell in *Narration in the Fiction Film* (1985), while the latter were surveyed and categorized by Bill Nichols in two key publications, namely *Representing Reality* (1991) and *Blurred Boundaries* (1994). The work of these two scholars will provide me with the terms and categories that are necessary for delineating the poetics of cinematic history in a fashion akin to the poetics of history found in *Metahistory*.

Starting with historical fiction films, we can reformulate what White calls the "explanation by emplotment" as an "explanation by mode of narration," wherein a mode of narration is defined as "a historically distinct set of norms of narrational construction and comprehension" (Bordwell 1985, 150). The three principal and most comprehensive modes of narration identified by Bordwell until the mid-1980s are the classical, the art-cinema and the historical-materialist narration.[12] To these three, I would like to add the post-classical mode that I formulated in my own research into filmic narration from the 1990s onwards (Thanouli 2009a). On the whole, in the course of a century of fiction filmmaking, we can trace at least four key modes of narration, each with specific and distinct formal characteristics that determine the ways that stories are depicted. So, what does it mean to explain history by mode of narration? It means that each mode of narration presents the historical facts and actions according to certain patterns that already contain an explanation of the ways that humans and their cosmos work. For example, a classical narration relies on a character-centered causality that places human initiative at the center of the action and foregrounds the accomplishment of a mission. When a filmmaker plots his historical account in the classical mode, he views history as a process dominated by human initiative and freedom of action. This view always already amounts to an explanation of how history works and what the meaning of it may be. On the other hand, when an art-cinema mode of narration is employed to depict a historical situation, the subject is no longer viewed as a free agent ready to act upon its surroundings; instead, other forces, like chance, coincidence, or subconscious drives carve an unpredictable path with no clear beginning, middle, or ending. The lack of clarity and purposeful action, on the contrary, is eliminated in the historical-materialist mode, which is the most openly political and militant one. The films of this kind adhere to the Leninist-Marxist doctrine, explicitly projecting this specific approach to the historical process and favoring collective struggles over personal and subjective goals. Finally, the post-classical mode of narration is a highly self-conscious breed that problematizes several of the classical plot elements and destabilizes the certainty about the power of individuality. Just like Satire in White's scheme, the post-classical narration multiplies the signs of representation in a way that denies any definitive take on what historical reality is and invites a more provisional and open-ended understanding of the historical past. Therefore, when dealing with historical fiction in the cinema, the first step is to identify the explanation by mode of narration, which provides an interpretation of the historical situation already through the formal elements of the film. It is the most palpable level of explanation, given that the narrative modes have been theorized sufficiently in the field and constitute systematic and reliable knowledge about how storytelling works in the realm of fiction.

When we switch to nonfiction narratives, we find the terrain sufficiently mapped by Nichols' research that spans several decades. Despite the remarkable influence of Bordwell's poetics on Nichols' work, the latter has formulated a typology of the nonfiction film that is less rigid, on the one hand, but equally inclusive and comprehensive on the other. From Nichols' various publications on the subject and the wide range of terms and categories that he has tried out in his effort to understand the workings of nonfiction filmmaking, I suggest that we single out his five main "modes of representation," namely the expository, the observational, the interactive, the reflexive, and the performative mode.[13] Nichols calls them "modes of representation" and not "modes of narration," as his categories combine narrative with rhetorical and ideological elements in a way that renders them less pure and less consistent compared to those of the fiction film. These five modes, however, can be considered as formal vehicles that, when dealing with a historical subject, they handle the facts and the raw data in ways that prefigure certain types of historical explanation. For instance, the expository mode presents a specific topic with the guidance of a powerful voice-over narration that creates a sense of coherence and unity. The causal relations of the events are spelled out by this authoritative voice and a full explanation is normally reached by the end of the film. Expository documentaries make up for the lack of spatiotemporal continuity with a tight cause-and-effect continuity that allows no gaps in the film's perspective. These formal characteristics, akin, to some extent, to the classical mode, render the historical event depicted intelligible and reinforce the faith in objective and impartial historical knowledge. However, the observational mode is a particularly difficult category to apply to historical subjects, as history defies its principal element, i.e. direct observation. And yet, the idea of recording history as it unfolds, for all its paradoxical nature, is often tried, particularly in the case of political events that are meant to be of historical importance. Therefore, observational documentaries, such as *Primary* (1960), the *War Room* (1993), or even Leni Riefenstahl's *Triumph of the Will* (1935) vaunt a formal structure characterized by spatiotemporal continuity and lack of authorial intervention that codify historical events as self-evident and self-explanatory. Moreover, observational documentaries place the human figure at the center of the action and emphasize the particularity of each moment, prefiguring thus the historical process as the study of unique occurrences. The interactive mode, instead, brings the filmmaker into the foreground and invites a more vivid and free-ranging exchange of views, at least in the first instance. Interactive documentaries are populated by interviews, dialogues, monologues, and accompanying visuals that result in a less unified structure compared to the expository ones, even though the various speaking positions voiced in them may ultimately promote a specific view on the historical matter at hand. When a historical documentarian opts for the interactive mode, they are open to a less stringent explanatory framework and approach the historical field as a complex and multi-faceted territory, despite the fact that the human figure may be the key force of action. Complexity is raised even higher in the fourth mode, the reflexive, which places particular emphasis on the documentary's constructional principles. Unlike the rest, a reflexive documentary calls attention to its means of production and problematizes, like Satire, our limited capacity of actually knowing what happened in historical reality. Through the use of irony, parody, and self-conscious stylistic techniques, it challenges the very process of accessing the past and forming interpretations out of relics and other historical data. As a formal explanation, the reflexive historical documentary destabilizes the centrality of Man in history, as it questions both his agency and his epistemological faculties, while it allows for other types of agency to come into play. Finally, the performative documentary substitutes objective knowledge, the quintessential feature of most nonfiction films, with subjective and personal perspectives on various historical matters. By doing so, it scales down the process of historical investigation from general history to micro-histories that emphasize the role of human subjectivity. As a result, it invites us to think about what Foucault termed "the practices of the self," i.e., all those opportunities, taken or missed, that each person encounters in the effort to become a subject and act upon the complex world around them.

All the modes of narration mentioned above, whether in fiction or in documentaries, can be related to White's other two types of historical explanation (formal argument/ideology) in the same manner as the modes of emplotment in every historical work are related to specific world-hypotheses and ideological implications. Even though filmmakers are not institutionally committed to put forth rhetorical arguments and abide by scientific principles, their historical films implicitly contain both hypotheses about how the world around us supposedly works as well as ideological orientations that prescribe specific ways for interpreting and evaluating human action. In other words, the formal structures of historical films are accompanied by types of explanations, argumentative and ideological, as those procured by Pepper and Mannheim's typologies respectively. The question, of course, arises about films, just as it did about written histories: Is every level of explanation tied only to specific options on the other levels or is every combination possible? White argues that there are "structural homologies" among various possible modes of emplotment, argument, and ideological implication, leading to certain "elective affinities" that render some combinations more amenable than others. For instance, in his schema, the Romantic mode tends to accommodate a Formist hypothesis and an Anarchist ideological view, while the Comic emplotment is better combined with an Organicist argument and a Conservative ideology. Despite these suggested combinations, White remains fairly open throughout his analysis about the possibility of other associations, especially when it comes to ideological implications, and he acknowledges the dialectical tension ensuing so often in complex historical works, such as those under scrutiny in *Metahistory* (White 2014, 28–9).

With these basic theoretical concepts and arguments in mind, I would like to develop a detailed methodological grid for analyzing historical films. In the two chapters that follow, I will explore further the relation between narration and historical explanations and I will examine in great detail how diverse modes of narration in fiction films and documentaries invite various types of explanations by argument and ideology. In fact, as my analysis will show, the cinematic forms seem to play a far more determining role on the historical explanations of a film, limiting considerably the possible combinations among the various types. At any rate, the merger of White's poetics of history with Bordwell and Nichols' formal categories will serve a two-fold task; first, to create a working taxonomy for analyzing and evaluating historical representations in the cinema and, secondly, to illustrate how the relation between history on paper and on screen is a complex play of similarity and difference. This is a development that we need not approach with caution and suspicion but with curiosity and insightfulness. History on film is another phase in the long history of historiography and it has a lot to tell us about the power of historical imagination and the role of historical knowledge in our current age.

Notes

1 Foucault is no longer with us to complete his own typology nor is it possible for us to imagine his reaction to White's reworking of the "epistemes" through linguistic tropes. However, from the 1980s onwards there is a vast literature on the idea of postmodernity which, despite its diverse and controversial nature, seems to corroborate the skepticism that Foucault identified in our current age toward the concepts and epistemological categories of the past, and particularly those of modernity.

2 See the conclusion.

3 See chapter 1.

4 A more detailed discussion of Jean-Louis Comolli's famous article is found in the conclusion.

5 The categories of true/false and fiction/nonfiction will be further discussed in the conclusion.

6 For a solid explanation of Foucault's complex relation to formalism, see Tanke (2013, 127–8).

7 I will be using the term "narration" and not "narrative" for my film examples, as it is the one employed by David Bordwell.

8 Trevor Whittock's book *Metaphor and Film* (1990) is emblematic in this regard.

9 In film theory and criticism, the term "genre" is largely applied to mainstream narrative films to describe a set of constructional elements as well as audience expectations. Famous genres include melodrama, comedy, gangster films, westerns, and musicals. In this instance, I am using the idea of a generic choice in a broader sense, as the one suggested by Alan Williams in his article "Is A Radical Genre Criticism Possible?" (1984). Williams pinpointed the significant difference of the term genre as applied in literary theory, noting that the categories of Romance, Comedy, and Tragedy are not equivalent to film genres like those mentioned above. Instead, he suggested the following: "It's mainly a question of terminology, of course, but I wonder if we ought to consider the principal film genres as being narrative film, experimental/avant-garde film, and documentary. Surely these are the categories in film studies that have among themselves the sorts of significant differences that one can find between, say, epic and lyric poetry" (121).

10 This issue will come into focus in the conclusion.

11 Here, I will be using the terms "nonfiction film" and "documentary" interchangeably. In the literature, however, the nonfiction film is often defined as a broader category. See Nichols (2010, 144–5).

12 In *Narration in the Fiction Film* Bordwell identifies a fourth mode of narration called "parametric," which applies only to "isolated filmmakers and fugitive films" (Bordwell 1985, 274). It is a loosely defined narrative category with a limited baseline that does not contain a distinct plot structure in relation to the other three modes. Therefore, I do not consider is capable of putting forward a separate form of historical explanation.

13 In his most recent work, Nichols added a sixth mode, "the poetic," while he also renamed the "interactive" as "participatory." I prefer to rely on Nichols' earlier work, as I do not consider these amendments significant for my own frame of research. The "poetic mode" is often a nonnarrative type of documentary more akin to experimental works than the narrative documentary that I am interested in here.

5

The Representation of History in the Fiction Film

Understanding historical fiction films has lain at the center of academic scholarship ever since Robert Rosenstone published his groundbreaking *Visions of the Past* (1995) and urged the community to study closely how the cinema had represented history for almost a century. His tentative categories, such as mainstream drama and innovative films, were helpful starting points that need to be expanded and reworked precisely through the historical knowledge of cinematic forms and expressions. Such knowledge as well as a reliable method of formal analysis can be found in David Bordwell's historical poetics. Historical poetics is an ambitious and wide-ranging research project that was conceived as "the study of how, in determinate circumstances, films are put together, serve specific functions, and achieve specific effects" (Bordwell 1989a, 266–7). It is a framework that poses questions about the films' formal and narrative construction, emphasizing the historical nature of cinematic forms and elevating formalism to an essential prerequisite for explicating other facets of the cinematic medium. The historical poetics' agenda has been exemplified in Bordwell's own prolific writings on hundreds of films and dozens of filmmakers, while its distinctive advantage over other theoretical approaches was explicated in his work *Making Meaning: Inference and Rhetoric in the Interpretation of Cinema* (1989). As the title suggests, the book explores the strategies of filmic interpretation and sets up an important distinction between the comprehension of a film, on the one hand, which focuses on referential and explicit meanings and its interpretation, on the other, which seeks implicit and symptomatic meanings hidden in the body of a film. Bordwell is critical of the vast majority of interpretative practices,[1] lining up several examples of exaggerated interpretations that take very little consideration of what actually appears on the screen in favor of what is supposedly repressed under the surface. As a remedy for this problematic course of film studies, he puts forward historical poetics as a research platform that will make both history and form relevant again and will constitute the basis for any worthwhile interpretative activity.[2] In the final pages of *Making Meaning,* he argues for the necessity of interpretation, provided that it retraces its steps back to the film form and its effects. His closing words are worth quoting below:

> In titling his 1923 study of conventionality in art *The Knight's Move* Shklovsky created an image rich in implications. One of them is the necessarily oblique development of art. Like the chess knight, art does not progress in a straight line. It gets deflected because it aims to be unpredictable in relation to reigning norms. Criticism can progress in a similar fashion. The greatest novelty, at this moment, will come not from new semantic fields (postmodernism, or whatever will follow) but from a sidestepped dislocation of interpretation itself. It is time for critics to make the knight's move.
>
> Bordwell 1989a, 274

I believe that deploying historical poetics as the foundation of the map of historical representation in the cinema could be regarded as such a move. Any attempt to analyze and interpret the historical films needs to begin by examining closely the shape and the function of the cinematic form in relation to the historical content. Hayden White did precisely that with written history, as we saw in the previous chapter, when he differentiated between five distinct elements in every historical account, i.e. the chronicle, the story, the mode of emplotment, the mode of argument and the mode of ideological implication. Notice how each element leads to another of higher abstraction; starting from the most tangible, the chronicle as a list of dates and events, moving all the way up to the most speculative, the ideological underpinnings of the historical work. Put differently, every historical account addresses two types of questions: first, "What happened, when and why?" and second, "What is the point of it all?" or "Where does it all lead to?" In this light, comprehension of the events (what, when, why) and interpretation of them (what is the meaning) appear as two separate and, yet, intricately interconnected activities that feed off each other.[3]

A similar trajectory needs to be followed for the historical films with some minor conceptual adjustments. In the case of the cinema, the chronicle and the story become part of the "narration," defined by Bordwell as the process whereby the film's plot and style interact in the course of cueing and channeling the spectator's construction of the story[4] (Bordwell 1985, 53). This comprehensive definition of the narrational process allows us to proceed from the narration of a single film to the "mode of narration" that comprises a set of narrational strategies that recur regularly within particular historical and institutional contexts. Bordwell developed the concept of the "mode of narration" in order to categorize a large number of films from various historical and geographical junctures according to their compositional characteristics.[5] As he explains in *Narration in the Fiction Film*, he selected the term "mode" for its ability to "reveal, at a certain level of generality, significant unity among historically specific narrational strategies" (150). A mode is more fundamental, less transient and more pervasive than a genre, while it even transcends schools of filmmaking, movements and entire national cinemas (ibid.). As such, compared to the four literary genres (Romance, Tragedy, Comedy, and Satire/Irony) deployed by White as modes of emplotment, the filmic modes of narration are simultaneously more historically specific, and yet broad enough, to accommodate numerous films from across the world and do justice to their shared formal particularities.

Therefore, for every historical fiction film we need to explore the "what, when and why" first as plot elements and then as integral parts of specific narrative configurations. Starting from the narration of the film, we can gradually move on to the explanations by mode of narration, mode of argument, and mode of ideological implications, just as White did for written history. For example, a historical film about the Second World War can represent this event in various different ways; it may have one protagonist or more, it may have a tight or loose causal logic, it may represent time and space realistically or not, and so on and so forth. The meticulous evaluation of all the aspects of its narration (plot, style, story) will allow us to categorize the film to one of the established modes of narration. Then, we are ready to pose the question "What is the point of it all?" at three different levels: the narration, the argument, and the ideology, each yielding a diverse range of explanations about the meaning of this historical world conflict to us today. In this complex process, the study of the narration constitutes the cornerstone of our analysis, holding together the comprehension and the interpretation of the historical film and allowing us to pass from one realm to another with sufficient consistency and justification.

The central goal of this chapter, consequently, is to flesh out this procedure and present the range of historical explanations available to historical films, depending on their narrative form. Before, however, proceeding to this task, I would like to make one last theoretical clarification regarding Bordwell's theory of narration. It pertains to the role of the author/narrator in filmic narration. Unlike a history book, a historical film does not bear the name of a single author who is credited with the historical representation contained in the work.

Admittedly, the director is most often identified, by critics and scholars alike, as the chief creator of the filmic historical images, but, at the same time, it is widely acknowledged that filmmaking is a collective process. One look at the credits is sufficient for understanding the complexities of the filmmaking business. Especially when it comes to historical filmmaking, it is regularly discussed how a number of other contributors, such as the studio, the producers, the writers, the historical advisors and the production designers, play significant and even definitive roles in the final outcome. As I argued in the previous chapter, this is an obvious difference between written and filmic accounts, even though attributing agency can be a complex matter for professional historians as well, depending on one's deeper views on agency and causality. For films, at least, these complications are manifest and invite us to be cautious about the ways we approach the cinematic rendition of a historical event in terms of its creating force. This is why the poetics of cinematic history cannot be grounded on some emblematic filmmakers akin to the way White developed the poetics of history, deploying figures like Ranke, Marx, and Burckhardt as exemplary cases. Instead, the poetics of history that I will formulate in the following pages will employ the mode of narration as its key unit. In fact, Bordwell's treatment of authorship within his narrative theory is in line with the ambivalent status of the filmmaker in the historical film. As he notes, "to give every film a narrator or implied author is to indulge in an anthropomorphic fiction" (62). More specifically, he insists that the narration in the fiction film does not entail the presence of a narrator and we should not be tempted to attribute the entire narrative edifice to a specific author. Instead, he invites us to understand narration as a process that presupposes a "message" and a "receiver" but not a "sender." Since the presence of a "narrator" as a tangible form in a film is not a permanent and ubiquitous feature, his narrative theory, as he argues, need not contain it as a built-in element. It is something we can identify on occasion, depending on the narrative mode and on various historical circumstances. Despite the severe criticism against this stance,[6] I believe that for the purposes of understanding historical fiction films and building historical interpretations, it is functional to consider the director merely as an extratextual agent, whose textual presence needs to be acknowledged only when the textual and extratextual parameters require us to do so.

With this important note in mind, I would like to investigate how the formal and narrative elements in a historical film help shape various historical explanations. I will take each of the key four modes of narration, i.e., the classical, the art cinema, the historical–materialist, and the post-classical, and I will examine how their narrative components host diverse arguments at the level of narration, argument and ideology regarding the meaning of history. Table 5.1 below summarizes my findings and presents an overview of the poetics of history in the fiction films. All the combinations of modes and explanations will be delineated and developed in two steps. First, I will present a general outline of the narrative modes and the types of historical explanations with which they can be correlated. Then, I will proceed to a series of case studies that illustrate in greater detail the explanatory mechanisms contained in every historical representation. Specifically, I will analyze films depicting two key historical events of the twentieth century, the Second World War and the Holocaust. In the literature so far, cinematic representations of these two signal moments in World history have occupied scholars extensively, spawning various readings and interpretations. In my own analysis, these films will be the litmus test for the poetics of cinematic history, shedding light on the ways in which we can connect narration to historical explanation and interpretation.

Modes of narration and historical explanations

The classical

Classical narration is a set of constructional principles that Bordwell identified in an extensive sample of American studio films from 1917 to 1960. During that period, the American film industry gradually established a set of creative options that became commonplace not only in American filmmaking but also across the world with various more or less deviations. It is noteworthy that in the monumental study *The Classical Hollywood Cinema: Film Style and Mode of*

Table 5.1

Mode of Narration	Mode of Argument	Mode of Ideological Implication
Classical	Formist or Contextualist	Liberal or Conservative
Art cinema	Organicist	Anarchist
Historical–materialist	Mechanistic	Radical
Post-classical	Contextualist	Liberal or Conservative

Production to 1960 (1985) Bordwell and his two co-authors, Janet Staiger and Kristin Thompson, argue that the invention of sound does not function as a milestone, as is usually the case; instead, all the elements of the classical narration were already in place by the end of 1910s. What is also noteworthy is that, despite the close ties of the classical mode of narration with Hollywood's mode of practice, the former continued in full force even after the latter's demise. One of Bordwell's key positions to this date is that the classical mode of narration remains the key model for fiction films, regardless of some minor technical and stylistic developments (Bordwell 2006). And he is quite right; the classical mode of narration, not only dominates most films coming out on our screens even today, but it also constitutes the dominant option for historical fictions. But let us see closely how this mode works.

Bordwell's succinctly describes a classical film as follows:

> The classical Hollywood film presents psychologically defined individuals who struggle to solve a clear-cut problem or attain certain goals. In the course of this struggle, the characters enter into conflict with others or with external circumstances. The story ends with a decisive victory or defeat, a resolution of the problem and a clear achievement or nonachievement of the goals.
>
> Bordwell 1985, 157

This compact description contains a number of key components of the classical narration that I would like to elaborate on, starting with the notion of the "psychologically defined individual." The cornerstone of the classical mode is the character-centered causality, i.e., the idea that the actions of the individual and his/her free will are the driving forces of the story. The character is an autonomous agent who bears specific traits, behaviors, and qualities, which are evidently established in the film from the beginning with the help of recurrent motifs. In the course of the film, the character participates in two separate but often intertwined plotlines: the accomplishment of a mission and the formation of the heterosexual couple. Each plotline contains goals, obstacles, and struggles that give the opportunity to the character to demonstrate his/her determination and resolve, even if the outcome is not always successful. Above all, it is the clarity of purpose and the tight cause-and-effect chain of events that guide the narrative logic and shape the spatiotemporal coordinates of the plot. This means that the construction of space and time in the classical film strives to accommodate the actions of the characters and offer the viewers the best possible view of the story world. To that end, filmmakers rely on the system of continuity editing for the creation of a continuous and unobtrusive movement in space and time, while they keep their stylistic flourishes to a minimum in order not to deflect attention from the progression of the story. Finally, linear chronology, ellipses, and smooth temporal transitions contribute to the overall unity between causality, space, and time that render the classical mode the most intelligible and accessible narrative option in the history of cinema.

When it comes to historical films, the classical mode is by far the most popular choice in historical filmmaking across the twentieth century. The classical narrative form has proven to be the most accommodating vehicle for the historical vision of numerous filmmakers who produced historical accounts with the help of the classical devices mentioned above. The fact that a historical film has a classical narration already tells us a few things about the film's approach to the historical process and the possible types of explanation that may stem from it. This is a point that will be fleshed out extensively in the analyses of the films that follow in the Case Studies section, but here I would like to provide an overview of the explanatory options available within the classical mode. Therefore, when a historical film is plotted as a classical narration, history is presented as an individual-driven process guided by the personal initiatives of the key protagonists. From this perspective, history is made by a few heroic figures that bear specific goals, ambitions, and visions, and who are willing to fight and even sacrifice for their cause. The key source of agency in these accounts is the human individual who may encounter other forces, such as natural phenomena, sociopolitical imperatives or even contingencies, but they will eventually master them and shape their own destiny. Take *Spartacus* (1960), for instance. The eponymous hero is a clearly defined individual with recurring character traits, presented right from the opening sequence, who manages to become a force of history and a symbol of free will. This clarity of purposeful action is further sustained by the unity of narrative space and time that shapes, in turn, our conception of historical time and space. When it comes to space, we tend to believe that it primarily functions as a terrain for human action, while it is characterized by consistency and permanence. Historical time, on the other hand, is presented as linear time that can be easily dissected into historical periods bearing an internal unity and logic. Thus, when a classical film like *Spartacus* depicts the ancient times on the screen, it presents, on the one hand, antiquity as an integral whole, while it also approaches historical time as real time; i.e., as a natural flow that progresses steadily to our current moment.[7]

These explanations by "mode of narration" are usually accompanied by an explanation by a "formal argument" in White's terms, which reveals a certain underlying world hypothesis, at least one of the four identified in Pepper's work (Pepper 1970). Even though historical films, compared to written histories, are meant to be more art than science, they, too, contain historical arguments that work in tandem with the formal choices at the level of narration. Thus, the classical mode of narration is best paired primarily with the Formist argument and secondarily with the Contextualist. Both arguments are feasible within the classical paradigm because their overarching theories are dispersive, paying attention to the specificity of things and allowing for a certain degree of chance and unpredictability, something that is excluded from the Organicist or the Mechanistic views. However, Formism is dominant in classical historical films, as they are committed to the description of particular characters and events in their uniqueness. As Pepper notes:

> All the Formist needs to observe (if he does observe it) is that as an empirical
> fact all concrete existences do participate in the physical laws of time and space,
> so that every concrete existent object is to be located at a date and at a place.
>
> Pepper 1970, 174

When we look at the historical situations depicted in Hollywood films we are overwhelmed by the emphasis on historical specificity that takes the form of a detailed construction of *mise-en-scène* (settings and costumes) as well as a meticulous delineation of the traits of the protagonists that act as unique individuals in a very particular point in space and time. In *Spartacus* again, the leading hero stands out more for his personal characteristics and his distinctive features than as a representative of the class of slaves. The classical character is precisely a "psychologically defined individual" because the film regards him/her as a unique human being and not as an average representative of a certain group or class, as is the case in the historical-materialist tradition, which we will discuss shortly. The option of a Contextualist argument, on the other hand, is possible in some cases, as we can see, for instance, in *Judgment at Nuremberg* (1961) or in Gavras' *Amen* (2002). In these cases, the films seek to embed the characters and their actions into a wider web of historical developments and agencies. Contextualism is an argument that becomes central in post-classical historical narrations, as I will argue, but we cannot exclude it altogether from the classical mode. When a classical narration opts for the Contextualist argument, we witness a multiplication of causal factors as well as an effort to connect specific individuals to their social, historical, and political surroundings.

Finally, a classical historical film can be related to an ideological argument that pertains more to extra-textual and extra-epistemological concerns. In White's poetics of history, which I introduced in the previous chapter, ideology is viewed not as a set of observations of the past but rather as a set of "prescriptions" about the present and future. In other words, the ideological implications in a historical work, whether on paper or on film, give away a specific value system according to which we judge aspects of social life and practice, such as reason, science, justice, or social change. The four options suggested in *Metahistory* via Karl Mannheim's work (Anarchist, Conservative, Radical, and Liberal) could possibly be expanded or complicated in view of current political and ideological conditions but I would like to maintain them as they are, as general markers of ideological preference. The connection of the previous two types of explanation, i.e., the mode of narration and the formal argument, with these four options of ideological implication is a fairly loose connection that takes us from the realm of comprehension to that of interpretation. In this sense, historical films may be open to multiple interpretations that vary depending on the audience and other external circumstances. However, there are certain limitations. A film like *Spartacus* is unlikely to be interpreted as Anarchist; instead, the chances are that its ideological preference is, first and foremost, Liberal with some possibly Radical undertones. Radicalism, however, cannot be dominant in classical narrations with Formist arguments. The most fitting ideological position for them is found in Liberal mentality. As Mannheim observes:

> The fundamental attitude of the Liberal is characterized by a positive acceptance of culture and the giving of an ethical tone to human affairs. He is most in his element in the role of critic rather than that of creative destroyer. He has not broken his contact with the present–the here and now. About every event there is an atmosphere of inspiring ideas and spiritual goals to be achieved.
>
> Mannheim 1979, 198

The Liberal emphasis on individuality, rational human agency, and the belief in progress and free will is best accommodated in the classical narrations, even though we cannot exclude cases of Conservatism, which does not oppose the idea of individualism but emphasizes the value of tradition and considers the "present" as a realization of utopia (206–11). In fact, Hollywood cinema has perennially been accused of a Conservative ideological agenda from critics at home and abroad based primarily on a crude distinction between the Left and the Right. Mannheim's categories, however, are more sociologically specific and go beyond party politics. If by the Left we mean something along the lines of Radical Marxism, then clearly most classical narrations are not fit for serving this purpose in the way the historical-materialist mode does. However, the emphasis on character-centered causality and individual freedom is an element shared by both Liberal and Conservative views, whether they envision progress or favor stability respectively. In fact, this common ground was picked up by Robert Ray in his famous analysis of the ideology in classical Hollywood cinema, arguing that:

> In retrospect, as a guide to American culture's relationship to contemporary events, these movies reveal persisting similarities between the apparently polarized Left and Right. Ultimately, of course, they both shared the same mythology, with its predisposition to regard events in terms of the reconciliatory pattern's abiding advocacy of individualism.
>
> Ray 1985, 300

As a result, the classical historical films, founded on the primacy of individual action and initiative are likely to portray the historical events as either a Liberal vision of progress and improvement of humanitarian ideals or as a Conservative celebration of the status quo, considered as an already accomplished ideal.

Overall, the classical mode of narration for an entire century has provided the formal molds for representing the historical past with a specific palette of historical explanations. From D.W. Griffith's *Birth of a Nation* (1915) with its classical, Formist and Conservative view on history to Nat Turner's *Birth of a Nation* (2016), an equally classical, Formist but Liberal approach to the same historical era, there have been thousands of films both in Hollywood and abroad, which engaged with the past deploying the classical narrative options and forming historical explanations within the argumentative and ideological range that I described above.

The art cinema

The art cinema is the second key mode of narration that Bordwell has identified in the poetic history of cinema, placing its emergence in the European soil after the Second World War and relating its existence to the flowering of the national cinemas and the various New Waves all over Europe in the late 1950s and the

1960s. Key examples of art films are found in the repertoire of great European auteurs, such as Alain Resnais, Federico Fellini, Michelangelo Antonioni, and Ingmar Bergman, to name a few (Bordwell 1985, 230). Compared to the classical mode, Bordwell's account of the art cinema rules of narrative construction is less rigorous and consistent[8] but it can help us, for our purposes here, identify a distinct set of historical explanations that are found in films following alternative narrative paths.

To begin to understand these different approaches to the idea of history, we need to look closer at the narrative options contained in this paradigm and examine how they initiate a distinct rationale not only with respect to the historical facts (what, when, where) but also as regards "the point of it all." According to Bordwell, the three main characteristics that regulate the narration of art films are objective realism, subjective realism, and authorial presence. Just like classical narrations, art films strive to appear realistic, adhering, however, to a modernist conception of reality. As Bordwell notes, "art-cinema narration, taking its cue from literary modernism, questions such a definition of the real: the world's laws may not be knowable, personal psychology may be indeterminate" (206). This core principle of art cinema forms a strenuous relation with the historical objective to represent a past reality, which, in fact, needs to be specific and concrete. For that matter, the option of an art cinema narration is not the most common or popular in historical fiction filmmaking. The art cinema norms often seem less compatible with our standard notion of historical knowledge, which dictates a clear engagement and a solid causal approach to the historical facts. However, there are several significant historical films cast in this mode, which put forward alternative views on the historical process. When we watch Bernardo Bertolucci's *The Conformist* (1970) and *1900* (1976), Liliana Cavani's *The Night Porter* (1974), Theo Angelopoulos' *The Travelling Players* (1975), or more recent films by Ken Loach, such as *The Wind that Shakes the Barley* (2006), we witness the resurrection of the past through a set of narrative conventions that carry with them their own underlying explanations and hypotheses about the meaning of history and the workings of this world.

Let us examine these conventions more closely. The objective realism of art cinema, as discussed by Bordwell, is translated into a loosening of the cause-and-effect logic of the events, an episodic construction of the plot and an open-ended resolution. It also carries a desire for verisimilitude in the construction of time and space, which is manifest in the preference for location shooting, natural lighting, and intervals or *temps mort* in the action. Furthermore, the art films place tremendous emphasis on a subjective realism, which focuses on the inner lives of the characters in the story and their personal struggles with their social environment. An art protagonist lacks the clear-cut traits, motives, and goals of the Hollywood counterpart, while his/her behavior is not always justified. Stylistically, the films seek to convey the personal wanderings and the psychological fluctuations by means of certain *mise-en-scène* techniques, like covert glances, static postures, or smiles that fade, whereas mental states are represented with subjective images, like dreams, hallucinations, and fantasies (208). Finally, the art cinema mode is characterized by the overt presence of an extra-filmic figure, namely the auteur. Unlike the classical films, which can stand on their own without resorting to the manifest gestures of their directors, the art films tell their stories by incorporating the commentary of the auteur in the plot. As a result, the act of narration becomes overt and self-conscious, drawing attention to the filmmaking process itself and the manipulation of the formal parameters. For instance, an odd camera angle or a mismatched cut or any strange manipulation of the spatiotemporal coordinates can be attributed to an extratextual authority, who intervenes and makes its presence felt to the audience. This last principle, as Bordwell notes, undercuts the desire for realism achieved by the other two realistic goals (objective/subjective). This difficult balance between realism, on the one hand, and authorial manipulation, on the other, is difficult to manage. In Bordwell's words, "a realist aesthetic and an expressionist aesthetic are hard to merge. The art cinema seeks to solve the problem in a sophisticated way: through ambiguity" (212).

When all these narrative and stylistic options are chosen for the representation of a historical event or a historical period, then the historical image flaring up on the screen bears remarkable differences from the one we discussed in the classical mode. At the center of the narration we still find a character whose trajectory, however, is not as goal-oriented or linear as that of the classical hero. The character is embedded in a highly determined historical and social milieu that seems too powerful and overwhelming. Take *The Conformist*, for instance. The presence of the fascist regime is ubiquitous even though Mussolini is hardly present. The fascist establishment is in charge and, yet, the power lies not in specific individuals in various ranks; they are only secondary to the idea of fascism penetrating the entire society. Objective realism in such a narration consists in the attempt to convey the complexity of a historical situation, the limited capacities of specific individuals and the difficulty of establishing a clear-cut causal logic connecting the historical events. Subjective realism, on the other hand, strives to engage with the individual as an equally complex entity driven by reason as well as other subconscious drives. A historical agent like Marcello Clerici (Jean-Louis Trintignant) is never sure of his actions, he doubts and dithers about the meaning of his activity, and he is the first to relinquish responsibility for his deeds. Historical change, such as the end of the fascist regime, is not the result of heroic action in the film; instead, every major historical event works as an incentive for us to ponder on the miniscule role of the individual in the large scheme of things.

A similar goal is found in the construction of time in most historical art films. The temporal scheme of this mode, which invites the frequent use of flashbacks and flashforwards as well as the manipulation of duration and frequency of the events, problematizes the notion of linear historical temporality and encourages us to reconsider the mediated relation of our present to the past. As Robert Burgoyne observes in his analysis of temporality evidenced in Bertolucci's films, with *1900* as his key case study:

> What is most unusual in this modeling of history is that the past acquires significance only as part of a theoretical practice in the present, as part of an ongoing polemic between past and present. Rather than attempting to fashion a new, more adequate representation of the past, the film asserts that the practice of historiography is one of criticism and confrontation—of the present with the past, of one social form or mode of production with another.
>
> Burgoyne 1991, 109

This emphasis on confrontation and self-conscious investigation of the complex relation between the present and the past is also served by the principle of the authorial intervention in the plot. Unlike the classical film, which makes great effort to convince the audience that "this is really what happened" by multiplying the historical details and their "reality effect," the art film draws attention to the very act of representation and its limited resources to provide a complete and unequivocal image of the past. The subjective realism, combined with the personal overtones of the auteur, demonstrate that any account of the past is bound to contain subjective elements that render the objective representation of history impossible.

All these explanations regarding historical knowledge, which stem from the art cinema mode of narration, are coupled with at least one world hypothesis that suggests an argument about how history works.[9] Specifically, of the four hypotheses in Pepper's taxonomy, the art cinema is best suited with the Organicist view. What characterizes the Organicist argument of history is the depiction of the particulars of the historical field as "components of synthetic processes" (White 2014, 15). As Pepper notes, "the organicist believes that every actual event in the world is a more or less concealed organic process. He believes, therefore, that a careful scrutiny of any actual process in the world would exhibit its organic structure [...]" (Pepper 1970, 281). In this light, the historical art film addresses the individual not for its singularity but for its participation into a greater whole, which is far more important than its constituent parts. The fact that art cinema characters often exhibit an inability to act and take control of a situation inevitably directs our attention to those forces from the social and historical environment acting upon them. In plain words, if the individual cannot act, then something else must be in charge. For all its subjective moments and inner explorations, a film like *The Conformist* approaches the principal character as a person embedded in larger ongoing processes beyond his control. Marcello's behavior is directly aligned with the historical and social reality of fascism and his adventure is nothing but a fragment of a wider historical process with its own teleology. It is important, however, to draw a distinction between Organicism's emphasis on the integration of the micro level into a macro level, on the one hand, and the search for universal laws and mechanistic causality, on the other. In my introduction of the art cinema, I quoted Bordwell explaining how this mode is premised on the idea that the world's laws are beyond our cognitive reach. Therefore, an art film that explores a historical event would be unlikely to argue that it knows the laws of the world or society and that it will proceed to portray them on the screen. Such a view is found in the historical-materialist mode, which I will present in the next section. In art cinema, though, a Mechanistic view of cinema is excluded. The presence of subjectivism, whether in terms of realism or authorial intervention, as well as the pervasive idea of ambiguity are not prone to endorse an argument that treats human and social interactions or events as predictable, determinate and scientifically explained. On the other hand, the same elements render art cinema incompatible with Formism and Contextualism as well. Unlike the latter, the argument that springs from a historical art narration is more integrative than dispersive. The characters, the settings, the actions and the historical time are not highlighted for their uniqueness but for their participation into greater entities. "Organicism takes time lightly or disparagingly," says Pepper (Pepper 1970, 281). And so it does with the specificity of existence, seeking to unearth the implicit organic whole found in each fragment (a person, a time, a space). Thus, the predicaments of specific individuals are portrayed in the historical art film not as self-serving autonomous occurrences but as pieces of a historical progress that is always larger than the sum of its parts.

What about ideology and art cinema now? After the explanation by mode of narration and mode of argument, we should consider the ideological options that we may encounter in the art film. As White observes, the ideological orientation of a historical work is tied to extra-textual and moral concerns. This means that it is important to take into account that the institutional framework of art films is significantly different from the industrial setting in which the classical mode developed and thrived. Particularly, if we consider the time of the emergence of art cinema, namely the end of 1950s and throughout the 1960s, we can understand why the dominant ideological current in European cinema was implicitly or explicitly related to left-wing politics. Thematically, subjects such as the revolution, communism, and collectivism were often prominent, while there was always present a critique of the bourgeoisie and the status quo. In addition, several art filmmakers were vocal supporters of the Left, a fact that bears direct influence on the narrative construction of their films, given the opportunities for authorial intervention that the art cinema mode provides. If, however, we have to work with Mannheim's four key ideologies, i.e., Anarchism, Conservativism, Radicalism, and Liberalism, I would argue that most historical art films veer much more towards Anarchism than Radicalism. A description of Anarchism from White's work will elucidate this point.[10] As he notes:

> [...] Anarchists are inclined to idealize a *remote past* of natural-human innocence from which men have fallen into the corrupt "social" state in which they currently find themselves. They, in turn, project this utopia onto what is effectively a non-temporal plane, viewing it as a possibility of human achievement *at any time*, if men will only seize control of their own essential humanity, either by an act of will or by an act of consciousness which destroys the socially provided belief in the legitimacy of the current social establishment.
>
> White 2014, 24; emphasis in the original

The nostalgia for an innocent past, the social critique, and the postponement of revolutionary action to an indefinite future trap the Anarchist ideology to a non-temporal perspective without any specific suggestions about the reenactment of change. Looking at *The Conformist* once more, we realize that when it comes to prescribing actions and supporting change, the art film is unable to offer specific solutions to the predicaments of social reality. When the film ends, Marcello does not follow the parades of the liberation; he stands alone, trapped in his presentness, unable to move in any direction. For all their critical rejection of the capitalist and bourgeois establishment, the art films do not easily yield to a Radicalist mentality, like the ones we find in the historical–materialist mode. Not even the films of Ken Loach, an openly political figure of the Left, do they support the idea of revolution as an imminent condition. Notice how both *Land and Freedom* (1995) and the *Wind that Shakes the Barley* (2006) paint a complicated picture as to the possibilities of Radical social change. Instead, they invite us to ponder on the conflicts of history and celebrate humanity in an abstract sense.

Overall, the art cinema mode of narration with all its formal idiosyncrasies and variations has proven remarkably hospitable to historical themes and has allowed filmmakers, particularly from Europe, to explore alternative views of history. The search for a new kind of realism combined with a high level of self-consciousness and authorial intervention have favored an Organicist view of history that aims to embed the protagonists' trajectories to larger ongoing processes and highlight the importance of "the big picture." Finally, despite their formal and argumentative differentiation from the classical mode, the implicit ideological positions of the art films seem more compatible with the Anarchist mentality, leaving Radicalism for those that I will discuss next.

The historical-materialist

The third mode of narration listed in Bordwell's poetic history is called historical-materialist and it originates in the works of the Soviet filmmakers of the period 1925–33. Compared to the previous two modes, the historical-materialist narration comprises fewer examples and it has a limited chronological and geographical scope. According to Bordwell, twenty-two Soviet films, such as *Strike* (1925), *Potemkin* (1925), and *October* (1928), exemplify a distinct set of narrational principles that are important enough to constitute their own paradigm. For our discussion of historical fictional filmmaking, these films are equally important, too. The prominence of historical themes in their plots, on the one hand, allows us to continue our exploration of the poetics of history on film, while their overall narrative setup, on the other, helps us to make manifest several of the issues that remained implicit in the films of the classical and art cinema mode. Specifically, a historical film of this tradition openly admits to supporting a specific argument and ideology, the Marxist-Leninist doctrine, which puts forth very specific tenets regarding the meaning and direction of history. Unlike the film examples that I have discussed so far, for which I had to infer their underlying philosophical and ideological implications, the films of the historical–materialist mode come already packaged as a narrative–argument–ideology, all in one piece. As Bordwell notes, "In Soviet cinema, the double demand of poetic and rhetoric shapes basic narrational strategies. There is the tendency to treat the syuzhet as both a narrative and an argument" (Bordwell 1985, 235). Thus, a historical film in this mode openly presents its didactic and persuasive goals in support of the Marxist-Leninist ideology, disclosing the intimate connection between the diverse types of historical explanation. Whereas the artistic, scientific, and moral concerns remained relatively separate in the other modes, the historical–materialist type binds them mechanistically.

Let us see how this new combination works. In terms of their narrative characteristics, the Soviet films are distinguished for their depiction of the character as representative of certain classes, social milieus, and political views. Instead of focusing on the individual as a unique existence, these stories choose characters as examples of collective identities. Take *Potemkin*, for instance. The mutiny on the ship is not attributed to the initiative of specific individuals whose names and attributes we care to acknowledge; instead, the sailors come forward as a group overwhelmed by the gushing current of revolution. Whereas a classical historical film singles out a protagonist for his/her unique personality and emphasizes the distinguished role they play in the historical process, the historical–materialist film submits the subject to the impersonal forces of history. What is also distinctive about these films is the clear distinction between plot and style, with the former adhering to limited and communicative patterns and the latter experimenting relentlessly with the film form. Specifically, the plots in the historical–materialist mode serve the core principles of the communist ideology; as such, they draw their thematic resources from a limited range of issues, such as the process of revolution and the struggle against the remnants of feudal or capitalist society. The repetition of predictable situations at the level of plot allows the filmmakers to experiment with stylistic devices, namely montage, in order to serve, yet again, the idea of struggle and conflict. Bordwell highlights the mode's overt and self-conscious narration, arguing that:

> This cinema goes beyond those narrational asides which we found in the art cinema; these films do not offer a reality (objective, subjective) inflected by occasional "commentary"; these films are signed and addressed through and through, the diegetic world built from the ground up according to rhetorical demands.
>
> Bordwell 1985, 239

Soviet filmmakers, with Eisenstein at the helm, developed techniques of montage that strived to visualize the ideological conflict at work in Soviet society and promote an alternative to traditional or bourgeois art. To that end, film form needed to escape the constraints of realistic representation and encourage the viewer to an active engagement with the work of art. Eisenstein masterfully combined his craft with theoretical writings on how film form could express abstract meanings, and predominantly the concept of conflict, through the graphic juxtaposition of filmic images (Eisenstein 2014). In *Potemkin*, each shot is built with intense inner graphic contrasts, while the editing of one shot to the next aims at a jarring effect that triggers complex associations in the spectator's mind. The famous Odessa steps sequence is not a momentary aberration in an otherwise classically edited film; *Potemkin*, as most of these Soviet films, is entirely conceptualized as a revolution against the invisible and seamless representationalism of traditional art. As a result, the narration, from beginning to end, defies the specificity of diegetic time and space and strives to generate "tropes of thought" and "tropes of speech" that will convey the basic tenets of their radical ideology (Bordwell 1985, 239). In this light, the "auteurist" experimentation of Eisenstein or Pudovkin with film form is not individually motivated but it is fully subservient to the rhetorical and ideological concerns of the political regime that commissioned them.

In this highly determined filmic mode, the argument that dominates the depiction of history is that of Mechanism. The underlying assumption of a Mechanistic historical argument is that history is governed by laws akin to those that govern nature. In White's account, Marx is considered primarily as a Mechanist philosopher of history,[11] as he is less interested in the particular qualities of historical figures, institutions, customs or art forms than in the species, class and generic typifications that they can be shown to exemplify (White 2014, 17). In the same spirit, the films of the historical-materialist mode can be viewed as instances of a Mechanistic approach to history, where individuals are merely instruments in larger social and historical processes that function according to specific laws. The sailors on the *Potemkin* are merely parts of a revolutionary machine, like cogs on the wheels of change. They do not instigate the revolution; they are not the primary agents of this momentous process. Instead, the revolution is bound to happen because the forces in the mechanics of history are designed in ways that render this evolution inevitable. Given their explicit political objectives, the historical arguments put forth in these narratives are clearly defined and easily related to the key principles of a Marxist approach to history.

Similarly, the ideological implications of these films are not pieces of a difficult puzzle that we need to solve. Unlike the classical and art cinema narrations, the historical–materialist films proclaim their Radical ideology as part of their plot, leaving no room for open or multiple interpretations. By making revolution as their primary theme, historical films in this mode advocate for radical political change, celebrate the Bolshevik Revolution and view the utopian condition as imminent. In other words, of the four dominant ideological positions, these films openly opt for Radicalism, emphasizing the importance of social structures for the effectuation of change and positioning the idea of progress in the form of revolutionary social transformation. Throughout the history of cinema, there have been hardly any other examples with more explicit, precise and fully prescriptive approach to history. The question now is what happens to Radicalism when Soviet cinema exits this brief historical–materialist phase and enters the one of Socialist Realism, which cuts down on the radical stylistic experiments in montage and establishes a more traditional narrative set-up. As Bordwell notes:

> In general, the historical–materialist paved the way for Socialist Realism in their use of referentiality, exemplary heroes, and the apprenticeship pattern. What was lost was the constant narrational presence and overt rhetorical address of the historical-materialist style. At the level of fabula structure, Socialist Realism is significantly different from the classical Hollywood cinema; but its narrational principles and procedures do not vary drastically.
>
> Bordwell 1985, 269

The fact that Soviet historical films from the 1940s onwards adopt an idiosyncratic narrational classicism is also, in fact, a sign of an ideological switch from Radicalism to Conservatism. Which is not surprising at all. Given that the revolution had established a new status quo, the films of that period would tend to celebrate it and defend it as a realization of utopia. There was no longer the need for revolution and change. Utopia was already there. To that end, the classical structures of clear causality and spatiotemporal coherence incorporated the exemplary hero and allowed for a more individualistic approach to narration and, consequently, to history.[12]

As a whole, the historical–materialist mode of narration is significant for the poetics of historical cinema for its unique formal features and the ways it openly combines them with the Marxist historical argument and ideology. This explicit correlation of narration with a specific rhetorical and ideological message also helps us reinforce the analogous correlations in other modes of narration that work with more subtle and implicit interpretative cues. Despite being incredibly short-lived, the historical–materialist mode exerted considerable influence on the younger generation of filmmakers with Marxist leanings. Yet, the growing awareness of the substantial problems of Communism in practice seems to have pushed them more towards the narrative ambiguity of art cinema and the temporal abstraction of Anarchism.

The post-classical

The post-classical mode of narration consists of a set of narrational principles that I identified in my own research presented in the homonymous book *Post-classical Narration: An International Poetics of Film Narration* (2009).[13] Its historical emergence can be roughly placed in the early 1990s but, unlike the classical and art cinema, its geographical base is more expanded, comprising films from the United States, Europe, Latin America, and Hong Kong. My account of this new mode was methodically modeled upon Bordwell's formulation of the classical, tracing a number of differences at the level of causality, time, and space. Regarding the causal axis, post-classical narrations enrich and complicate the classical character-centered causality with the depiction of multiple protagonists, manifold plot paths as well as the foregrounding of chance events and coincidences. The key difference, however, lies not only in a varied approach to the characters' trajectory but also in an entirely different realistic motivation, which I called "hypermediated realism" (Thanouli 2009a, 45). Post-classical films do not abandon the need to appear realistic to the audience but strive to do so by multiplying the signs of representation and favoring hypermediacy over transparent realism. As a result, the axes of time and space become highly mediated, allowing filmmakers to openly experiment with temporal and spatial devices, such as recurrent flashbacks, slow motion, freeze-frames, intensified continuity, spatial montage, and other special effects. In addition, the exceedingly self-conscious construction of the filmic images is further increased by the deployment of parody as an integral part of the films' narrative logic. A post-classical film playfully enters a dialogue with the history of the medium, drawing inspiration from films, genres, auteurs, scenes, dialogues, or even stylistic devices from the cinematic repertoire of the past. Overall, the post-classical mode is a fairly recent mode of narration that forms a complicated relation with the other established paradigms, but it stands on a ground of its own, a ground that seems to expand more and more with the passage of time.

But what about post-classical *historical* films? Admittedly, the dominant characteristics of post-classical narration, i.e. hypermediacy and parody, may appear at odds with the standard notion of history and its emphasis on precision, clarity and objectivity. Indeed, the post-classical will probably never become a popular choice for historical themes in the way that the classical mode has been for over a century. However, just like art cinema, the post-classical can offer an alternative view of the historical process and promote new ways of thinking about the historical past. Oliver Stone is the filmmaker who resorts to the post-classical options the most, offering us historical films, such as *JFK* (1991), *Nixon* (1995), *World Trade Center* (2006) and, more recently, *Snowden* (2016). Steven Spielberg, on the other hand, prefers the classical mode for his historical dramas with *Munich* (2005) as a significant post-classical exception. Moreover, Stanley Kubrick's *Barry Lyndon* (1975) is an intriguing example of post-classical narration, which was recently scrutinized for its historical representation (Pramaggiore 2013). Finally, an emblematically post-classical filmmaker like Quentin Tarantino tends to avoid historical matters but when he decided to deal with history in *Inglourious Basterds* (2009), he certainly did it in the post-classical way.

Let us now see how the narrative options contained in this mode already point to a different set of explanations about the meaning of history. Starting with the modified use of character-centered causality, the post-classical historical film maintains the focus on individual activity but it chooses to problematize the traditional notion of agency by demonstrating how individual agency is part of a complex web of acting forces, including other individuals, societal groups, or norms as well as chance events and contingencies. The use of spliced plots, forking paths, and episodic structures loosens the causal chain and allows the filmmakers to handle competing agents in ways that multiply the connections and defy the classical linearity of purposeful action. By embedding the individual hero into a wider net of historical actors, the narration produces a multi-perspectival historical explanation that relieves the historical subject of his/her sole responsibility for the turn of events. Take *Munich*, for instance. Despite the undertaking of a mission, namely to take revenge for the Munich Massacre at the 1972 Olympics, the protagonist and his collaborators are not classical agents. They reluctantly plan their assassinations but the outcome is always contingent upon other parameters, whether other secret agents or mere chance. The film loosens the causal chain and slackens the characters' determination in order to depict a complex historical predicament and not an example of heroic action.

At the level of style, the hypermediated realism that permeates the post-classical narrative logic inevitably spills over to the axes of time and space, welcoming a level of manipulation and self-consciousness that would never fit into the classical. The flaunted constructedness of the images always already points to the fact that whatever access we may have to the events of the past is bound to be partial, mediated and, thus, to a greater or lesser degree fabricated. This is an admission that runs against the invisibility of the classical narration and its ensuing implication that the historical film shows us the past "as it really was." Instead of multiplying historical details to fake accuracy and produce the desired "reality effect" à la Barthes, the post-classical historical film multiplies the signs of representation, demonstrating that any attempt to resurrect the past is inevitably constructed and, therefore, open to criticism and revision. In *Munich* again, from the hypermediated depiction of the massacre, pasting real footage into dramatized sequences, to the recurrent flashbacks and the ironic signaling of terrorism through the final shots of the World Trade Center, the narration does not hide its fabricated nature. It merely concedes to the fact that it provides one possible version of the historical past.

The explanations that stem from a post-classical mode of narration seem particularly compatible with the Contextualist argument from Pepper's taxonomy. The principle characteristic of a Contextualist view of history is that a historical event cannot be examined autonomously from its context; instead, we need to examine every historical occurrence in conjunction with other events and agents in the historical field and to reveal the specific relations between the diverse participants in the scene that have rendered the event possible. Thus, Contextualism combines an emphasis on particular historical elements, not for their unique existence, as was the case in Formism, but for the ways these elements interact with each other to produce certain results or fulfill specific functions. At the same time, however, the detection of these results or functions does not make the next step to formulate general goals (Organicism) or universal laws (Mechanism). Contextualism refuses to integrate every circumstantial historical observation into a greater interpretative scheme. It chooses to remain particular and dispersive. As Pepper notes:

> Contextualism is accordingly sometimes said to have a horizontal cosmology in contrast to other views, which have a vertical cosmology. There is no top nor bottom to the contextualistic world. In formism or mechanism or organicism one has only to analyze in certain specified ways and one is bound, so it is believed, ultimately to get to the bottom of things or to the top of things.

> Contextualism justifies no such faith. There is no cosmological mode of analysis
> that guarantees the whole truth or an arrival at the ultimate nature of things.
>
> Pepper 1970, 251

The ultimate truth about the past, viewed from a Contextualist point of view, will never be revealed. What we have is a "here and now" and we can make approximations as to what may have happened. Our analyses are never definitive truths; they are investigations that begin and end in a rather arbitrary manner and they are open to change and revision, whenever new elements come into the picture.[14] This historical relativism is indeed a key aspect of post-classical films, which seek to challenge the very means through which we produce historical knowledge. The certainty and the aspired objectivity of a classical account of the past is not part of the post-classical rhetoric. Quite the contrary. The latter may even deploy historical relativism and the critique of official knowledge within the plot itself, as in *JFK* or *Snowden*. But even in the case of less controversial subjects, such as *The Big Short* (2015) or *300* (2006), the emphasis of post-classical narration on the context of things, instead of their unique singularity, is quite remarkable.

Finally, the ideological implications of the post-classical mode are more likely to fluctuate between the Liberal and the Conservative views. The Anarchist ideology requires a level of vagueness that is improbable in these historical films, while the Radical position commands a level of precision and determinism that is equally unlikely. Just as in the case of the classical mode, the power of the character-centered causality in post-classical fictions, however modified, draws our attention to individual actions and centers our attention primarily on the power of human activity. Unlike the classical counterparts, nonetheless, the post-classical histories on screen deprive us of the optimism and the unconditional faith in human values. The ingrained skepticism of these narrations, whether of a Liberal or Conservative perspective, problematizes the audience about the very possibility of utopia, rendering our pursuit of knowledge and happiness more self-conscious than ever. In contrast to the formal self-reflexivity of the art cinema, which appealed to the unknown as a means of celebrating an abstract sense of utopia, the relentless specificity of post-classical self-consciousness, does not leave plenty of room for dreaming. Thus, garnering historical knowledge becomes a hazardous and contingent process that stares at the present and the future with reservation and cynicism; humans are flawed entities who exist in a complex environment that not only contains other agents, but it is also subject to chance or other uncontrolled forces. In this situation, the belief in a utopia of any kind is admittedly jeopardized but humanism is not necessarily abandoned altogether. It is either Liberalism, as in *Snowden*, or Conservatism, as in *World Trade Center*, that still offer a platform for human action that will try to "do the right" thing, no matter what.

In conclusion, the post-classical mode of narration closes off the list of narrative modes of fiction filmmaking and the historical arguments that each hosts in the depiction of the historical past. In the case study section that follows, I will revisit these general connections between narration, argument and ideology through more detailed textual analyses and more comparisons between diverse historical approaches captured on film.

Case Study: The Representation of the Second World War and the Holocaust

I have chosen these two important and intricately connected historical events of the twentieth century because their representation in the cinema is itself exceptionally fascinating and thought-provoking. Despite their chronological proximity, filmmakers did not engage with these events in an even way. In fact, the Second World War and the Holocaust have had an almost antithetical cinematic treatment. The former was, right from the start, excessively present in the moving images, while the latter remained conspicuously absent for years after it ended. Before moving on to our specific film analyses, I would like to present a historical framework for the filmic portrayal of these two landmark moments in human history.

The Second World War stands out as an intriguing period in the history of Hollywood cinema. After the bombardment of Pearl Harbor and the American involvement in the war in 1941, the Hollywood industry was eager to express its wholesale commitment to the imperatives of the operation. As Tomas Schatz observes, "never before or since have the interests of the nation and the movie industry been so closely aligned, and never has Hollywood's status as a national cinema been so vital" (1998, 89). Hollywood's prompt mobilization, combined with the prominent role of cinema as the dominant mass medium at the time, turned the war into the most thoroughly documented and dramatized event in history (Doherty 1993, 6). Since television and the twenty-four-hour transmission of images were not yet available, it was the motion pictures that brought the war to the wide public through the vast production of newsreels, documentaries, and dramatic features. The abundance of fiction and nonfiction images, however, did not amount to a multi-vocal perspective. Rather, the message was one and only: it is a just war that needs to be fought and won over at all cost.

The representations of armed forces in wartime movies encompass a wide range of films which feature soldiers, sailors, and airmen both in combat and non-combat situations. Especially at the outset of the war, the "war themes" were integrated into the already established film genres, such as the musical and the comedy, where the uniformed men functioned merely as props in crowd scenes, in the streets, in night clubs, and train stations (Shull and Wilt 1996, 162). However, according to Schatz, "the term *war film* took on steadily narrower connotations as Hollywood refined specific war-related formulas" (1998, 103). These formulas comprised espionage films, occupation films, home-front dramas depicting military training, or the daily experience of the wartime Americans, and above all, combat films, which constituted the core of the genre.[15]

In the aftermath of the war, the filmic representations not only dwindled in numbers but also toned down their heroic mood. Although the combat film remained the dominant formula for another two decades, the films looking back at the Second World War adopted a more moderate stance toward the enemy and tried to provide a less biased account of the war. Some of the most frequently debated films that exemplify this revisionist turn are *Attack!* (1956), which portrays a conflict within the American army, *Tora Tora Tora* (1970), which tries to shed light on the circumstances that led the Japanese to attack Pearl Harbor, and *Patton* (1970), which provides a very controversial portrait of a modern hero (Solomon 1976). *Patton* was actually the last commercially successful and critically appraised epic of that era. The outbreak of the war in Vietnam combined with the ascent of television as the popular mass medium shifted people's expectations in relation both to war and cinema. For two decades, until the making of *Saving Private Ryan* and *The Thin Red Line* in 1998, the Second World War would remain an unpopular and distant subject.[16]

A rather opposite trajectory is found in the case of the representation of the Holocaust. Despite the filming of the concentration camps immediately after the war by the forces of the liberation, the portrayal of the horrors taking place therein would evolve into a complex problem of aesthetic, conceptual, and moral dimensions. Unlike the simplicity of the message of the Second World War, as a heroic war against fascism or a Manichean battle between light and darkness, the Holocaust could not easily fit into snap tags and slogans. The event itself defied easy answers. Its very name, the Holocaust, has been subject to controversy, as it is overloaded with implications not only regarding the identity of the victims of this genocide but also regarding the meaning and purpose of their extermination (Magilow and Silverman 2015; Kerner 2011). The major dispute surrounding the Holocaust, however, concerns the capacity and the moral imperative of representation to address an event of such proportions. In other words, can and should such atrocities be depicted in art? To those who responded negatively, there were always more, asking "how can we not to"?

The dilemma "to show" or "not to show" slowly crystallized into a purely cinematic opposition, that between Claude Lanzmann and Steven Spielberg. These two filmmakers became metonymical figures for the two opposing views on the matter of Holocaust's representability in general (Elsaesser 1996). The former, with his almost nine-hour documentary called *Shoah* (1985), stands for all those who argued that any representation of this ineffable tragedy is a violation; it is a disrespectful distortion that creates presence in the place of absence. The latter, on the other, with his Oscar-winning box office hit, the *Schindler's List* (1993), represents all those who regard cinema's visual power as a force of redemption. By representing this dark moment in history, Spielberg's film familiarizes a wide audience with the Nazi atrocities; it stimulates empathy with the millions of victims, while it amalgamates the survivors' memories into one powerful classical narrative. These two divergent philosophical and moral positions on the issue of representation still fuel much of current public debates whenever a Holocaust film garners publicity.

Looking at the history of the Holocaust representation in the cinema, we realize that during the first two decades after the war the theme was still fairly marginal. The few dramatic features that stand out from the 1950s and 1960s include *The Diary of Anne Frank* (1959), *Judgment at Nuremberg*, and *The Pawnbroker* (1964). The life and the killings at the camps, however, were not extensively dramatized until the screening of the famous eight-part TV series, *Holocaust*, in 1978. This was a landmark production with worldwide impact, which triggered passionate public debates about the limits of representation. Despite the heavy criticism, especially from Jewish survivors, *Holocaust* paved the way for hundreds of dramatic features both in the United States and in Europe, which kept pushing the public debate further and further. Especially from the 1990s onwards, the theme of the Holocaust was embedded in various established generic formulas, including those of comedy, horror and even pornography (Kerner 2011). Just as in the case of the Second World War, the Holocaust gradually proved to be a very malleable historical subject, which could unfold in very different narrative plot paths and through different representational techniques.

In the pages that follow I will analyze a series of critically acclaimed historical films to show how their narrative elements generate various historical arguments and ideological implications. My analysis will follow a standard structure, moving from narration to argument and ideology in the same way in each film, to facilitate their comparison. It is not meant to be exhaustive, however. Each axis (narration, argument, ideology) can be considerably extended and developed, along the lines I indicate. My goal is to offer a blueprint for the reading of the historical film and to demonstrate how the formal, the philosophical, and the ideological elements feed off each other in a consistent and predictable manner. From the enormous filmography of these two major historical events, I have chosen to work with the following: *Saving Private Ryan* (1998), *The Thin Red Line* (1998), and *Dunkirk* (2017), which depict aspects of military operations during the Second World War. From those portraying the Holocaust, I have selected *Life is Beautiful* (1997), *The Son of Saul* (2015), and *Inglourious Basterds* (2009). It is a selection of American and European fiction films, which will allow us to discuss very diverse modes of narration and examine a wide range of historical explanations, elaborating further on the poetics of filmic history, as I laid it out above.

The Second World War

Saving Private Ryan (1998)

Spielberg's 1998 war epic signaled a return to the history of the Second World War and renewed the public interest in that historical era. The reviews, the commentaries, and the analyses of this fascinating combat drama are profuse and, unsurprisingly, contradictory.[17] At any rate, it is a remarkable addition to Spielberg's historical dramas and an invaluable example of filmic history, whose particularities stand out even more when juxtaposed to those of *The Thin Red Line* and *Dunkirk*. This cinematic triptych is illuminating as to what history on film "can do" and my comparative analysis here will emphasize how the different narrative mode of each film results inevitably in a different philosophical and ideological argument about the meaning of history.

Saving Private Ryan is a classical historical film. Despite the impulse to characterize it as something new and unprecedented—primarily thanks to the depiction of D-Day in the beginning—a careful consideration of the entirety of the narration attests otherwise. I would like to briefly mention the key compositional, realistic, and generic motivations of the film, which confirm its narrational classicism.[18] Compositionally, the narration relies on a very clear-cut logic, which involves the accomplishment of a difficult mission, namely to find and rescue Private James Ryan (Matt Damon). The principal hero in charge of this mission is Captain John H. Miller (Tom Hanks) who selects eight more soldiers to assist him. Miller and his company, as it is customary in combat films, carry on their assignment, facing obstacles and setbacks until its final resolution. Despite the casualties and the heavy toll in human lives, the mission is successful; Ryan is not only saved but also lives long enough to accomplish another mission, that of "earning" his salvation and proving worthy of the sacrifices of the others. Captain Miller is also a fairly classical hero. The entire Omaha Beach scene not only works as an important representation of a historical battle but also as an introduction to Miller's bravery and unique skills. Each sequence from then on adds, little by little, the pieces of his personality and constructs him as Bordwell's typical "psychologically defined individual." Miller expresses doubts about the moral premises of his mission but he also honors his role in the military service. He commits himself to Ryan's rescue till the very end and he considers his and his men's sacrifice meaningful, as long as Ryan turns out to be a decent human being. In other words, Miller gradually internalizes the mission and makes it his own. This is how he manages to reign over the occasional resistance of the others and inspire them to go on.

The tight cause-and-effect logic of the events in the plot and the clear temporal and spatial progression of the story are also combined with a strong realistic motivation. It may not be the realism of classical Hollywood in the 1940s and 1950s, but it is a realistic portrayal of the events, nonetheless. The landing on Omaha Beach on June 6, 1944 is contained in a twenty-seven-minute sequence shot with swift cutting, intense camera movements, graphic close-ups of human bodies, and powerful sound effects. Like most war films in the past,[19] Spielberg took advantage of the latest technologies to portray the violence, the immeasurable brutality as well as the strategic planning involved in warfare. Every shot, every movement, and every action contained in this part of the Normandy invasion seeks to be realistic and create the feeling of actually "being there." A similar, even if more conventional, realistic principle pervades the rest of the film, which follows the classical paths of shot composition and continuity editing. What is also fairly classical is the film's generic motivation. As the expert on the combat film, Jeanine Basinger, notices in her reading, Spielberg revisits almost all the standard plot elements of the combat genre, including the dynamics between the hero and his team, the absence of women, the reminiscing over past lives, the exchange of letters and the alternation between moments of tragedy and humour (Basinger 2003, 259–61). Thus, on all fronts (compositional, realistic, and generic), *Saving Private Ryan* remains fairly within the boundaries of the classical narration.

But what does this formal classicism mean for the historical representation that ensues? The choice of the classical mode for the portrayal of this particular historical moment already defines the limits of interpretation regarding the significance of the historical events contained therein. *Saving Private Ryan* tells a fictional story about the rescue mission of Private Ryan due to his family's tragic predicament; the death of all four of his brothers in the battlefield. The real-life inspiration came from Stephen Ambrose's historical book, *Band of Brothers* (1992), and particularly the case of the Niland Brothers.[20] As in all historical dramas, the plot treads an intricate path between fact and fiction, seeking to multiply its reality effects by drawing on historical sources and maximizing the details of its iconography. For example, the references to Abraham Lincoln and the Bixby letter, on the one hand, and the meticulous choreography of the D-Day invasion, on the other, create a historical image where the line between truth and fiction becomes irrelevant. Unless we are one of those pedants playing "Everett's Game,"[21] we should analyze Spielberg's historical representation not in order to tell fact from fiction but to understand how its narrative elements point to specific historical explanations regarding the significance of the war for us today.

Cast through the form of a classical narration, the historical representation of D-Day, of the life in rural Normandy, of the German enemy, of the Second World War combats, and of specific military policies is predestined to possess certain characteristics. The mold of the classical narratives already predetermines the lens through which history will be gazed. The character-centered causality dictates the emphasis on the individual as the driving force of history. Even in complex situations, such as warfare, where the power of the military hierarchy and the official mandates are visible, the classical mode still accentuates the importance of human initiative and personal decision-making. Even in the most chaotic situations, such as the Omaha beach sequence, the classical camerawork and editing will find a way to rise above the noise, the speed, the bullets, and the splattered bodies, in order to single out and linger on those few selected individuals, like Captain Miller, who are brave and unique enough to survive. As the film moves on to the mission, the individuality of each team member is even further explored, rendering their deaths as heroic acts. For instance, the death of the first soldier, Adrian Caparzo, is viewed less as an accidental occurrence than as a personal choice; he deliberately and willfully placed the safety of the little girl over his, despite the others' vocal warnings. In addition to the character-centered causality, the classical narratives opt for a linear chronology of the events and a clear closure. Spielberg contains most of the story in a flashback initiated by Ryan at the present moment, but like most classical flashbacks, it is a highly motivated and stylistically signposted device to turn back the time. It does not create, in other words, any confusion nor does it raise any questions about the events' temporality. Just like in any traditional historical account, the historical time is represented as a natural flow that moves smoothly from the past to the present, while the historical events possess a beginning, a middle, and an ending. The classical narrative temporality is particularly hospitable to the idea that history progresses linearly and that historical events are clearly defined entities with temporal as well as spatial and causal characteristics. In fact, the temporal and spatial organization of the classical narratives are serving the overarching consistency of the narrative logic. The Second World War is portrayed as a specific event in recent history, with a clear beginning and ending, with specific participants in the roles of heroes and villains, and with a victorious outcome, which was the result of the heroic actions and sacrifice of millions of individuals.

These explanations by mode of narration accommodate Formist historical arguments, as we argued in the previous section. Like most classical narratives, *Saving Private Ryan* puts forth a Formist argument in the sense that its historical recounting aims at transmitting the vividness and the powerfulness of each particular element, instead of pushing for broader generalizations. Spielberg's film aims at capturing the uniqueness of a historical moment, such as D-Day for instance, depicting with painstaking detail the human and material elements clashing with each other on that particular day. For a Formist historical argument, the value of the description is of immense importance, as it reveals the particularities of a historical situation. All a Formist historian needs to do is observe the concrete existence of persons and objects at a particular place and time. In a classical film like *Saving Private Ryan*, the verisimilitude of the *mise-en-scène*, the careful choreography of the camera, and the seamless effects of continuity editing strive to underscore the uniqueness of each landscape, each moment, and each personality. Particularly, the character delineation strives to emphasize how each historical agent is a unique individual that stands in its own right. Notice, for example, how Spielberg frames one of the final moments, when Ryan stands over Captain Miller's grave at the Normandy cemetery. Ryan's point of view shot focuses on the cross bearing Miller's name, while hundreds of other crosses lie indistinguishable in the background. What matters is not so much the sacrifice of the many, but, rather, the secret bond that unites those two. What matters is whether Ryan proved worthy of Miller's sacrifice. The underlying philosophical argument of this representation is dispersive; it does not seek to build general observations regarding the meaning of history nor unearth any laws of the historical process. Unlike an Organicist or Mechanistic account, the Formist argument is analytical, placing emphasis on particular elements, while remaining dispersive; in other words, it steers away from the need to integrate those elements into a higher-level entity. Like most classical historical films, *Saving Private Ryan* articulates such an argument through the representation of a small fragment of the Second World War. In its historical take, it does not seek to explain the war as a result of wider socio-political structures, as an Organicist or Mechanistic would, nor does it raise any skepticism regarding the very fabric of history, as a Contextualist might. Instead, the film paints an elaborate picture of the Second World War warfare, of character mentality and patriotic courage that stands sufficiently on its own.

Finally, in terms of the ideological implications of the classical narrative mode, I argued that the two dominant options are Liberalism and Conservativism. In fact, Spielberg's film has received both interpretations by different commentators (Morris 2007; Burnetts 2016). In my view, however, the film veers clearly toward the Conservative side. The main defining characteristic of Conservativism is not its emphasis on human values; this emphasis is shared by Liberalism as well. What a Conservative ideology seeks to emphasize, according to Mannheim's typology, is the value of the status quo and its accomplishments as a realization of utopia. In this light, the portrayal of the Second World War in *Saving Private Ryan* is viewed as a commemoration of a great American War.[22] Despite the brutality, the immeasurable human pain, the doubts, the fears, and the complex moral dilemmas of its characters, the historical representation does not question the perennial premise of the Second World War, namely that it was a just war. Despite the chronological distance that separates this film from the vast majority of Second World War films made in the 1940s, the underlying notion of the American powerful nation fighting for a rightful cause against the evil forces of Nazism is not all that different. Admittedly, most films during the war focused more on the Japanese, rather than the Germans. It was the "Japs," as they called them, who personified evil at the time.[23] Yet, the general ideas of American exceptionalism, of patriotic commitment, and of principled military conduct remain almost intact.

All in all, in this brief analysis of *Saving Private Ryan* as a historical representation we witness a standard combination of a classical narrative with specific historical explanations of a Formist and a Conservative kind. Most historical films throughout the twentieth century to date have relied on the classical narrative formulas for recounting major historical events. The "invisibility" of the classical style and the transparency of a classical narration often cause us to consider these formal options as natural vehicles for storytelling. Thanks to Bordwell's work, we know that they are merely historical options, which arose out of economic, technological and other cultural developments at the beginning of the twentieth century. The "naturalness" of the classical mode, however, also prevents us from realizing the philosophical and ideological arguments that lie underneath its historical representations. These arguments become significantly more visible when we look at other modes and the history that they create. The historical explanations of Spielberg's film, in other words, become more demonstrable when we compare them to those of Terrence Malick in *The Thin Red Line*.

The Thin Red Line (1998)

The Thin Red Line is a three-hour epic about the Second World War, directed by Malick, who made his comeback to the film industry after twenty years with a subject that had been neglected, as we saw, for almost as long. The film is based on James Jones' novel, published in 1962, which was first adapted for the big screen by Andrew Marton in 1964, rather unsuccessfully. For many years, the book seemed to defy cinematic adaptation due to its deliberately choppy storyline, its lack of a single heroic protagonist, and the multiplicity of perspectives (Macnab 1999). Malick tried to overcome these obstacles by creating a film which broke "most of the commercial rules about narrative and drama," as a critic observes (MacCabe 1999, 10). As we will see, however, the film did not need to reinvent the wheel. All these "commercial rules" had been broken before, particularly by those European filmmakers in the 1950s and 1960s whose works consolidated under what Bordwell called the art cinema narration. *The*

Thin Red Line adopts the narrative strategies of this mode for the representation of World War II and it matches them with the Organicist historical argument and the Anarchist ideological implications.

Let us start with the narration.[24] *The Thin Red Line* is set on the Guadalcanal Island in the Pacific Ocean in 1942 and depicts the attempt of the American army to seize control over the island against the Japanese occupiers. Unlike in a classical film, the military mission here is merely a pretext for a series of fragmented episodes that feature different soldiers and different plights. Instead of building the plot with a tight cause-and-effect logic around a central purpose, Malick presents a series of personalities and incidents that are only loosely connected with each other. The goal-oriented soldiers of the classical combat films are replaced with deeply tormented individuals who typify art cinema's cornerstone, the boundary situation. As Bordwell notes: "The boundary situation is common in art-cinema narration; the film's causal impetus often derives from the protagonist's recognition that she or he faces a crisis of existential significance" (1985, 208). The opening of the film blatantly plunges us into a situation of this kind by introducing Private Witt (James Caviezel); a soldier absent without leave (AWOL) on an unspoiled island in the Pacific. Witt observes the life of the natives, pondering upon the meaning of nature and violence, while feeling unable to reconcile his military duties with his esoteric needs. And he is not alone in this predicament. The film presents all the characters in a boundary situation, which, in fact, becomes their only connective thread. Unlike a standard combat film, which presents the collective activities of a unit, *The Thin Red Line* never shows us the main characters in action together. We do not know how they are related or even if they know each other. We glimpse one character's life for a few moments only to move on to another in the next scene. We hear their parallel monologues or occasionally some conversations but the narration never builds any sense of comradeship, which was so essential in the war films of the past. The battlefield is a landscape scattered with random people, sharing only a feeling of hopelessness and despair.

The film's objective realism (episodic structure, loose causality, and boundary situation) is coupled by a conventional use of art cinema's subjective realism. The narration is rife with meditative voice-overs, daydreams, and fantasies that disrupt the already slow progression of the story. Particularly, the use of the voice-over track is striking, as it accommodates the thoughts of diverse soldiers, even of those who are not so appealing, like Colonel Tall (Nick Nolte). The revelation of the innermost ruminations of various characters contributes to the fragmented plot structure and prevents the viewer from identifying with them in any depth. As soon as gain some insight into one individual, the narration switches focus to someone else. This unmotivated arrangement of the plot renders Malick's authorial presence quite prominent, as is typical of art films. Unlike classical narrations, which conceal the traces of their makers, an art film like *The Thin Red Line* capitalizes heavily on Malick's creative idiosyncrasies. At the level of *mise-en-scène* and editing, the blatant juxtaposition of human faces with landscapes, on the one hand, and warfare with wildlife, on the other, result in metaphorical compositions that betray the auteur's philosophical preoccupations on the theme of war and human nature.

All these formal characteristics of *The Thin Red Line* determine a very specific range of historical explanations regarding the battles in the Pacific Ocean during the Second World War. In this portrayal, military operations are construed as unfathomable abstract processes with devastating results and immeasurable human losses. The fragmented plot structure and the loose causal chain of events depict war as a chaotic event without any sense of coherence and, certainly, without any clear beginning, middle or ending. Compared to the clarity of purpose and the temporal framing of the war in *Saving Private Ryan,* Malick's account refuses to create a specific causal or temporal perspective on the historical events. The supposed mission to take over the Guadalcanal Island is never explained nor completed by the end of the film; after almost three hours of viewing, the battle rages on without any sense of direction and meaning. Above all, however, the film denies the individuals their role as driving forces of those historic moments. The soldiers are hardly portrayed as agents of rational and purposeful action; instead, they can only react to strenuous external circumstances by closing in on themselves. Instead of partaking in the heroic mission of their nation, they question their presence in the chaos of war and find refuge in their memories and dreams. As typical art protagonists, they cannot act; they can only react to a harsh reality beyond their control. In this sense, they cannot take part in the historical process as empowered individuals. History is too formidable, too overwhelming, and too confusing for the human mind; its true forces lie somewhere in the dark, way beyond its reach.

This type of historical explanation, which is tied to the art cinema mode of narration, is easily paired with the Organicist argument on history, as I have already argued. An Organicist approach to the historical process does not pay attention to the specificity of historical agents and events but, rather, seeks to unearth the general rules that may apply to a historical situation. It is a synthetic and integrative type of thinking, as it accumulates a multitude of elements in order to configure them in ways that form a certain pattern. In *The Thin Red Line* nobody is exceptional or unique; they are all pawns of larger historical processes. When we look at the suffering or the hallucinations of a certain soldier, like Private Witt for instance, we are not interested in his particular personality nor do we try to establish his uniqueness or superiority, as we did with Captain Miller in Spielberg's film. Instead, his presence or his thoughts point to a greater truth beyond individual experience. When he says phrases like, "I see another world" or "Maybe all men got one big soul," the intention is not to turn our gaze onto his own predicament but to point us to a bigger picture. In fact, Malick's argument on war is limited neither to a particular historical period nor to the Second World War per se. The latter merely stands as an archetype of War, as the epitome of Evil, both with capital initials. As the opening narrator puts it, "This great Evil. Where does it come from? How is it still in the world? What sea, what route did it go from? Who is doing this? Who is killing us? Robbing us of life and laughter?" Occasionally, the film flirts with the Marxist theory of history, as when Sergeant Welsh cries out loud: "Property! The whole fucking thing is about property!" but, overall, it avoids providing very concrete historical materialist answers. What matters is to emphasize that a man alone means nothing to history. It is the whole into which human lives integrate that matters. The core of the film's Organicist argument may, in fact, be summarized in one of the voice-overs: "Maybe all men got one big soul where everybody is a part of. All faces of the same man. One big Self."

Finally, the film's Organicist argument is congruent with the Anarchist ideology and its utopian vision. The opening sequence featuring the idyllic life of the natives on the island is the very definition of the Anarchists' dream state; "a remote past of natural-human innocence from which men have fallen into the corrupt 'social' state in which they currently find themselves," to remember Hayden White's words on Anarchism once more (2014, 24). Private Witt's recurrent insistence on "seeing another world" is indicative of Malick's broader ideological implications, namely the need to seize control of what is essentially human and protect it from the corruption of the current state of affairs. Admitted, like all Anarchists, Malick does not provide very specific solutions for this return to unspoiled human nature nor does he specify a temporal frame for such a shift to occur. The abstract nature of the philosophical questions that the characters pose, the lack of specificity in the historical agencies and events involved in the portrayal of the Second World War as well as the loose temporality of the action contribute to an Anarchist vision of "another" world without any compass to help us actually get there.

Overall, *The Thin Red Line* has been hailed by scholars and commentators as an idiosyncratic combat film on the Second World War, breaking several of the classical traditions of the Hollywood genre. As I tried to illustrate, its fundamental difference from films like *Saving Private Ryan* stems from its adoption of the art cinema conventions. As soon as a military story is molded through the formal principles of this distinct mode, the range of historical explanations at the level of narration, argument and ideology is limited to the options I described above. This proves, once again, how closely linked form and content are and how each historical interpretation in the cinema needs to depart from an informed understanding of filmic narration. Even though an absolute equation between modes of narration, on the one hand, and philosophical and ideological arguments, on the other, may not be feasible, the possible and probable correlations among them are not infinite either. The next case study, *Dunkirk*, will strengthen this central premise, presenting a different configuration of historical explanations in yet another representation of the Second World War.

Dunkirk (2017)

Christopher Nolan has repeatedly expressed his admiration for *The Thin Red Line* (Mottram 2002) but when it came to directing his own war film, he opted for a post-classical narration. *Dunkirk*, his latest blockbuster about the evacuation of the British armed forces from Dunkirk in 1940, features an intriguing plot structure as well as other constructional elements, which led me to classify it within the boundaries of the post-classical mode.[25] Nolan seems too grounded on classicism to give in to art cinema's flair for subjectivity and ambiguity. The choice of the post-classical options allows him to build a representation of history, which differs equally from a classical (Spielberg) and an art cinema (Malick) portrayal of the past,[26] as it yields its own set of historical explanations. Specifically, as my analysis will illustrate, *Dunkirk* combines its post-classical mode of narration with a Contextualist argument on history and a Conservative ideological take on the significance of the Second World War.

The story of the heroic enterprise, which took place in Dunkirk in late May and early June 1940, is presented in an episodic manner through three distinct plotlines. The first portrays the experience from the land, and particularly from the beach where thousands of soldiers await their rescue. This segment is entitled

"The Mole" and its story duration is one week. The second depicts the operation from the sea, focusing on the participation of hundreds of British private vessels, which were requisitioned by the Royal Navy and sailed to Dunkirk at great risk. This story is called "The Sea" and lasts for one day. Finally, the third episode captures this historic event from the air, concentrating on three RAF Spitfires and their dogfights with the German planes in the area. "The Air" episode is very powerful but only lasts for an hour. Each plotline contains its own protagonists, with their own goals and aspirations as well as their own successes and failures, creating an intricate tapestry of human action and fate against the backdrop of what Winston Churchill called "a colossal military disaster." Like all post-classical narrations, *Dunkirk* does not cancel out character-centered causality but it chooses to complicate it considerably through the deployment of a fragmented plot structure and the multiplication of the protagonists. Instead of a classical hero—or a classical military unit in the case of the combat genre—which can develop diegetically into a set of psychologically defined individuals, Nolan populates the storyworld with a wide range of characters who are imbricated in an overwhelming war situation, leaving very little room for classical exposition and character development. However, we are not facing an ambiguous or vague situation akin to that of *The Thin Red Line*. The masterful intersection of the three episodes through crosscutting combined with the ingenious dissection of the diegesis into the smallest particles may initially cause confusion; eventually, however, the viewer is allowed to put the pieces of the puzzle together, even if upon a second or third viewing. The multiple storylines and their fragmented arrangement loosen the classical cause-and-effect chain of events, while they allow the forces of chance and coincidence to come into play. What matters, overall, is that *Dunkirk* combines complexity with communicativeness and allows the viewer to comprehend how its story progresses and how it resolves.

The connections of the three episodes are primarily non-diegetic; crosscutting is effectuated by an extra-diegetic force, which chooses each time which plotline to display.[27] The initial clarification via intertitles regarding the story duration of each episode helps us realize early on that the switch from one scene to the next is not dependent on relations of simultaneity, as is often the case with crosscutting.[28] We know, for instance, that Tommy's (Fionn Whitehead) struggle for survival on the beach is not directly related to Farrier's (Tom Hardy) attempts to shoot down the German bombers. The relentless change of focus at the plot level, from land to sea and air and back, as well as the intensified continuity built through the editing and the camerawork create in tandem a hypermediated sense of realism. This type of realism, instead of effacing the traces of representation, chooses to multiply them for a heightening effect. In contrast to classical realism, which strives to pass off as immediate and transparent, hypermediated realism in post-classical narratives combines hypermediacy[29] with the need to really be there in the action. Nolan's relentless crosscutting, unlike Malick's interventions, does not seek to draw attention to his authorial presence. On the contrary, the abrupt passages from one part of the operation to the other create suspense and contribute to the development of the key compositional elements of the plot. As it is typical of post-classical films, *Dunkirk's* narration handles a high level of self-consciousness with communicativeness and realistic motivation. This is a combination that cannot be sustained either within the classical or the art cinema mode.

But what does it mean for a historical film to employ the post-classical mode? How is this historical representation of the Second World War different from those we discussed above? The key distinction lies in the explanations that can be accommodated within the post-classical forms, especially at the level of narration and argument. Starting with the former, we notice that the story of the evacuation of Dunkirk is not a classical tale of heroism or an abstract exploration of the human psyche. In their place, we find an elaborate and complex portrayal of a military enterprise in multiple layers and from a wide range of perspectives. We are encouraged to glimpse into the enormous scale of such a historic event, instead of focusing on a single personalized storyline. By encompassing all three major military divisions (army, navy, and air force), Nolan seeks to address the complexity of war operations and the careful planning (or lack thereof) entailed in their execution. Operation Dynamo, as it was called, was a miracle performed by a magnitude of forces, human and nonhuman. The loosened character-centered causality allows the film to distribute agency across a wide range of parameters, including pure chance. In this sense, history is not made by great individuals and their exceptional courage but by a massive involvement of people who sometimes act purposefully, while at other times are merely swept along by other factors. The modified character-centered causality strikes a delicate balance between the classical notion of agency and other approaches found not only in art cinema but also the historical-materialist mode.

Let's take Farrier's trajectory, for instance. Farrier may be characterized as a heroic figure who is willing to sacrifice himself to accomplish his mission, namely to take down a German bomber, then land his fuel-less plane with safety and surrender to the enemy. This is an all-too-classic premise, which could easily develop into a classical dramatic plot. Except that it does not. Farrier's episode is embedded into a series of several other accounts, losing thus the opportunity to establish this character as the center of our attention and to endow him with all the necessary recurring motifs and motivations, transforming him into a classical agent. His purposeful achievements are a little more than a drop in the ocean compared to the overall pattern of action that arises from the fragmented episodes and their intricate configurations. At the same time, however, Farrier is not presented as a typical representative of military personnel, as one would expect in a historical-materialist narration. His class or professional identity is not deployed as illustrative of a larger social formation, which is supposedly in charge of the situation. Both stylistically (close-up framing) and plot-wise, he maintains his individuality and his proportionate place within a larger scope.

Moreover, like all post-classical histories, *Dunkirk* combines the traditional "reality effect" (abundant and realistic details in the *mise-en-scène*) with the "reality effect plus" of hypermediated realism. The choice of the relentless crosscutting and the puzzle film structure, Nolan's trademark, aims less at arguing that "this is really how it happened" and more at saying "hey, this is one hell of a way of putting things together." In his work, the systems of narrative space and time become considerably more prominent, challenging their traditional subordination to causal logic. On the one hand, he gives us the opportunity to see how each centimeter or each second matters in combat situations, while, on the other, he demonstrates emphatically how historical representations are built on the manipulation of space and time coordinates. By treating historical time and space as malleable entities, he opens up the possibilities of treating them otherwise. In other words, Nolan's *Dunkirk* always already tells us that its story can be told in many other ways. The distance separating the historical explanations of the post-classical from the classical forms becomes palpable, if not abysmal, when we compare Nolan's version of Operation Dynamo to Leslie Norman's in the homonymous *Dunkirk* (1958), filmed almost sixty years earlier. There, the classical devices of character-centered causality, linear chronology, and continuity editing, among many, built a solid and unequivocal image of the historical situation dependent on the notion of traditional heroism and self-sacrifice.

The differences between the two films obtain, quite predictably, at the level of historical argument, too. Whereas the classical version of the Dunkirk evacuation supports a Formist argument, the post-classical opts for a Contextualist. As I explained in the first section of this chapter, the Contextualist argument is at once synthetic and dispersive. In its approach to history, it favors an aggregate perspective that encompasses a wide range of agents in the historical field and evaluates their interrelations. It does not single out one or two elements for their uniqueness, as the Formist counterpart does. Rather, it examines the specificity of historical elements for the ways in which they interact with each other in a particular context. In *Dunkirk*, the excessive crosscutting and the painstaking dissection of each plotline into hundreds of little pieces allows us precisely to view this historic military operation as a puzzle of forces that had to lock into each other in order to work. From start to finish, nobody and nothing could stand on each own. All characters and all places were ceaselessly dependent on each other, intersecting and influencing one another in many anticipated or unexpected ways. The historical miracle of Dunkirk is not presented as the result of unique and unprecedented forces but rather, as a complex and unpredictable merger of human initiatives, natural forces and sheer luck. Yet, the goal of a Contextualist argument is not to pile up all these factors in order to build a general theory of history. Quite the contrary; Contextualism emphasizes the fact that such a generalization is not possible. To remember Pepper once again, Contextualism, unlike all other world-views, bears a horizontal cosmology; it does not believe that it can get to the bottom or top of things (Pepper 1970, 251). In other words, it resigns itself to the fact that we cannot get to an ultimate historical truth. In this light, we can understand why *Dunkirk*'s historical argument is of the Contextualist kind. In its portrayal of history, the film seeks to examine as many parameters as possible without, however, pointing to a general law governing human action. Unlike the Mechanistic views of historical-materialist films and the Organicism of art cinema narrations, Nolan's work does not phase out the specificity of the historical moment for the sake of broader ideas. His war is not just any war, as in Malick's case. It is a very specific point in time and a very special moment in the chronicle of the Second World War. Instead of taking the classical road and its accompanying Formist argument, nonetheless, he trades the emphasis on uniqueness with comprehensiveness and synthesis. Thus, he creates a historical image which is, in some respects, as flat as a blueprint. If we could straighten out his plot and glue the bits and pieces together in a linear fashion, then we would be left with a very detailed and thorough representation of a specific but immeasurably complex historical situation. Not a model of the historical process nor a mechanism of how history works. Simply, a provisional graph of what probably happened those days in the shores of Dunkirk where hundreds of thousands of lives were at stake and various historical actors (the government, the military, the privates, the pilots, and the civilians) did their share with many failures but many more successes.

The ultimate success of Operation Dynamo and Nolan's evocation of the miracle right from the opening title is what, I believe, determines the film's ideological implications and its Conservative take. The expectation of a miracle and the slow progression towards its realization generates a reassuring feeling and a comforting faith in the moral principles on which the war was fought. In *Dunkirk*, just as in *Saving Private Ryan*, there is no question as to which side one must stand on. There is not even a question of whether the sacrifices were worth it. As Mr. Dawson (Mark Rylance) puts it at one point, "If we don't help, there won't be any home." Similarly, other characters at various junctures get the opportunity to express their commitment to the war and their pride in serving their country. Unlike the soldiers in *The Thin Red Line,* their presence in the battlefield is not felt as meaningless or futile. In fact, their commitment is even greater than the one we found in Spielberg's film. There, the violence and the cruelty of war often steered feelings of frustration and disenchantment. In *Dunkirk*, however, the British nation appears in complete unison. Despite the brutality and the absurdity with which death and destruction spread around them, the British people are portrayed as solid patriots who are united by a common heroic spirit. Finally, the closure with Churchill's famous "We shall never surrender" speech seals the film's dominant Conservatism and generates a profound feeling of righteousness and satisfaction. Nolan pays tribute to the spirit of Dunkirk and transforms this historic event into an opportunity for the British nation to learn from their heroic past. Of course, the ideological interpretation of this or any film, as I have previously explained, is not solely dependent on formal parameters; rather, it is conditioned by moral and extra-textual concerns, which are subject to change over time. At the period of its screening, *Dunkirk* was received favorably by Conservative commentators, such as Niall Ferguson, while it was openly correlated with the current Brexit affair, which torments and divides the British nation, even as I am writing these words (Ferguson 2017; Roberts 2017). Its future readings may differ but they will have to move within the Liberal-Conservative range, as the post-classical mode excludes the possibility of a Radical or Anarchistic ideological agenda.

The Holocaust

Life is Beautiful (1997)

Roberto Benigni's film about the persecution of Jews in Italy and the life in the concentration camps is not only a historical dramatic feature on this vexed topic but also one that chooses comedy as its primary genre. The controversy that followed its screening was, admittedly, foreseeable. As Aaron Kerner notes, "Not since the 1978 NBC miniseries *Holocaust*, or Spielberg's 1993 *Schindler's List*, had a film about the Holocaust roused the praise and the ire of so many" (Kerner 2011, 96). The idea to represent the German atrocities through fiction was already controversial enough, as I explained above, but the genre of comedy seemed to add insult to injury. White had tackled this issue in his article "Historical Emplotment and the Problem of Truth" where he discussed Art Spiegelman's comic *Maus: A Survivor's Tale*, as an example probing us to reconsider the relation between emplotment and events, between form and content (White 1992). Ironically enough, Spiegelman rejected Benigni's film as "overreaching," despite its good intentions, while he shuddered at the idea of people considering the two works comparable (Taylor 2007, 194). However, *Life is Beautiful*, just like *Maus*, can elucidate the workings of emplotment and help us grasp precisely what it is that bothers, or in other cases soothes us, in the representation of history in general, and of this exceptional event in particular. Especially when juxtaposed with *The Son of Saul* and *Inglourious Basterds*, Benigni's work gives us a blueprint of the most common form of historical fiction, namely the classical historical film.

The story of *Life is Beautiful* contains two distinct parts: the life in the small town of Arezzo in fascist Italy around 1939 and the life in a concentration camp for a short period until the liberation by the Allied forces. The protagonist, Guido Orefice (Roberto Benigni), is a lively and imaginative character who arrives in Arezzo to work as a waiter at the restaurant of an expensive hotel. From the opening scene, Guido meets and falls in love with Dora (Nicoletta Braschi), a teacher who moves in the aristocratic circles of local society. It takes Guido several attempts and many more coincidences to win over her heart but he finally succeeds; Guido and Dora get married and have a son named Giosuè. The second part of the story begins on Giosuè's fifth birthday when he and Guido are rounded up, together with all the Jewish population of the area, and transported to a concentration camp. There, Guido takes on a new mission; he struggles to protect his son from the madness of the new reality surrounding them.

Despite the critical attention drawn into the second part of the film, the first one is equally bold for its portrayal of the fascist rule in Italy in the 1930s. Benigni creates a textbook case of classical narration, employing all the standard tropes of Hollywood comedies: repetitions, recurring motifs, and coincidences, all collaborating seamlessly to form the heterosexual couple. And all these formal devices become meticulously invested with the most representative elements of that historical era, namely the fascist ideology, bureaucracy and racial discrimination. Like Charlie Chaplin in *The Great Dictator* (1940), Benigni turns comedy's excess and spectacle into a magnifying glass over the most common absurdities of totalitarianism, such as the salutes, the flags, and the daily distortions in human communication. The secondary characters and the comic stunts are openly related to the social and political reality, forming a scathing critique of that era. The petty bourgeois bureaucrat and the arrogance of the civil servants, the extravagant orientalist engagement party, the racist speech in the classroom and the growing discrimination against Jews are all semantics of that particular historical time in Italy. The second chapter at the camp is also very classically constructed. Guido's mission here is to keep his little boy interested and distracted from their harsh and inhumane routine. Every scene and every dialogue is planned as a representative sample of the life in that dreadful place, as we have already known it in other representations. The dormitories, the uniforms, the tattooed numbers, the food, the forced labor, the gas chambers, the Nazi social gatherings, the piles of clothes and shoes; all become an integral part of Guido's world and his interaction with his son. The fact that he distorts the meaning of these places, signs, and objects for the sake of humor does not eliminate the ties of their representation to historical reality. Just as any dramatic feature which emplots the same events through the conventions of other genres, Benigni's comedy carries the same representational weight. What differs, in fact, is the light in which these events are cast and the underlying moral assumptions that it invites us to make.

The historical explanations of *Life is Beautiful* at the level of narration are those of the classical mode, as we have discussed them so far in other examples. The classical plot in both parts places the human individual at the heart of any historical development. The protagonists appear strong and independent enough to take matters into their own hands and change their place in history. Dora's case is remarkable in this respect. In spite of the fact that her allocated place was not on those wagons, she was bold and decisive enough to change that. The same holds true for Guido, too. He defined his place in the camps in the way he wanted to, defying the dreadful circumstances. Just as he had always done from the start. Despite all odds, he managed to marry the woman he loved, to open his bookstore, and raise his Jewish kid according to his own magical rules. The power that the narration invests in these characters is distinctive of the classical mode and its character-centered causality. Equally typical are the tight cause-and-effect logic of the events and the multiple motivation of every single element in the narration. For instance, Giosuè's miracle survival from the gas chamber is attributed to his already established aversion to taking baths. Despite the comic treatment of this ineffable tragedy and the importance of chance and coincidence within the comedy genre, Benigni's film employs a strict intrinsic causal logic that renders the impossible premise of the plot—game playing in a death camp—fairly consistent and poignant. It is a historical representation of the Holocaust that celebrates the strength and the resilience of the individual and transforms sacrifice into a heroic act.

Admittedly, this is the point that exasperates many of the Holocaust specialists and commentators of the film. Apart from Spiegelman, Lawrence Langer wrote passionately about how in reality "Life isn't Beautiful" and how Benigni is disrespectful to all those who did not survive (Langer 2006). But let us not forget that every classical narration on this subject is bound to represent the Holocaust experience from a personalized perspective, even when the comic overtone is replaced with the most dramatic. All classical dramas, from *Pawnbroker* and *Sophie's Choice* (1982) to *Schindler's List* and *The Pianist* (2002) are compelled to approach the Holocaust involvement in that manner. When Sophie stands on the platform and has to choose at the threat of the gun which child to save, what shutters us is a mother's impossible decision. Not the suffering of the hundreds that remain out of focus in the background and certainly not the millions dying in other places. This is how the anthropocentric framing and the character-centered causality work in the classical mode and there is not a way for a classical film to portray it otherwise. Hence the perennially negative response from those critics who expect from such films to do justice to the entirety of a historical event.[30]

The mode of narration also determines the range of arguments, which can be expressed within this formal vehicle. Thus, at the argumentative level, *Life is Beautiful*, like most classical narratives, is confined to a Formist argument of history. Its historical portrait is analytical and dispersive at the same time; it aims at capturing the particularity of each moment, each event and each action as instances of an unrepeatable process. The focus of a historical account like this lingers persistently on the uniqueness of the historical agents. Guido experiences the discrimination, first, and the persecution, later, as a personal affair that needs to be handled accordingly. The film does not invite us to ponder upon the collective experience of the Holocaust nor examine the broader conditions that led to this monstrous enterprise. The classical formal devices, from the narrative logic down to the *mise-en-scène* and the editing, demand that we maintain our perspective on the specificity of the protagonists and their surroundings, while they depict in minute detail every scene and every experience as unique moments in time and place. It is neither a greater whole that matters nor a general rule that may dictate the occurrence of the events in the story. We do not seek to understand any overarching theory of evil or adopt any mechanistic conception of history where the individual would be merely a cog in the wheel. Even when we see Guido carrying anvils along with other prisoners, he is the one to stand out and expose, in his parodic manner, the brutality of the task. Moreover, it is the Formist argument of history, as we argued before, which leaves room for chance and unpredictability in the unfolding of events. The comic effect of the narration relies heavily on the role of chance, building a creative tension between Guido's intentions and the hazards in his environment, not only in the camps but also before. What finally prevails, though, is Guido's ingenuity. In the closing moments, we witness the realization of his fantasy; Giosuè exits the concentration camp in a tank and reunites with his mother, yelling triumphantly "We won!" The freeze frame holds the image of the mother and son, projecting it as a definitive closure. What seems to matter in this representation of a tiny fragment of the Holocaust experience is the uniqueness of this story and its astonishingly happy ending.

The victorious spirit embalmed in this final image is emblematic of the film's ideological implications and the moral significance that Benigni wants to cast on this sensitive historical topic. And it is precisely what scandalizes critics like Langer and Spiegelman. Much more than the choice of comedy, what they find insulting is the optimism ingrained in Benigni's Liberal vision. The former accuses him of fabricating "the durable illusion of a hopeful future," while the latter finds sinister Benigni's idea to banalize the Holocaust "so that we can get on with our lives" (Langer 2006, 40; cited in Taylor 2007, 193). Having narrated this particular story in a classical mode, Benigni had two options regarding the ideological orientation of his work; the Conservative and the Liberal. A classical film, as I previously argued, cannot accommodate the Anarchistic ambiguity regarding the realization of utopia nor can it express the mechanistic precision required in the Radicalist vision. Choosing the Liberal mentality, in this case, means that the film stresses the importance of free will and envisions the future as an improvement on the past. It chooses to focus on those who survived and lived to tell their stories, helping us learn from past mistakes and urging us to make a better world for future generations. Looking back at the Holocaust with optimism and preferring laughter over tears is undoubtedly a sensitive moral decision open to controversy. It is not impossible though. It is a decision that has nothing to do with historical accuracy but it has everything to do with the extratextual parameters that determine our interpretation of this moral stance. This ideological/moral issue is going to become clearer, as we compare *Life is Beautiful* with two more films, starting with *The Son of Saul*.

The Son of Saul (2015)

In his film debut, László Nemes offers an idiosyncratic depiction of the life at the concentration camps and delves right into the hot debate about the representation of the Holocaust, namely the dilemma to show or not to show it. *The Son of Saul* takes the middle road, flaunting a narration that shows as much as it hides, that tells us as much as it keeps secret.[31] No wonder why Claude Lanzmann, the famous proponent of the "not to show" side, sang the praises of this work. As he noted, "I think it's a very new film, very original, very unusual" (cited in Donadio 2015). Part of Lanzmann's excitement probably stems from Nemes' reversal of a number of classical Hollywood storytelling devices. From the first seconds of the film, we realize that this is going to be a strange viewing experience. Yet, its overall formal make-up is not that unprecedented. *The Son of Saul* can easily fit into the, admittedly, spacious category of the art cinema narration,[32] which thrives on the idea of ambiguity, as we saw in the case of *The Thin Red Line*. Nemes, in fact, vocally embraced the expressive value of ambiguity, while lamenting the mainstream trend "to make sure that the audience understands continuously and totally" (ibid.). Art cinema narration offers him a range of creative options that could accommodate his artistic vision, while articulating an Organicist argument about the meaning of history and an Anarchistic vision about the place of hope and utopia in today's world.

Let us start with the main narrational elements of the film. The opening frame informs us about the word "Sonderkommando," which designates a special group of prisoners who worked at the concentration camps for a few months before being executed. The next shot is a blurry image of a space in the woods; we hear the birds sing, we discern some figures moving in the background but the entire field is persistently out of focus. The scene lasts long enough to make us uncomfortable, when eventually a figure approaches the camera and stops right in front of it in close-up. It is Saul Auslander, a Hungarian Jew and a member of the Sonderkommando. From then on, Saul becomes our guide in the diegetic world, which is filmed in long takes, hand-held camera, and an extraordinary shallow focus, all resulting in an intensely jarring effect. The main story revolves around Saul's struggle in the camp to give a young child, who may or may not be his son, a proper Jewish burial, instead of sending him in the ovens with the rest of the bodies. We follow Saul in his obsessive quest for a day and a half until he is executed along with other prisoners. As a typical example of art cinema narration, *The Son of Saul* is built on the three aforementioned principles: objective realism, subjective realism, and authorial commentary. In the category of objective realism we can include elements such as location shooting, natural sounds[33] and lighting, loose causality, the character in a boundary situation, a fragmented plot structure, and the presence of chance encounters and coincidences. As subjective realism, on the other hand, we can consider the dominant and overwhelming use of the shallow focus throughout the film. In fact, it is a stylistic element that can be accounted for either within the limits of subjective realism or the authorial presence. From the perspective of the former, we could argue that Saul's vision subconsciously blurs his surroundings in order for him to bear to perform his duties as Sonderkommando. In this scenario, the frame is simultaneously co-habited by a diegetic and a focalized level of narration. If, on the other hand, we consider the shallow focus and the persistent close-up framing as an author's gesture, then we find the film's realistic motivations clashing with the authorial intrusion. This is hardly a problem for the art film, though. The notion of ambiguity allows these competing expressive strategies to co-exist.

What are the historical explanations that Nemes' film suggests for the experience of the Holocaust at the level of narration? It is intriguing to compare it to *Life is Beautiful,* given the sketchy similarities at the plot, namely a father's (with and without quotation marks) struggle to provide for his son. In the classical mode, a highly-motivated hero with a full-blown personality sought to outwit and outmaneuver the harsh conditions at the camp and save his child. And he succeeded even at the cost of his own life. In the art mode, an obscure protagonist, whom we know almost nothing about, is fixated about burying the body of a dead child for reasons that remain unknown. The word "son" in the title may indicate a real blood relation or it may be simply symbolic. At any rate, his determination comes across as irrational and obsessive, given the chaos reigning around him. In the end, he is defeated; the boy's body drifts away in the river, while his life is terminated, too, soon thereafter. As a typical art cinema anti-hero, Saul has a very limited capacity to act and change the conditions around him. His efforts to accomplish his mission are constantly thwarted and finally blocked. In its image of the Holocaust, *The Son of Saul* does not elevate human actors to powerful historical agents. There is nothing Saul or the Sonderkommandos or, much less, the thousands who enter the gates of Auschwitz can do to change their place in history. The reality of the camps is incommensurable. The shallow focus over the piles of bodies or the blurry images of their agonizing faces as they enter the showers strip them of any sense of power. Everybody in that place, including the Germans, appears like an automaton; others kill and others die but nobody is presented as a rational human agent with personal judgment and critical thinking. It is a depersonalized account of the Holocaust that points to larger historical forces, without however finding a way to identify them.

Evidently, the art cinema mode of narration is once again paired with an Organicist argument of history. The lack of specificity in this filmic rendering of the Holocaust experience indicates its emphasis on the historical events as large-scale entities reduced to abstraction. Saul is not chosen for his unique particularities but rather as "a character representing something universal," as Nemes explains[34] (cited in Ganjavie 2015). Just like the soldiers in *The Thin Red Line*, his predicament is not merely a personal affair. Death and destruction are spread in the camps, as previously in the combat zone, as symptoms of a greater evil in the world. The gas chambers, the killings, and the ovens are all too hazy to be tied down to specific historical circumstances. Names, dates, and other traditional historical markers are blatantly absent. Hence, Manolha Dargis's characterization of the film as "radically dehistoricized" (Dargis, 2015). In her rationale, history is predominantly of the Formist kind. This is why she laments that Nemes' work transforms "all the screaming, weeping condemned men, women and children into anonymous background blurs" (ibid.). In Organicist historical approaches, however—no matter how much rarer they may be—history is a process governed by general rules and principles that remain stable across various historical junctures. In this sense, historical elements do not interest us for their unique occurrence but for the ways in which they can coalesce and integrate into greater ensembles. Thus, *The Son of Saul* does not aim to document specific prisoners or offer proof of particular facets of the Holocaust enterprise. All that has been done before by classical films, like *Schindler's List*. Instead, it portrays the Holocaust as an experience so ghastly and unfathomable that can only be rooted in metaphysics. To the same end, the subplot regarding the resistance planned within the ranks of the Sonderkommando also intends to capture the principles and ideas circulating among them rather than offer a conclusive account of such attempts in the past. The choppy presentation of their actions and the constant reversals of their ploys brings forth the mechanisms with which humans seek to cope with unspeakable evil. Like Saul, they devise their rebellious schemes as a means for survival. Eventually, they are all executed together off screen. Each with their own delusions, as the force of reality sweeps them by. In its Organicist take, *The Son of Saul* sacrifices specificity for the sake of scope. In Nemes' own words, "[…] when you show frontally, you only reduce the scope of it. So making it small actually makes it much bigger" (cited in Donadio 2015).

Finally, as it is common, the Organicist argument is coupled with the Anarchist ideology. In Saul's story, the desire for redemption and salvation is very tangible, while its potential is postponed to an indefinite future. Surely, the ideological readings of any film may differ, especially on such a contentious matter; but I believe Nemes' film epitomizes art cinema's penchant for the Anarchist mentality. Particularly around the issue of survival, the film opts for a complex metaphysical approach that reworks the Holocaust's second most important dilemma, namely to show *the survivors* or not. In *Life is Beautiful*, we saw how the tale of survival provoked indignant responses. In *The Son of Saul*, nobody survives but the human desire for survival is not cancelled out. The entire film is premised on a fierce inner desire to battle against the relentless external forces. In this light, Saul's tale is also one of hope, even if hope has to come in the shape of madness. In a long interview, Nemes insists on the "absolutely hopeful" message of the film. As he explains, "In the face of a situation in which there is no possibility of hope, Saul's inner voice commands him that he must survive, to be able to do a thing that bears meaning" (cited in Ganjavie 2015). This is not a Liberal optimism, however. It is not a restored faith in humanity and rational judgment. It is an optimism grounded in the vague depths of the human nature, awaiting to be discovered and take charge at some indeterminate point in time. As I have shown with previous examples, such as *The Conformist* and *The Thin Red Line*, the formal elements of the art cinema mode delimit the ideological options to the Anarchist type, due to the amalgam of ambiguity and subjectivism. All other ideological categories in Mannheim's scheme require a level of specificity and purposeful human activity (either at the level of the individual or a class), which are not easily embedded in art cinema's compositional structure. Thus, in *The Son of Saul* the vision for a better world, one where the acts of horror in the camps have no place, is bound to remain abstract and remote.

Inglourious Basterds (2009)

Closing the case studies with Tarantino's cinematic extravaganza feels appropriate for the ways it highlights the intimate relation between history and cinema. *Inglourious Basterds* is almost a play at Godard's theorem, discussed in chapter 1. It is a *"Histoire(s) du Cinéma"* tackling the theme that Godard considered as cinema's weak spot, namely the representation of the Holocaust. Unlike other approaches, however, Tarantino does not address Jews as victims of Nazi persecution but recasts them as perpetrators of acts of violent revenge and retaliation. And he does not depict how Jews were exterminated behind closed doors or violently gunned down so that they can burn later in the ovens of a concentration camp. Instead, it is the high-ranking Nazis and their wives who are desperately banging on the locked doors of a cinema theater, running and screaming in confusion, while Jews execute them with machines guns and explosives before, ultimately, setting them on fire. It is a reversal of roles that Tarantino believes cannot go unnoticed. In his words, "But now that we're so knowledgeable about the Holocaust, when you see that film now, you can't *not* see it" (cited in Sordeau 2009; emphasis in the original). In a twisted way, both *The Son of Saul* and *Inglourious Basterds* take our knowledge of the Holocaust as a given. Only here, Tarantino opts for the post-classical mode. Whereas art cinema allowed an emphasis on abstraction and subjectivity, the post-classical narration offers the most apt formal means for a blatant re-writing of history, raising skepticism about the very process of historical representation. *Inglourious Basterds,* like most post-classical films, approaches its historical theme with a high degree of self-consciousness that binds the historical explanations of the narration with a Contextualist argument as well as a Liberal ideological orientation.

The film tells two entirely separate stories of Jewish revenge against the Nazis. In the first, a young woman called Shosanna (Mélanie Laurent) decides to avenge her family's violent death caused by SS officer Hans Landa (Christoph Waltz) as soon as she runs into him again in Paris three years later. In the second, the Basterds, a group of Jewish American soldiers led by Lt. Aldo Raine (Brad Pitt), are dropped behind enemy lines in Occupied France in order to kill and scalp as many Nazis as possible. These two stories are contained in distinct alternating episodes, while they converge in the last one called the "Revenge of the Giant Face." Even though Shosanna never gets to know the Basterds, their shared goal to exterminate all the attendants of a big film premiere, including Adolf Hitler, is met with triumphant success. Despite losing their lives, Shosanna and most of the Basterds manage to end the war and change the course of world history. The episodic structure in the film allows the presentation of a long list of idiosyncratic characters, such as Archie Hicox (Michael Fassbender), Bridget von Hammersmark (Diane Kruger), Hugo Stiglitz (Til Schweiger), and Fredrick Zoller (Daniel Brühl), each representing a different thread of action in that particular historical moment. The complex tapestry of characters and the pursuit of their missions are visualized through the extensive use of hypermediated realism generated by the constant manipulation of narrative time and space. Apart from the techniques of intensified continuity, the plot relies on recurrent flashbacks as well as spatial montages that increase the density of the filmic image and expose its malleability. The tremendous self-consciousness of the images and sounds in *Inglourious Basterds*, however, stems from Tarantino's excessive use of parody. As Eyal Peretz aptly puts it, "every frame and gesture in *The Inglourious Basterds* are marked as belonging to *cinema* rather than to a supposedly representational, natural reality" (Peretz 2010, 65; emphasis in the original). Indeed, there is not a single element in the film, from the characters and their lines to the most minute camera movement that does not come across as a citation of an earlier cinematic moment or as a reference to other art forms (Setka 2015). Thus, what appears to be motivated compositionally, i.e., as an element of the plot, is also motivated artistically, i.e., as a self-reflexive nod towards aspects existing outside the text. The result is a historical representation that merges realism, on the one hand, and authorial intervention, on the other. Yet, this time the contradiction is not resolved through ambiguity, as in art cinema, but through high communicativeness, as it is typical of the post-classical.

The *Inglourious Basterds'* narrational strategies transform an already controversial historical subject into an exercise in historical representation. First of all, the striking resolution in Tarantino's tale immediately undermines the film's status as a historical film. Admittedly, all historical fictions portray imaginary stories against the backdrop of real historical developments, rendering it difficult—as we have seen so far in all previous examples—to differentiate strictly between fictional and nonfictional elements. However, the startling twist of events in the finale blows up this predicament out of proportion, illustrating how the cinematic signifiers have the power not only to rewrite history but also re-imagine it altogether, using the knowledge of the present. In this light, the warped temporality of historical discourse that always already takes cues from the present is openly exposed through the retroactive causality bestowed upon the acts of revenge. The post-classical narrative devices, and particularly the fragmented storylines, the multiple protagonists, the complex temporality of the plot and the pervasive role of parody, complicate the forces of causality that operate both within and outside the cinematic image. They call attention to the materiality of the historical image and beg us to realize that the historical narrative is not something that historians discover but something they creatively construct according to certain formal as well as ideological principles. The stylistic flamboyance combined with the reversal of the historical roles in the plot, as I described them above, seek to capitalize on the excessive representation of the Holocaust and Nazism and to raise skepticism about cinema's relation to historical reality. Given that we are unlikely to believe that Hitler was violently murdered in a movie theatre, Tarantino feels quite comfortable repurposing the long history of cinema and retrofitting the famous historical characters.

When it comes to character delineation and the attribution of agency, the fragmented storylines, the plurality of eccentric characters, and the use of parody result in a modified character-centered causality that delimits the power of personal initiative. Whereas the classical psychological motivation built strong individual protagonists driven by their personal desires and goals, the post-classical uses and abuses this classical premise by injecting it with overriding extratextual motivations. The characters, their dialogues, their postures, and their entire behavior are not merely governed by the diegetic prerogatives but also by Tarantino's artistic concerns. Thus, purposeful action becomes one layer of agency underneath several others, depending on how complex each intertextual reference is. Aldo "the Apache" Raine, for instance, is not just a brave soldier dedicated to killing Nazis but also a figure carrying an enormous representational weight. As Tarantino explains:

> I had a whole history with Pitt's character, Aldo. Aldo has been fighting racism in the South; he was fighting the Klan before he ever got into World War II. And the

fact that Aldo is part Indian is a very important part of my whole conception, even of turning Jews into American Indians fighting the unfightable, losing cause. So that lead guy is legitimately an Indian.

Cited in Setka 2015, 149

Like Aldo, all the characters in the film are designed to play multiple "roles," one designated by the diegetic needs while others dictated by Tarantino's fascination with history of all kinds. As a result, the classical notion of the "psychologically-defined individual," is undermined to an extent that diminishes, in turn, the impact of rational agency. A similar effect was achieved in *Dunkirk*, even though not through parody but through Nolan's puzzle structure. There, we discussed how the complex plot and its multiple threads, on the one hand, and the relentless non-diegetic crosscutting, on the other, reduced the individuality of the characters and the value of their purposeful actions. In all post-classical cases, whether they favor plot complexity or parody (or both), the individual characters might still possess goals and pursue missions, but the overarching pattern of causality exceeds their personal initiatives.

As a result, the underlying philosophical assumptions of this post-classical mode belong to the Contextualist kind. In *Inglourious Basterds*, the historical explanations regarding the meaning of history may be characterized as Contextualist on two counts; the blueprint of action in its plot and the historical relativism of its retroactive causality. As far as the former is concerned, we realize that the film chooses to portray the issue of Jewish revenge from multiple perspectives, instead of focusing on the singularity of just one. The Americans, the British, the French, and the Germans take part in this tale of revenge in a way that stresses more their cultural and ideological interactions rather than the actual actions. Notice the length of the scene in the basement of the French tavern where the meeting of Bridget von Hammersmark with Hicox and the Basterds goes awry. Through a complex play of cultural signifiers, the film dwells on the interactions of the characters, while it also reveals the power of contingency in the course of the action. Had Hicox ordered his beer differently, he and his team would have been saved from a brutal and bloody death. Moreover, the spectacular finale and the execution of Hitler are presented as the outcome of a few somewhat antagonistic forces. Shosanna planned her part, two of the Basterds managed to join in, while the ultimate success of the plan was sealed by Hans Landa, who not only allowed the film premiere to go on but also placed the explosives underneath Hitler's seat. This coexistence and simultaneity of such diverse agents and motivations are beautifully underscored by Tarantino with the use of crosscutting and spatial montage in the final moments. From this perspective, the end of the Second World War is presented not as the result of heroic action but of a mix of sacrifice (Shosanna), passionate revenge (the Basterds), and cynical calculation (Landa). At the same time, the portrayal of such an alternate ending for this historical world conflict illustrates the power of the cinematic language to rewrite history whether with a negative or a positive intent. On the negative side, one may consider revising history as an act of distortion and propaganda, while on the positive, one may invite such historical retrofitting as a form of speculative history that seeks to underline how everything in the past could have taken a different course. The latter is, in fact, a part of what is called "alternate," "virtual," or "counterfactual" history, a small branch of academic historical practice which engages with "what if" questions and unravels the assumptions of historical determinism (Ferguson 2011). As a playful and, yet, quite knowledgeable exercise in a "what if" scenario, *Inglourious Basterds* expresses a key Contextualist conviction, namely that no historical analysis can get to the bottom or top of things to reveal their true essence. The historical field is a terrain with complex forces at play, while our access to it is fragmentary, partial, and mediated through our expressive means. Re-writing history in such a self-conscious manner illustrates our capacity to acknowledge the creative power of our formal tools as well as the absence of governing laws in history. Being able to imagine a different path for human action means precisely to defy the Organicist and Mechanistic views of historical causality. It also means to thwart the need to reduce historical entities to metaphysical needs. The characters in *Inglourious Basterds* are not representatives of some greater forces of good and evil like Saul was in Nemes' film. They are specific earthy creatures that make decisions, plan, and occasionally die in circumstances shaped by them *as well as* others. It is this paradoxical dispersive specificity that forms the gist of Tarantino's Contextualist argument, which I believe is accompanied by ideological implications of the Liberal kind.

Again, deciphering the ideological orientation of a historical work, whether on paper or film, is the interpretative task the least attached to shape of the form. Despite the fluctuating external circumstances, however, a mode of narration does set boundaries to the ideological range of its reading. As a post-classical film, the *Inglourious Basterds* were likely to be viewed either as Conservative or Liberal. And indeed, different commentators have stressed either the one or the other direction (Peretz 2010; Setka 2015; Burnetts 2016). To me, the latter seems more prominent. If we decide to maintain the notion of hope and survival as markers of ideological orientation, as we did in the previous case studies, then Tarantino's resolution certainly seems to restore faith in humanity in a very immediate and concrete manner. The graphic materialization of Jewish revenge in the final moments as well as the Basterds' persistence to inscribe the swastika on Landa's forehead illustrate that justice and righteousness remain two human virtues capable of overpowering evil. This positive and hopeful finale is akin to Benigni's emphasis on survival. In both cases, at the end of the war, the survivors celebrate the victory and earn the right to envision a better future. Unlike *The Son of Saul*, where salvation could exist only within the mental realm and hope was pushed to an indefinite future, the *Inglourious Basterds* and *Life is Beautiful* dare to address Nazism and Holocaust in a playful manner that demystifies the rhetoric of their ineffability and generously allows goodness to prevail above all evil. The only major difference between these two cases of Liberal optimism can be traced in the inherent skepticism of the post-classical forms and the historical relativism that the latter tend to advocate. This means that, despite the peculiar happy ending in Tarantino's work, its self-conscious portrait of history cannot establish a definitive and final closure on this historical matter. Unlike the unconditionally happy moment between the mother and the son in the final freeze-frame of *Life is Beautiful,* the inexhaustible cynicism of *Inglourious Basterds* cannot freeze the past and settle accounts with it once and for all. The film, indeed, places its bets on those who survived and scarred irrevocably the face of Nazism, but it cannot but acknowledge that the relation of the past with the present is an open one, always prone to revision, over and over again.

A concluding note

Historical fiction films are magnified miniatures of historical books that seek to explain the past in the process of narrating it. Whereas the process of explanation through narration in written forms of history may go unnoticed thanks to their scientific, or more broadly academic, credentials, the same process in the cinema becomes easily identified and exposed. This means that what Hayden White tried to demonstrate in his poetics of history, by discerning the role of emplotment, argument, and ideology in every historical work, is significantly clearer in the historical film due to the magnifying effects of the cinematic form. In fact, the enterprise of formulating the poetics of filmic history is even easier thanks to David Bordwell's historical poetics and the formal precision that characterizes the modes of narration in the fiction film.

As I have tried to illustrate throughout this chapter, the cinematic forms that assume the task of representing the past determine specific constraints regarding the meaning of history that they project on the screen. Each mode of narration delimits the options of historical explanations that can be expressed within its formal range, exemplifying the intricate ties between form and content. White's graduated taxonomy, from the emplotment to the ideological implications, allows for the refinement of these ties from the textual to the extratextual elements, helping us carve a steady trajectory in the reading of the historical film. A notable difference, however, between White's suggested combinations of historical explanations and the ones that I presented here (see Table 5.1), is that mine are considerably more restrictive. While White merely describes "elective affinities" between the diverse modes in written history,[35] my research into historical fiction films showed that the mode of narration imposes more precise limits. In other words, the form in a historical film tends to control the content of the historical representation in more definitive ways. I suspect the reasons for this important difference between a written historical work and a historical fiction film are both intrinsic and extrinsic. The former regards the fact that a historical film condenses and exaggerates the narrating act in a way that vests the cinematic form with more formative powers than in a written account. For instance, the mold of the classical narration controls very tightly the compositional and the realistic elements that a filmmaker can include in a historical representation, restricting, by consequence, the range of arguments and ideological implications that can be fitted therein. The second reason is extrinsic because it has to do with the terminology we employ to describe the phenomena in question. As I explained in the opening of this chapter as well as in the previous one, White relies on the four genres of Romance, Comedy, Tragedy, and Satire to describe the historical work at the level of emplotment. These formal categories, however, are remarkably broader in their scope and much more inclusive in their technical repertoire than the modes of narration in the cinema. As a result, the discussion of narrative form in written history becomes more spacious and grants historians with greater freedom to combine forms of emplotment with a wide range of arguments and ideological implications. The importance of terminology in the way we map our historiographical options, whether on paper or on screen, becomes even more palpable in the next chapter, which examines the historical representation in the documentary. There, we will see how Nichols' terminology, by being less formally rigorous than Bordwell's, gives the opportunity for more combinations between the various modes of explanation in the historical documentary.

Notes

1   Bordwell is particularly critical of the use of what he calls "SLAB Theory" (Saussure, Lacan, Althusser, and Barthes) to interpret mere instances and fragments of any film in order to corroborate the theory's key tenets (Bordwell 1989a).

2   According to Bordwell, such examples we find in the works of André Bazin, Noel Burch, Rudolph Arnheim, and Sergei Eisenstein (Bordwell 1989a, 261).

3   Admittedly, the significance of interpretation and meaning in (historical) representation is part of long philosophical discussions that exceed the scope of my work here. For a comprehensive overview of these discussions, see Ankersmit (2012).

4   Bordwell's original definition is this: "the process whereby the film's syuzhet and style interact in the course of cueing and channeling the spectator's construction of the fabula" (1985, 53). The terms "syuzhet" and "fabula" originate from the works of Russian literary formalists and are adapted for the cinema in Bordwell's theory of narration.

5   Despite my own disagreement and criticism on some of Bordwell's arguments, especially the infinite spaciousness of the classical mode of narration from the 1990s onwards and the relative spaciousness of the art cinema, his contribution to historical poetics in the cinema is immense and the value of his work is unquestionable. His narrative theory and the modes of narration present us with the most comprehensive method and models, respectively, for handling cinematic forms. Any discussion about the relation between form and content in historical cinema cannot but be premised—to a lesser or greater extent—on his theories.

6   Indicatively, see (Burgoyne 1990; Chatman 1990; Thanouli 2009a and 2013b).

7   Notice how Kracauer insightfully observes that the same process is at play when it comes to general histories. He writes: "Temporal continuity is inseparable from meaningful togetherness. In addition to bolstering that continuity, the general historian will therefore automatically try to make any period of his concern appear as a unity. This calls for adjustments of story content, enabling him to blur the discrepancies between coexistent events and turn the spotlight instead on their mutual affinities. It is almost inevitable that, as a matter of expediency, he should neglect intelligible area sequences over cross-influences of his own invention" (Kracauer 1969, 173).

8   For my criticism of Bordwell's art cinema narration, see Thanouli (2009b).

9 Notice that my discussion of the philosophical and ideological arguments of art cinema focuses only on the historical art films and does not apply to art films in general. The philosophical and ideological range of art films with nonhistorical plots is much more diverse and expanded.

10 Note that according to Mannheim, the fourth type of ideology next to Liberalism, Conservatism, and Radicalism is what he calls the "Orgiastic Chiliasm of the Anabaptists" but he notes that in contemporary times "the anarchism of the Bakunian variety comes closest in our opinion to continuing the Chiliastic outlook in the modern world" (Mannheim 1979, 196). In White's work, the fourth type is directly labeled as Anarchism.

11 In his analysis of Marxist theory, Hayden White identifies a partly Organicist and partly Mechanistic logic (White 2014, 286).

12 The employment of classical narrative devices in cinemas outside Hollywood is a fascinating issue that has hardly been explored in depth. I have tacked it to some extent for a small number of Greek films from the 1950s and 1960s (Thanouli 2012). At this stage and with what we know so far, I would be hesitant to include all these variations within the classical mode. Especially when it comes to historical filmmaking, we need to consider the mode of narration in conjunction with the arguments and ideologies with which it can be combined, so that the specific correlations between mode, argument and ideology remain solid and effective.

13 Bordwell has not discussed the post-classical mode of narration in any of his own publications so far. He has repeatedly rejected, and rightfully so, the idea of postmodern cinema as distinct from classical cinema based on a mélange of arguments that blend formal matters with social and ideological developments. My account of the post-classical was meant as a continuation of his historical poetics work and as an addendum to his four modes of narration.

14 In *Metahistory*, White presents Jacob Burckhardt as the emblematic Contextualist historian. It is not accidental that Kracauer, in *The Last Things Before The Last*, puts forward Burckhardt as his ideal historian, explaining how his work overcomes the limitations of other historical approaches, including the realistic tradition of Ranke or the scientific tradition of Marx (Kracauer 1969). It is not accidental either that Burckhardt has been hailed as the "first postmodern historian" by recent reviewers and critics (Jones 1998).

15 The combat movies provided the most direct and all-encompassing treatment of the war by dramatizing the actual battles and inaugurating a new sense of realism and historical immediacy in the Hollywood films. They depicted battlefield situations on sea, land, or air, and described the violence, the hardships, and the courage of the soldiers in the front. The largest number of combat films produced during the war take place in the Pacific theater of operations and some of the most legendary

examples include *Wake Island* (1942), *Bataan* (1943), *Guadalcanal Diary* (1943), and *30 Seconds Over Tokyo* (1944), to name just a few. See Shull and Wilt (1996).

16 As Thomas Doherty notes, "By the early 1990s conventional Hollywood wisdom considered the 1941–45 background 'box-office poison' because multiplex mall crawlers and the crucial 18-to–24-year-old demographic find Frank Capra's Great Struggle as remote and irrelevant as the Peloponnesian Wars" (1993, 297).

17 For the most comprehensive overview of the film's reception, see Morris (2007).

18 For the explication of the term "narrative motivation," see Bordwell (1989b).

19 As Robert Burgoyne notes, "*Saving Private Ryan*'s innovative use of technology places it in a long tradition of war films that have broken new ground in terms of special effects, creative camera work, and mass choreography in the service of realism and emotional power. *The Longest Day*, *All Quiet on the Western Front*, *The Birth of a Nation*, and the aviation warfare film *Hell's Angels* all established new camera and optical techniques, and set new standards for realism in film" (2008, 51)

20 The incredible irony is that the screening and publicity of the film brought to the surface a significant mistake that Ambrose had made in his historical account regarding the Niland case. This is a perfect "parapraxis," a term I will introduce in the conclusion, which illustrates the relation of both cinema and written history with the idea of representation as failure. About the historical mistake, see Kodat (2000).

21 See chapter three.

22 As Robert Burgoyne observes, "*Saving Private Ryan*, in contrast, insists on commemoration. Like earlier World War II films in which there is always someone who survives to remember and tell the story, the film closes with an explicit recall of the sacrifices that the soldiers have made" (2008, 71).

23 In the combat films of the 1940s, the portrayal of the Japanese as duplicitous and barbaric "subhumans" had no precedent. As Bernard Dick notes, "in contrast to the 'good German' and the occasional good Nazi, good Japanese were almost unheard of" (1985, 231)

24 For a more detailed analysis of the narration in this film, see my article "*The Thin Red Line* and the World War II Hollywood Tradition" (2005). At the time, however, my connections between the formal, philosophical and ideological elements of the film were more intuitive than substantiated by a concrete theory of the poetics of filmic history, as the one I have attempted to develop here.

25 In his analysis of the film, David Bordwell takes careful notes of the deviations of the narration from the classical norms, and yet, in his conclusion he insists on including it within what he perennially calls "the boundaries of difference." In his words, "In all, Nolan has taken the conventions of the war picture, its reliance on multiple protagonists, grand maneuvers, and parallel and converging lines of action, and subjected it to the sort of experimentation characteristic of art cinema. (As, in a way, Bowman's time-grid in *Beach Red* anticipates the rigor of the Nouveau Roman.)

Nolan exploits one feature of crosscutting: that it often runs its strands of action at different rates. He then lets us see how events on different time scales can mirror one another, or harmonize, or split off, or momentarily fuse. As a sort of cinematic tesseract, *Dunkirk* is an imaginative, engrossing effort to innovate within the bounds of Hollywood's storytelling tradition" (Bordwell 2017). For my criticism of the "the boundaries of difference" rationale, see Thanouli (2009a).

26 Very often, people who are not familiar with the post-classical mode of narration (or people who are reluctant to acknowledge it as an equal mode among Bordwell's other four) claim that films like this are something *between* the classical and the art cinema mode. This idea of "in-betweeness" is practically and conceptually useless. Film forms develop and cluster in various configurations across time and the number of narrative modes is not limited. The narrative elements identified as parts of the classical and the art cinema mode are free to re-arrange and expand endlessly, without any attachment of any kind to these two initial theoretical categories. The existence of a distinct and autonomous mode simply requires a consistent and recurring combination of narrative forms, which do not need to be hetero-determined by other modes. For my arguments on the autonomy of the post-classical mode, see Thanouli, (2009a).

27 For an introduction to the concept of "diegesis" see Thanouli (2013a) and for the levels of narration see Edward Branigan's narrative theory (Branigan 1992).

28 I find Bordwell's analysis of crosscutting in *Dunkirk*, as always, thorough and historically informed, despite my objections to his final conclusion about the film's overall narration (Bordwell 2017).

29 According to Bolter and Grusin the logic of immediacy has a twin logic, that of hypermediacy. As they note, "If the logic of immediacy leads one either to erase or to render automatic the act of representation, the logic of hypermediacy acknowledges multiple acts of representation and makes them visible" (Bolter and Grusin 1999, 33).

30 Furthermore, when they compare films to written histories, they fail to notice that the latter shape the historical events through emplotment just as well. The difference being, of course, that emplotment becomes all too obvious in a historical fiction film whereas Hayden White had great difficulty in convincing the historians' community of the existence of this element in historical discourse.

31 Filmmakers working on the topic of the Holocaust have to tackle a remarkable level of self-consciousness when it comes to the act of representation. Nemes was confronted head-on with the question about his own moral decision about what to show and what not. His response was this: "If you want to show too much then you might end up with less but at the same time, if you show too little then you might downgrade the impact of the horror of the Holocaust. The moral question then was how to balance these two facts" (cited in Ganjavie 2016).

32 See note 6.

33 The sound design in the film is extraordinarily complex and layered but the impression that it strives to achieve is one of spontaneity and naturalness.

34 The narrative analysis of the film and its ensuing interpretation does not need to be corroborated by the filmmaker's statements in articles and interviews. It can stand autonomously, regardless of the auteur's intentions. In Nemes' case, however, it is remarkable how his ideas and arguments are in line with the method I'm applying here on the historical film at the level of narration, argument and ideology.

35 See chapter 4.

6

The Representation of History in the Documentary

History has been an integral part of the cinema, not only in the dominant genre of fiction but also in its low-profile sibling, the documentary. In fact, nonfiction films are more easily related to works of written academic history, given the shared commitment[1] on the part of their makers, documentarians, and historians respectively, to respect the truth and report it objectively. Here, I will continue my investigation into the cinematic forms of historical representation, by looking closely into the ways in which the documentary tradition has approached historical topics and by discerning the types of historical explanations that it has projected on the screen. The primary guide in this journey will be Bill Nichols' work, and particularly his two books *Representing Reality* (1991) and *Blurred Boundaries* (1994). His extensive research into the forms of documentary is invaluable, on the one hand, for helping us map the poetics of the historical documentary while bringing together, on the other, the impact of all the three key figures that featured prominently in this book so far, i.e., Michel Foucault, Hayden White, and David Bordwell. Nichols' common concerns and affinities with these scholars allow us to carry on this long and extensive investigation into the workings of history on the screen, maintaining an increased level of consistency and rigor, as we move from one level of generality to the other. In this middle level that we have reached at this point, it is important to acknowledge how all these diverse ideas and arguments, ranging from the philosophy of history all the way down to narrative devices, can connect in systematic ways and warrant a necessary sense of coherence. In plain words, the ideas of Foucault, White, Bordwell and, now, Nichols are not meant to work here as a casual collage in the spirit of "anything goes." On the contrary, each and every one of them provides another invaluable piece of a puzzle that forms a complex but logical and intelligible argument regarding the functions and forms of cinematic history throughout the twentieth and twenty-first centuries.

When it comes to defining the documentary and, thereby, differentiating it from fiction films, Nichols is careful to avoid an essentialist position. As he argues, "Documentary as a concept or practice occupies no fixed territory. It mobilizes no finite inventory of techniques, addresses no set number of issues, and adopts no completely known taxonomy of forms, styles, or modes. Documentary film practice is the site of contestation and change" (Nichols 1991, 12). The Foucauldian overtones are already evident in this key passage that opens the section "Defining Documentary" in his book but the adoption of Foucault's anti-essentialist philosophy becomes even more explicit further on, when Nichols quotes him lengthily to suggest that we should define the documentary in exactly the same way as madness (16–17). Consequently, Nichols' attempt at a definition, on the one hand, remains deliberately open-ended, while, on the other, is premised on a loose configuration of discursive and non-discursive practices, including the community of practitioners and their institutional settings, a corpus of texts, and a constituency of viewers. Clearly, however, of all these parameters the weight of his work falls on the documentary as text and the formal procedures at work in an extensive sample of nonfiction films from the very first steps of the cinematic medium.

Once he has calibrated the focus of his investigation, Nichols leans regularly on White's writings on historiography to explain how several concepts, such as tropes, argument, and ideology, take shape in the documentary form. Even though the parallel between White's poetics of written history and the poetics of documentary does not come center stage,[2]—not least because documentaries are not always historical—the idea that a documentary presents a part of reality in order to suggest an argument and promote a certain ideology is critical. In fact, one of the key distinctions that Nichols attempts to build between fiction and nonfiction is based on the importance of the argument in the latter. As he notes, "Documentaries take shape around an informing logic. The economy of this logic requires a representation, case, or argument about the historical world" (18). And further on, he insists that:

> Even if the images forfeit their claims of congruence, even if the documentary constructs what occurs in front of the camera as a representation of what occurs in the world, as do the films *Night Mail, Louisiana Story, Nanook of the North, Letter from Siberia*, and *The Thin Blue Line*, we still persist, as long as we assume it is a documentary that we are watching, in inferring an argument about the world. The documentary viewer employs "procedures of rhetorical engagement" rather than the "procedures of fictive engagement" that guide the viewing of classic narrative film.
>
> Nichols 1991, 25–6

Thus, the construction of an argument is considered by Nichols as the emblematic function of every documentary. In his frame of thought, the relation between "narration" and "argument" is viewed primarily as one of opposition, each indicative of the level of fiction or nonfiction respectively. In other words, the more narration a film has, the closer it is to fiction and the more difficult it is for us to discern its argument. Notice how he juxtaposes fiction and documentary, extending the opposition to "story versus argument."

> We enter a fictional world through the agency of narration, that process whereby a narrative unfolds in time, allowing us to construct the story it proposes. We enter the world in documentary through the agency of representation or exposition, that process whereby a documentary addresses some aspect of the world, allowing us to reconstruct the argument it proposes.
>
> Nichols 1991, 112–13

This clear-cut distinction, however, is repeatedly undercut throughout his analysis of various types of documentaries that combine "narration" and "argument" in various degrees, rendering not only their separation but also their supposed antagonism practically untenable.[3] Besides, if Nichols had kept his arguments a little closer to White's ideas, he could have acknowledged the notion of emplotment in any documentary as an absolutely integral part. Then, he could have explored how different types of narration are accompanied by a gamut of arguments and ideological positions, just as in any historical work.

A similar problem arises when we delve deeper into the ways Nichols deploys Bordwell's work. On the one hand, he relies heavily on his observations not only on film form but also on the viewers' activity, clearly modeling his work upon *Narration in the Fiction Film*. Unlike the latter, however, Nichols' construction of the five modes of representation[4] does not proceed from a solid and thoroughly formulated theory of documentary narration. The definition of "narration," "representation," "argument," and even "ideology" is slippery enough to allow for various contradictions and loose ends that render the five modes relatively harder to work with, especially when we want to combine them with White's poetics of history and, particularly, the three types of historical explanation. Nevertheless, these theoretical and conceptual discrepancies should not overshadow Nichols' tremendous effort to systematize and categorize an enormous and diverse body of documentaries from across the world and for the span of almost a century. In his two aforementioned volumes, Nichols presents us with the most comprehensive account of documentary form and puts forward five modes of representation (expository, observational, interactive, reflexive, and performative) that help us organize a vast terrain of nonfiction filmmaking. His modes, just like Bordwell's, rise above individual creativity or national sensibility, containing a hierarchy of conventions and norms that remain flexible enough to accommodate diverse styles and arguments, without, however, "losing the force of an organizing principle" (23). Modes, as he explains, may rise as a movement but they tend to persist "beyond a particular time and place, adding new variations in structure and content" (ibid.). Even though his method is not as strictly empirical as Bordwell's, in the sense of choosing a historically demarcated sample of films with chronological geographical or institutional specificity, the result is not very different. In other words, Nichols' looser application of the historical poetics' principles on the documentary may contain more conceptual pitfalls and formal inconsistencies than Bordwell's account of the fiction film but it succeeds in maintaining a level of comprehensiveness and applicability unparalleled to this date. This is why I consider Nichols' work as safe scaffolding for exploring the historical representation in nonfiction filmmaking and for construing the historical explanations that this type of cinema generates and communicates to the world. The table below (Table 6.1) summarizes the results of my exploration and it presents schematically the various configurations of modes of representations with modes of argument and ideology in nonfiction films.[5]

As in the previous chapter, my exposition will consist of two parts; first, I will present an overview of the modes of representation and the types of historical explanation that each may contain. Then, I will proceed to a series of case studies that aim to present in greater detail how the formal and narrational principles of a documentary relate to diverse explanations about the meaning of history.

Table 6.1

Mode of Representation	Mode of Argument[6]	Mode of Ideological Implication
Expository	Organicist (synthetic)	Liberal, Conservative, or Anarchist
Observational	Formist (analytical)	Liberal or Conservative
Interactive	Organicist or Contextualist (synthetic)	Liberal, Conservative, or Anarchist
Reflexive	Contextualist (dispersive)	Liberal or Anarchist
Performative	Formist or Contextualist (dispersive)	Liberal or Anarchist

Thematically, my examples will derive from nonfiction films that address two separate topics; the Vietnam War and the biography. My choice attempts to complement the filmography of the fiction film so that the overall sample covers some of the most fundamental historical issues addressed in the literature so far. By adding the Vietnam War and the biographies to the Second World War, and the Holocaust, I seek to offer a comprehensive account of the ways in which cinema, whether in the form of fiction or documentary, has represented the past with moving images.

Modes of representation[7] and historical explanations

The expository

The expository mode characterizes the most common type of documentary that comes to our mind whenever we think of this genre. A voice-of-God commentary addresses us as viewers and assumes the task of guiding us through a certain topic of the historical world. It takes us "by the hand" and gradually exposes all the necessary evidence for us to understand the matter in question and reach a specific conclusion. In expository films, the nonsynchronous sound of the voice track dominates over the visual elements; images serve whether as illustration or counterpoint for something that has been verbally expressed in the soundtrack. However, the commentator is not merely somebody who describes a situation but, rather, an authority who puts forward a concrete argument aimed to convince us of its truthfulness and validity. As Nichols observes, "The rhetoric of the commentator's argument serves as the textual dominant, moving the text forward in service of its persuasive needs" (Nichols 1991, 35). Persuasion in this mode is primarily achieved through the impression of objectivity and comprehensiveness that contribute to a well-substantiated argument. It is also achieved by a tight causal logic. Just like the classical fiction film, the expository documentary presents its key theme as a puzzle or a problem-solving procedure, which is carefully executed without gaps, ambiguities, or other fissures that could probe questions or skepticism. In this mode, continuity needs to be sustained not between spatial or temporal elements but between rhetorical propositions. Each shot or sequence is organized around the needs of the central argument, which is progressively developed until it reaches a final closure.

The formal structure of the expository documentary, even if described in sketchier terms than the formal structure of a mode of fiction film, already suggests a specific approach toward the acquisition of knowledge. Specifically, when it comes to history, a historical documentary of the expository kind, irrespective of its chosen subject, creates the impression that our view of the past can be rationally constructed on the basis of historical evidence and their objective evaluation. The continuous commentary on the soundtrack becomes an authoritative voice that we are meant to trust and believe. The tight cause-and-effect logic that relates the visual proof leaves no time for hesitation or pondering on our own. The unity of logic and the consistency of the explanatory frame in every expository documentary invest on a solid idea of rational interpretation, of objective thinking, and of conclusive interpretation. The historical accounts of the past that we witness through the expository mode contain clear-cut answers to complex historical processes and provide us with a sense of closure and fulfillment that can only be compared to the experience of the classical fiction film. Let's take as an example a relatively lesser-known documentary entitled *Cinema Combat: Hollywood Goes to War* (1998) directed by Edith Becker and narrated by Martin Sheen. The very presence of Sheen in the voice-over serves the primary purpose of the expository mode to build trust around the commentary as it guides us through the exploration of its key theme, which is the representation of war in Hollywood cinema. What is fascinating, however, is that the history of the combat film becomes inextricably linked to the American history of the twentieth century, demonstrating how cinema and history can no longer be separated in our public imagination. As the commentary puts it, "In just one hundred years, film has changed the way we look at war, the world and ourselves." This admittedly complex agenda is served through an elaborate and systematic examination of a wide range of interconnected parameters, such as the film industry, particular films and filmmakers, audience and institutional responses as well as official documents, historical moments, and figures. Images, archival materials, film clips, and sound bites are meticulously combined to craft a chronological account of key historical events and their cinematic representation that starts from the destruction of the battleship *Maine* in 1898 and ends with the war in Iraq in 1996. The solid structure of the narration, its clear chronological order, and the coordinated equivalence between words and images create a detailed and unequivocal account of the close relation between cinema and history throughout the twentieth century. When the film ends, we feel that we have seen and heard all there is to see and hear about the subject. The seamless commentary and its tight cause-and-effect logic generate a very traditional image of history with clear-cut beginnings and endings, with all the necessary milestones (dates and figures), and, of course, a specific underlying rationale that drives human action, which, in this particular case, is none other than patriotism and the protection of the American values.

Apart from the historical explanation that stems from its narrative structure, the expository documentary tends to sustain explanations by argument of the synthetic kind, i.e., either Organicist or Contextualist, as Pepper classifies them (Pepper 1970). The meticulous assembly of images and their careful visual orchestration around a dominating commentary are more likely to accommodate arguments that focus on clusters of elements and favor synthesis. The specificity of each person or moment documented is often surpassed by the general logic that binds all evidence together. In most cases, this synthesis breeds generalizations causing the argument to veer toward the Organicist side. Formally, we cannot exclude the possibility of a voice-over commentary that puts forward a Contextualist argument; yet, such a move would gravely undermine the key purpose of the expository mode, namely to present a solid version of truth and objectivity. On the other hand, expository documentaries would not veer toward an absolute historical determinism either. A Mechanistic approach to historical truth would not be easy to communicate. For all their certainty and argumentative coherence, most documentaries of this mode settle for a little ambiguity as to the ultimate mechanisms of history. Thus, the Organicist view of history becomes the most suitable historical argument, which allows them to gather a large number of historical elements as indices of larger ongoing processes. In *Cinema Combat*, for instance, its Organicist argument projects the idea of the "American nation" as the unifying force of all the particular elements contained in its narrative. First of all, the official American history provides the signposts that determine the temporal, spatial, and causal parameters of the investigation into cinematic representation. We hear about the breaking of the First World War, for instance, then we see relevant evidence (newspaper clips, newsreels) and, then, we turn to cinema to find out about the directors and the films that addressed the historical events or became part of the history themselves in one capacity or another. The particulars in this documentary, i.e., specific stars, producers, film scenes, are accumulated as components of a wider process at work, namely their service to the American nation. This service, however, is not restricted to acts of patriotism or heroism in times of war but it is also accompanied by the effort to understand the American psyche and distill the human values that make America great. To all those films and filmmakers that have pondered upon the nature of war, humanity and American values, the film attributes a unifying agency that overwhelms the specificities of their existence. Notice, for example, how the commentary approaches the dramatic change in Hollywood's stance towards American politics from the Second World War to Vietnam. It does not view it as a radical discontinuity that should ultimately problematize the ties between the film industry and political power. Instead, it suggests that we should regard it as a progressive step toward understanding the complexity of the human individual and the moral ambiguities entailed in the enterprise of war. Thus, like in most Organicist accounts, each new phase of Hollywood war films is integrated into a greater organic process, i.e., the service of the American nation, adding yet another layer of events that works toward the same goal. As Sheen puts it in his final words, "documentary images of war and the dramatic interpretations offered by Hollywood's best filmmakers form an important record of our past and a guidepost to our future."

The same phrase bears significant ideological weight that takes us to the third type of historical explanation that we borrowed from White's theory, namely the explanation by ideology. Establishing the ideological implications of a documentary like *Cinema Combat*, just like any other work of history, is an act of interpretation that is always contingent upon extratextual factors that may change over time. If we limit ourselves to Mannheim's four broad categories— the Anarchist, the Liberal, the Conservative, and the Radical—we could argue that all positions may be accommodated in the expository form. *Cinema Combat*, for instance, can be construed as a moderately Liberal documentary that welcomes complexity and self-reflection as a means to improve American society without demolishing the accomplishments of the status quo. The formula of the voice of God commentary combined with images strung together in a tight causal logic may well serve other agendas whether on the Conservative or the Radical side. When it comes to the latter, however, we notice that films in favor of radical ideas, such as communist ideology, veer toward Anarchism when they deploy the expository mode. Just like art cinema in the genre of fiction, expository documentaries that sympathize with radical politics, such as Frédéric Rossif's *Mourir a Madrid* (1963),[8] tend to resort to the atemporal utopia of Anarchism rather than to a "call for arms" suited to the Radical ideology.

The observational

The observational mode of representation emphasizes the direct observation of an ongoing real situation, rendering it a quintessential example of "life caught unawares."[9] Films that belong to this category seek to emphasize the nonintervention of the filmmaker, eschewing voice-over commentary, non-diegetic music, reenactments, or any material that may appear external to the events that are recorded by the camera (Nichols 1991, 38). As I noted in chapter 4, this mode is problematic when it comes to the discussion of historical representation, since history is not something that can be directly observed. Thus, we could either consider the observational mode as non-applicable to historical subjects or we could reserve it as a possibility for events of a highly official or political nature that de facto grants them the status of "history in the making." I will opt for the second option on two grounds;[10] firstly, the three famous observational documentaries that have recorded such historical events, namely Leni Riefenstahl's *Triumph of the Will* and D.A. Pennebaker's *Primary* and *The War Room* (with Chris Hegedus) are considered landmarks in the history of documentary and have been influential in numerous theoretical debates, whether in politics or aesthetics. Secondly, the idea of observing history as it unfolds is reminiscent of Arthur Danto's "Ideal Chronicler" who is able to record everything that happens the exact moment it happens (Danto 2007, 149). Filmmakers aspire to become ideal chroniclers of a certain situation, whereas, in fact, the final outcome proves once again Danto's point that this is not what history is about. A careful scrutiny of observational documentaries illustrates that history is inevitably about selection (an angle, a moment etc.), narration (plot/style) as well as about hindsight.[11] In this sense, the observational documentaries offering direct recordings of historical events contain a representation of history that bears no specific privilege on objectivity nor offers a unique access to the past. Just like all the other modes, an observational film can be analyzed into specific narrative procedures that host historical explanations on several levels.

Starting with the level of narrational construction, we notice that the observational documentary consists of recordings of an ongoing situation and creates the impression of an unmediated access to the historical world. It opts for long takes, minimal editing, and an unobtrusive use of the camera, so that the people involved act without reserve or self-consciousness. The implications of these formal techniques regarding the significance of history are primarily related to the cherished value of objectivity, immediacy and, above all, disclosure. In contrast to the official visual documentation of political or other major historical events, the idea to "look behind the scenes" or be present for a long duration while events are still unfolding is a possibility that written historiography cannot easily provide. It is a fantasy, however, that observational documentaries tend to sustain. Let's take *The War Room*, for instance. The film follows Bill Clinton's two chief strategists, James Carville and George Stephanopoulos, and their activities between the New Hampshire Primary and the presidential election in 1992. It is a historical record of Clinton's political campaign, presenting private and group meetings as well as other key events, such as public speeches, strategy maneuvers, and personal moments of crisis. It contains material that professional historians can draw on in order to narrate a part of American political history, while viewers have the chance to experience it firsthand during the film's viewing. It gives them a front seat in history and promises to deliver it "*wie es eigentlich gewesen*," realizing not only Ranke's wish but also Griffith's vision.[12] The immediacy of the recording, the linear temporality, and the spontaneity of the scenes fuel the idea of history as a natural and self-evident process; history is something we can all witness in real time. *The War Room*, like all observational documentaries, argues that immediate visual access to a historical event guarantees both knowledge and comprehension of it. The fact that scholars can take a documentary like *The War Room* and literally take it apart, exposing its formal and ideological construction,[13] does not cancel or even diminish the historical explanation that the observational documentary mode promotes to the average viewer. Its formal and structural devices create the impression of history as a linear process that evolves in a specific spatiotemporal frame according to a clear causal logic that we can all easily grasp.

These formal implications are also coupled with a specific type of argument, which is none other than the Formist argument of history from Pepper's list. The observational documentaries observe people and situations as unique occurrences that take place in a very specific place and time. They capture moments and segments of life that are sometimes important, while other times they maybe casual or trite. Their direct recoding of reality allows the possibility for chance or unpredictable incidents, an element that is excluded from other modes. In addition, the visual and aural attachment to individuals in their settings prevents us from reaching broader generalizations that would fit other integrative arguments, such as the Organicist or the Mechanistic. Instead, an observational film like *The War Room* remains adhered to a persistent indexicality and literalness that foreground the historical specificity of the depicted situation. What also causes the observational mode to veer more toward Formism, rather than Contextualism, which is also dispersive, is their difference described by White most aptly below:

> Here [in Contextualism], as in Formism, the historical field is apprehended as a
> "spectacle" or richly textured arras web which on first glance appears to lack

coherence and any discernible fundamental structure. But, unlike the Formist, who is inclined simply to consider entities in their particularity and uniqueness— i.e., their similarity to, and difference from, other entities in the field—the Contextualist insists that "what happened" in the field can be accounted for by the specification of the functional interrelationships existing among the agents and agencies occupying the field at a given time.

White 2014, 17

In a film like *The War Room*, the actions of the two key personalities, Carville and Stephanopoulos, come center stage and establish a strong character-centered causality that accentuates the importance of individual actions. The faces of the protagonists dominate, construing them as unique historical actors and powerful rational individuals that act upon the world. In the observational mode, the filming style and the overall narrative structure leave no room for the examination of contextual parameters. Context is nearly impossible to film directly, so the weight of the argument falls entirely on the Formist side.

Finally, the next question that arises regards the types of ideology that historical observational films are more likely to express.[14] The two most common positions that can be easily combined with the narrative and argumentative characteristics analyzed above, are the Liberal and the Conservative. What binds these two ideological traditions, as I previously argued,[15] is their foregrounding of individuality as a significant historical agent. In this sense, the direct observation of specific historical subjects may, on the one hand, serve a Liberal vision of progress and an exaltation of humanitarian principles, or, on the other, it may reiterate its faith in traditional values and the accomplishments of the established order. Both *Primary* and *The War Room* could be interpreted as Liberal accounts not only because they both support democratic politics but also because they introduce a progressive conception to politics and the role of the media in political campaigning. On the other hand, others may view them as Conservative in the sense that they do not question the flaws of the democratic process and allow the camera and its fictional potential to play a decisive role. Since any text is open to multiple interpretations, depending on the viewers or analysts' agenda, I believe both readings are possible. It would not be possible, though, to view these films as Radical or Anarchist.

On the whole, the very few examples that are available in this category prevent us from evaluating the full potential of the observational mode with respect to ideology, while Riefenstahl's *Triumph of the Will* certainly probes us to exceed Mannheim's four dominant ideologies. In fact, Mannheim did acknowledge "fascism" as a type of modern political consciousness,[16] even though he did not elevate it to an entire utopian mentality. In his treatment of the subject, White chose to leave fascism out of his own scheme due to the term's strong anachronistic effect (Mannheim 1979, 104; White 2014, 22). Indeed, when viewing *Triumph of the Will* today, its fascist ideology appears blatantly self-evident to us but, at the time of its initial release, fascism would not have provided an established ideological frame. At any rate, the idiosyncratic case of the *Triumph of the Will* illustrates how the process of interpretation, especially when it comes to ideology, can never take a definitive shape. Despite the fixed nature of the formal parameters and the argumentative premises they may contain, the ideological implications of a film are always more susceptible to change and revision in the course of time.

The interactive

The interactive mode is constituted by films that rely heavily on the use of interviews with various social or historical actors and allow the participation of the filmmaker in the events that are recorded by the camera. In fact, the interaction between the filmmaker and his subjects, as the name suggests, is its key characteristic. As Nichols writes about the filmmaker's role, "the possibilities of serving as mentor, participant, prosecutor, or provocateur in relation to the social actors recruited to the film are far greater than the observational mode would suggest" (Nichols 1991, 44). Departing from the norms of both the expositional and the observational mode, interactive documentaries bring the filmmaker into the picture in various degrees so that he or she can investigate the chosen topic through an engagement with the people that have some kind of direct experience or involvement. Especially when it comes to historical subjects, witnesses or participants of a historical event come center stage as sources of invaluable knowledge. Their contribution may come in the form of a monologue, a dialogue, or a conversation, all of which introduce "a sense of partialness, of situated presence and local knowledge" (ibid.). Evidently, these options obtain only when it comes to historical events of the recent past and not of earlier periods that are accessible only through archival work. As a result, the two major events of the twentieth century, the Holocaust and the Vietnam War, gave us some of the most intriguing interactive documentaries, such as Claude Lanzmann's *Shoah* (1985), Marcel Ophuls' *Hotel Terminus* (1988), Emile de Antonio's *In the Year of the Pig* (1969), Michael Rubbo's *Sad Song of Yellow Skin* (1970) and, more recently, Errol

Morris' *The Fog of War* (2004). In addition to the interviews, the filmmaker is allowed to present information from other archival sources in various forms, such as intertitles, images, or documents that may corroborate or contradict the words of the interviewees. Nichols considers such juxtapositions as a "key tool in the filmmaker's discursive repertoire" that indicates how the latter may exert his/her influence on the argument that springs from the overall work (45). In other words, the interactive mode presents an argument and an ideological stance about the historical world, just like any other mode, and the final word rests, again, on the filmmaker. For all their grass roots material, interactive documentaries shape various explanations regarding the meaning of history and the workings of this world that we could explore at the level of narration, argument, and ideology, as we have done so far with the other modes.

The predominant role of the interview in the interactive mode sets up a narrative account that revolves around the verbal recounting of specific historical agents. The interviewees become characters who are bound to approach history from their own point of view, according to their own criteria and their own personal agenda. Unlike professional historians, the witnesses that appear in front of the camera do not bear any commitment to objectivity and sober evaluation. On the contrary, they are invited to share their subjective stories and their intimate recollections, which are inevitably partial, fragmentary, and even unreliable at times. The history that comes out from their shared experiences is not negligible though; rather, it is a microhistory[17] that pays close attention to the role of the everyday individual and their participation in wider historical processes. By elevating memory to a significant form of history,[18] these narratives seek to reverse the established hierarchy of the historical profession, which singles out individuals only if they possess an official capacity.[19] In this bottom-up approach to history, individual voices not only have a merit of their own but can also shed light on historical circumstances that would otherwise be inaccessible to us. Such is the case of *Shoah* and its exploration of the Holocaust experience from three different points of view, namely the Jewish survivor, the Polish bystander, and the German perpetrator. In this historical work that runs for more than nine hours,[20] Lanzmann combines interviews with Jewish, Polish, and German people, each talking about their own involvement in the Holocaust. Lanzmann's presence during the interviews is fairly dominant, as he probes the subjects with challenging questions that often set them off balance. His interaction is particularly felt with the Polish and German witnesses, whose accounts bear an additional moral weight. With his persistent probing, their testimonies reveal inconsistencies and contradictions that sometimes feel deliberate and other times unintentional. In all cases, however, the interviews reveal the power of remembering as well as forgetting. They also reveal how imagination blends with reality to build a personal interpretation of past events that are always conditioned by present circumstances. The example of *Shoah* indicates how historical interactive documentaries, by deploying the method of the interview and by allowing the interference of the filmmaker, display three key aspects of the historical process; firstly, they advocate the importance of everyday individuals as participants in history and as generators of knowledge. Secondly, they illustrate the partiality of the testimony, the subjectivity of memory, and the creative force of the imagination. Finally, they allow us to bear witnesses of the impact of the present condition on the interpretation of the past. Unlike the seamless continuity of the expository mode and the supposed objectivity of the observational kind, the microhistories of the interactive mode emphasize the value of individual cases, while portraying the complicated nature of personal memory.

Apart from the historical explanations that are related to the compositional elements of the interactive documentaries, this mode is able to host more general arguments regarding the role and function of historical agents in their surroundings. I would like to suggest that, despite their emphasis on individuality, the core argument of interactive historical films is of the synthetic kind, i.e., either Organicist or Contextualist. This is a paradox that needs unraveling. Interactive documentaries, like written micro-histories, give voice to the individuals and take note of their particularities not in order to stress their uniqueness, as a Formist would do. Instead, they delve into individual experience in order to generate safer generalizations about the historical world. As Carlo Ginzburg explains the purpose of microhistory, "Evidence must be collected according to an agenda which is already pointing towards a synthetic approach. In other words, one has to work out *cases*, which lead to generalizations" (Ginzburg 2012, 113; emphasis in the original). A similar point is made by Nichols who underlines the importance of a general argument, which stems not from a coherent voice-over commentary but from the interaction between the filmmaker and his historical actors. As he notes, "The individual identity, autobiographical background, or idiosyncratic qualities of those interviewed become secondary to an external referent: some aspect of the historical world to which they can contribute special knowledge" (Nichols 1991, 53). In this light, an interactive documentary like *Shoah* collects numerous individual testimonies to build three general speaking positions, namely the victim, the perpetrator, and the bystander. Lanzmann builds an Organicist argument that integrates each personal testimony into a greater whole that represents the entire Holocaust experience from three different standpoints. For all his seeming literalness and specificity, Lanzmann's consistent interventions testify to his underlying assumptions about his subjects and contribute to the synthetic purpose of his work. As the filmmaker himself confesses, "I built a structure, a gestalt! I didn't tell one personal story—the subject of the film is the extermination of the Jews— not the handful of survivors" (cited in Bruzzi 2006, 99). On the other hand, interactive documentaries may be Contextualist too. Whether the synthesis will point to integration or dispersion is open. The formal devices in this mode allow both possibilities. A Contextualist argument, for instance, is found in *The Fog of War*, which will be analyzed in greater detail in the next section. What suffices here to say is that Morris combines McNamara's interview with other archival materials to locate McNamara's figure into a very detailed historical context that elucidates the interrelations between diverse historical agencies. At any rate, whether Organicist or Contextualist, interactive historical documentaries capitalize on the presence and the creative power of the filmmaker in order to investigate a part of the past, employing personal memory and experience as a signpost to a more complex historical reality.

Ideologically speaking, such endeavors may embrace any position, except for the Radical one. The elevation of memory into a significant source for historical understanding runs, first and foremost, counter to the scientificism of the radical perspective on historiography and, particularly, its Marxist undercurrent.[21] Thus, to place subjective testimonies at the forefront of a historical argument would inherently contradict the radical agenda, i.e., the search for the laws of historical structures and processes. As a result, the range of ideological implications, which can be accommodated in a historical interactive documentary, includes only the Liberal, the Conservative, and the Anarchist views. *Shoah*, for instance, may be ideologically construed as an Anarchist account that is trapped in a non-temporal plane, unable to envision the future in any meaningful way.[22] Lanzmann's central argument helps him to organize fragmented personal experiences into coherent speaking positions,[23] which are condemned, nonetheless, to exist in what Stella Bruzzi calls a "perpetual present" (102). In Lanzmann's words, "The film is the abolition of all distances between past and present; I have relived the whole story in the present" (cited in Bruzzi, 101). *The Fog of War*, on the other hand, could go either way in terms of its interpretation.

It could be viewed as a Liberal treatment of a difficult historical personality, such as Robert McNamara, seeking to understand the role of human initiative in complex military decisions and shed light on issues of moral responsibility and rational agency. The discontent of many Liberal critics, however, in the reception of the film shows that Morris' documentary may be considered as tame and Conservative in the way it handles McNamara's controversial role in American politics and the way it justifies the workings of key political and military institutions.[24] The multiple ideological readings that have been put forward in regard to both *Shoah* and *The Fog of War* indicate a common predicament of interactive documentaries. Their formal and argumentative complexity welcomes contrasting views and fosters ambiguities that trigger diverse and, at times, entirely antagonistic ideological implications.

The reflexive

The reflexive mode of representation in Nichols' typology is an inclusive category that contains all those documentaries that employ self-conscious narrative devices and draw attention to the process of representation.[25] In these films, the presence of the filmmaker is exceptionally felt not as a means of interaction with a chosen subject, as was the case in the interactive mode, but, rather, as a play aimed toward the audience. In other words, reflexive documentaries seek to raise the viewer's attention in relation not only to a certain topic but also to the expressive tools selected for its exploration. As Nichols explains, "Whereas the great preponderance of documentary production concerns itself with talking about the historical world, the reflexive mode addresses the question of *how* we talk about the historical world" (Nichols 1991, 56–7; emphasis in the original). The increased narrative self-consciousness and the overt manipulation of the filmmaking process intend to question the very basis of nonfictional representation and its key principle, namely the objective and truthful access to reality. As a result, reflexive documentaries amount only to a small fraction of the overall production, which is dominated by films of the expository and interactive kind.[26] Particularly when it comes to history, the reflexive mode is a difficult choice for filmmakers and viewers alike, as both ends need to face head-on serious epistemological questions and address the complexity of historical knowledge. However, when reflexive documentaries do rise to the occasion, they challenge critics and theorists to rethink their categories and expand their vocabulary. Such was the case with films like Jill Godmilow's *Far from Poland*

(1984), Trinh Minh-ha's *Surname Viet Given Name Nam* (1989), Ross Gibson's *Camera Natura* (1984), as well as with notable biographies, such as Maximilian Schell's *Marlene* (1984), Chris Marker's *The Last Bolshevik* (1992), and François Girard's *Thirty-Two Short Films About Glenn Gould* (1993).[27] The classificatory problem with films that break new ground and subvert dominant narrative conventions is that they resist categorization and render it difficult for the analyst to group them into one coherent model of representation. Nichols places them under the rubric of the reflexive mode but the formal variety of these examples undermines the consistency of the mode on all grounds, whether narrative, argumentative, or ideological. Unlike self-reflexivity in the fiction film, which Bordwell scaled down into specific narrative devices, proposing, for example, the differentiation between the art-cinema and the historical-materialist films,[28] the reflexive mode for nonfiction films is a mixed category that shares only one key element, namely the desire to shatter the illusion of realistic representation and problematize the process of acquiring knowledge about the historical world. Whether this central premise is specific enough to warrant necessary and sufficient conditions for films to be included in the reflexive mode is not for me to debate here. What I would like to do, however, is to investigate the range of historical explanations that may be harbored in reflexive documentaries, keeping an open mind about possible exceptions and irregularities.

If we start with the historical explanations that derive from the narrative construction of the reflexive documentaries dealing with historical matters, we could observe that a common characteristic is the disruption of the clear causal logic of the historical events. Notice the difference from the other modes; the expository films employ a voice-over commentary to "explain" what happened and why it happened; the observational films record what happened and let us see for ourselves, while the interactive ones seek people who could tell us what happened, whether truthfully or not. Against these options, the reflexive films not only avoid explaining the causality of the historical events but also often question the very ontology of these events. Let's take *Marlene*, for instance. Schell struggles to portray the life and personality of Marlene Dietrich, employing the interview as his main investigative tool. Dietrich, at the age of eighty-three, agrees to be interviewed in her apartment in Paris but she refuses to be filmed. This critical obstruction compels Schell to evoke her presence only though photographs, scenes from her films and a few stand-in actresses but it mainly helps him to address the impossibility of knowing who Dietrich really was. Not only does he emphasize her refusal to appear in front of the camera but also he explicitly discusses, for the sake of the audience, how the lack of her image contradicts the very essence of cinematic representation and its ocular-centric nature. In a way, Dietrich's absent presence emulates the very quandary of historical cinema, namely to build the presence of something long gone. It reminds us that knowing what *really* happened is nothing but a chimera; we are bound to reimagine the past just as much as we are to discover it. Yet, this predicament does not discourage Schell nor does it lead him to consider the task futile. Through a relentless antagonism with his defiant subject, through endless contradictions or disagreements even about the most tangible evidence from her life, such as the existence or not of a sibling, Schell convinces us that the effort to get to know Marlene Dietrich was truly worth it. By employing a wide range of formal tools, such as complex chronology, ironic juxtapositions of images and sounds as well as graphic editing, Schell builds a remarkably rich portrait of Dietrich that denies us, however, both closure and causal clarity. Such is, in fact, the task of most reflexive documentaries about history; they manipulate all narrative parameters (causal, temporal, spatial) in ways that establish all types of answers, whether ontological, rhetorical, or moral, as merely provisional. Thus, the narrative structure of the reflexive mode invites us to ponder upon the nature of history as an open-ended process that tests our epistemological tools and allows us to construct multiple, and often conflicting, observations and interpretations.

This increased historical relativity of the reflexive narratives is more readily paired with a Contextualist argument of history.[29] Contextualism was a secondary option for the interactive mode too, given a filmmaker's interaction with an array of interviewees may pursue explanations of the synthetic type and highlight the complex interrelations of various agents in a particular historical field. Here, in this mode, Contextualism becomes a primary option not so much for its synthetic potential but, rather, for its dispersive approach. As I explained in my discussion of the post-classical historical narratives, which were also highly self-reflexive, a Contextualist approach to history is the only world-hypothesis that can handle disorder and tolerate the idea that the "whole truth" or the "essence" of this world may not be attained. Instead of trying to get to the bottom or the top of things, Contextualism flattens the scope and examines the relations of historical agents in their provisional context. Instead of searching for general rules or laws that govern human action and the workings of this cosmos, as Mechanism and Organicism do, a Contextualist thinking refuses to even acknowledge the existence of such a totality, let alone master it. In *Marlene*, for instance, Schell knows that Dietrich is such a complex personality that no film or book could ever succeed in containing her. In fact, the interview regularly underlines how most of her numerous written biographies have gotten various facts wrong whether about her films or her personal life. What he aims to achieve, nonetheless, is to capture Dietrich in a very specific moment in time and space, and to give her the opportunity to think back on her immeasurably rich life and reinvent it once more. Most reflexive documentaries ascribe to this relativist mentality and draw the viewers' attention to the effort entailed in the exploration of the past. Instead of pretending to discover the essence of things past and deploying realism to represent it, the reflexive mode explores the enormous expressive capacities of the cinematic medium in order to break the illusion of transparency, on the one hand, while focusing, on the other, on specific historical events or personalities for the fragmentary and contingent traces they have left behind.

When it comes to their ideological implications, reflexive films may cover the entire ideological spectrum, given that their tendency to break realistic conventions may be put to any ideological use. Notice how White explains the function of Irony, a key tool in the reflexive repertoire. As he writes:

> Irony can be used *tactically* for defense of either Liberal or Conservative ideological positions, depending whether the Ironist is speaking against established social forms or against "utopian" reformers seeking to change the status quo. And it can be used offensively by the Anarchist and the Radical, to pillory the ideals of their Liberal and Conservative opponents.
>
> White 2014, 37; emphasis in the original

Even though technically and tactically, reflexive strategies bear the capacity to serve all ideological positions, the history and practice of documentary filmmaking has shown that the Conservative and the Radical options are equally unlikely for the opposite reasons. A Conservative worldview is threatened by the concept of formal subversion and argumentative relativism, while a Radical perspective finds them too tame and too fastened to specificity.[30] Liberalism and Anarchism, on the other hand, can anchor on the reflexive mode their frustration with the status quo and envision social change either as a thing of the future, as in Liberal optimism, or as thing of the past, as in Anarchistic pessimism. The latter is pervasive in *The Last Bolshevik,* which, as I will discuss in detail in the next section, is compelled to address the ideological failure of Communism both at the national and the personal level through Alexander Medvedkin's life. *Marlene,* on the other, is neither disillusioned nor haunted by the past. The final zooming in on Dietrich's most recent image from *Just a Gigolo* (1978) reasserts the film's pervasive acceptance of the limits of knowledge and its affirmation of life over death. For all his frustrations and failures, Schell's choice to cast his documentary in the reflexive mode is meant to express both his respect and his appreciation for Marlene Dietrich, a historical personality that is bound to disintegrate in the multitude of images, books, and sounds of her life.

Overall, the formal diversity accommodated in Nichols' reflexive mode of representation forces us to investigate the historical explanations that stem from reflexive documentaries with more caution and flexibility than in the other modes. What helps us delineate their key characteristics is a comparative approach that sets reflexive films aside from all others. When filmmakers choose to explore a historical event or a historical individual through a consistent use of self-conscious narrative devices, then they are keen on engaging in a direct dialogue with the audience just as they are in revealing the historical subject per se. Reflexive documentaries use and abuse the dominant devices of all other modes, such as the commentary, the direct observation and the interview, in order to establish the provisionality of historical knowledge and foreground the complicated access we are bound to have to the past. The skepticism ingrained in this ironic abuse of the classical documentarist tropes promotes a Contextualist argument of history, while it may be underpinned by a Liberal optimism or Anarchist pessimism about the state of the human condition.

The performative

The final mode of representation in documentary filmmaking was added by Nichols in his book *Blurred Boundaries*, complementing his previous work in *Representing Reality*. Performative documentary is a category that surfaced in the 1980s and 1990s through a complex reconfiguration of all the key documentarist devices that dominated in the other modes. For example, in lieu of the confident and authoritative voice-over of the expository kind, performative films employ a verbal commentary with a subjective and personal tone. From the observational mode, they borrow recording techniques that aim less at proving the strong referential ties to the historical world than stressing the "qualities of duration, texture and experience" (Nichols 1994, 95). Moreover, the interactive devices in the performative mode bring forward the personal involvement of the filmmaker not as a probing tool for other people's experience but for his or her own emotional expression. Finally, performative documentaries do not hesitate to explore reflexivity not for the sake of estrangement but, rather, for celebrating the performative quality[31] of the filmmaking process. As Nichols explains, "Reflexive techniques, if employed, do not so much estrange us from the text's own procedures as draw our attention to the subjectivities and intensities that surround and bathe the scene as represented" (96). This eclectic relation that the performative mode forms with its predecessors is anything but random. It demonstrates, on the one hand, a critical awareness of the long history and theory of the documentary practice, while it constitutes, on the other, an attempt to re-establish a new rapport between fiction and nonfiction by bringing subjectivity center stage. Thus, the key shift between the performative and all the other modes is the shift from the objective to the subjective; the common denominator of all these formal borrowings is to forfeit the documentary's exclusive privilege to objectivity (in relation to the fiction film) and to introduce the power of subjectivity and emotion in the nonfiction genre. Yet, why would that be important for a contemporary documentarian? According to Nichols, a major implication of this shift "is the possibility of giving figuration to a social subjectivity that joins the abstract to the concrete, the general to the particular, the individual to the collective, and the political to the personal, in a dialectical, transformative mode" (94). I would also add, in tandem with Nichols' Foucauldian spirit, that the performative mode is as close as one can get to representing what Foucault called the "practices of the self," as we discussed them in chapter three. In plain words, performative documentaries seek to address the ways in which individuals can exercise their free will and carve their personal trajectory within socially and historically defined pathways. Particularly when we look at historical performative documentaries, such as Ari Folman's *Waltz with Bashir* (2008), Isaac Julien's *Looking for Langston* (1991), Rea Tajiri's *History and Memory* (1991), and Barbara Sonneborn's *Regret to Inform* (1998), we are invited to experience history as a tension between the personal and the collective and as a power struggle between the intimate and the public. These historical accounts generate historical explanations, just like any historical documentary, which I would like to distinguish at the level of narrative, argument and ideology.

Performative documentaries that seek to explore a historical event often take the form of a personal quest or journey taken by the filmmaker. The latter's involvement in the historical process triggers a more expansive exploration of the historical field that strives to correlate the personal experience with large-scale events. The formal depiction of this mission is not committed to a consistent temporal or spatial logic nor does it rely on the referential power of the cinematic image. When we watch a performative film, we do not expect to discover a solid image of the past but to witness diverse and scattered personal experiences of it. In other words, these films are less about "what happened" and more about "how it is remembered." For instance, *Waltz with Bashir* employs animation to portray Folman's deeply personal reconstruction of his role in the Lebanon War in 1982. The problem of memory and its traumatic blockage is the main theme of his film and its fragmented plot, comprising mainly of flashbacks, does not promise to deliver an accurate account of the events in question. The exact course of events and, even more so, their precise causality, will forever remain open to dispute. What is indisputable, though, is the death and devastation they left behind. Folman's decision to bookend his animated images with photographs of the real bodies of the massacre in the Sabra and the Shatila refugee camp shows that no matter how one chooses to remember or explain history, its force and impact on real lives are tremendous. The same purpose is found in *Regret to Inform*, which I will discuss in detail shortly. Sonneborn's journey to Vietnam and her personal quest for emotional closure for her long-lost husband becomes the impulse for exploring the Vietnam War from the perspective of its survivors who had to deal with destruction and loss. In these two performative cases, we find the device of the interview as well as the presence of the filmmaker serving a different purpose than the one we found in the interactive and the reflexive mode respectively. In contrast to *Shoah*, for instance, *Regret to Inform* is not accumulating testimonies in order to construct solid subject positions; instead, it presents us with a series of testimonies to help us understand the experience of these people and empathize with their agony. Unlike Lanzmann, Sonneborn does not aim to probe her subjects or bring out contradictions or weaknesses so that she can reach any historical truth. She is interested, rather, in bringing out the personal toll that the Vietnam War took on these lives and emphasize the subjective dimension of such national tragedies. In a similar vein, Folman does not embrace reflexivity in order to question historical truth, as one would expect in a reflexive documentary. The animated sequences and the episodic plot in *Waltz with Bashir* bring forward the subjective dimension of reality, the ruptures of memory, and the complex issue of historical causality and moral responsibility. Despite the difficulty in telling whose fault it is, the use of the performative mode by Folman is not meant to question the events themselves or their moral condemnation. As Nichols notes about performative documentaries:

> [...] the referential aspect of the message that turns us toward the historical world is not abandoned. Such works then, through expressive, stylized, and

evocative, also constitute a fiction (un)like any other. The indexical bond, which can also prove an indexical bind for the documentary form, remains operative but in a subordinated manner.

Nichols 1994, 98

These narrative characteristics help sustain an argument of a highly dispersive nature, which could be either Formist, as in *Regret to Inform* or Contextualist, as in *Waltz with Bashir*.[32] When we compare the role of testimony, which is a shared characteristic of interactive and performative documentaries, we realize that, while the former delve into personal experiences to form more precise generalizations, the latter's tendency is to let these experiences exist in their uniqueness. In this sense, the widows of the soldiers who died in Vietnam are not chosen by Sonneborn to build a "micro-history" in Ginzburg's sense. Her argument remains dispersive until the very end. The more she insists on how every single person matters the more she feels incapable of shaping precise explanations about general categories, such as nation/enemy, hero/victim, or duty/free will. Equally dispersive is Folman's argument, even though it belongs more to the Contextualist kind. His film does not seek to derive any laws or principles of historical causation, as his observations remain partial and tentative. He does strive to establish, however, a certain particularity in space and time when his actions took place, while he also tries to connect himself with the other historical agents in place. This tendency to join the pieces of the puzzle together, while also resigning to the fact that his task is bound to remain incomplete, is precisely what makes his use of the performative mode veer more toward Contextualism. At any rate, whether Formist or Contextualist, the complex reconfiguration of previous formal devices found in this final mode, combined with the acknowledgement of the limitations of the documentary in the exploration of the past, leads performative filmmakers to opt for a dispersive approach to history, accentuating the importance of individual agents and steering clear from any broad generalizations.

Finally, when it comes ideology, the performative documentary also feels burdened by the ideological stakes raised by the established modes in the past. And again, the reaction of this mode to the documentary traditions that surround it is not one of rebellion or opposition but one of recalibration. Given that these films surfaced at a time when "late capitalism" became, despite its flaws, the only dominant established order and any notion of "revolution" was no longer deemed plausible, the ideological range that remained available for any idea of change was limited to Liberalism and Anarchism. Nichols does not adopt this terminology but he is really close to it when he writes, "By restoring a sense of the local, specific, and embodied as a vital locus for social subjectivity, performative documentary gives figuration to and evokes dimensions of the political unconscious that remain suspended between an immediate here and now and a utopian alternative" (106). This suspended temporality is evidenced in both films that we discuss here as examples of the performative mode. In *Waltz with Bashir*, on the one hand, the confrontation with the past does not seem to lead to any promising future nor does it point to any chance for redemption. *Regret to Inform*, on the other hand, seems more hopeful. Sonneborn's journey does succeed in bringing a closure of sorts for the women who lost their husbands and learned to cope with fear and loss. The dialogue between American and Vietnamese women in some cases brought about a mutual understanding and respect that was therapeutic for both sides. Unlike Folman's more Anarchistic outlook on the meaning of history, Sonneborn maintains a humanistic perspective that allows her to cling to Liberal optimism about the future and the potential for change. Overall, performative documentaries resemble the reflexive ones when it comes to their ideological implications. The Conservative and Radical positions on the role of the historical process are unlikely to be endorsed by the performative devices, as they are too reflexive and too focused on subjectivity to serve any of these two agendas. Anarchism and Liberalism, on the contrary, are two frames of thinking about change and utopia, which are in line with the formal characteristics of performative documentaries and their effort to highlight the complex role of human subjectivity in the historical field.

Case Study: The Representation of the Vietnam War and the Biography

The Vietnam War has been a divisive political and military issue in American history that continues to this day to fascinate American filmmakers. As I write these lines, Ken Burns and Lynn Novick's latest documentary called *The Vietnam War* is broadcast on PBS, contributing another eighteen hours of footage to the long list of documentary material on this historic conflict. Unlike the solid patriotic image of the Second World War, the Vietnam War has been represented by diverse groups and individuals who have communicated critical and opposing views on the meaning of America's involvement in Vietnam. In the majority of these representations, what tends to stand out is the personal perspective of those who were directly involved or affected by "the Vietnam experience." As John Carlos Rowe observes:

> Although every war has produced fiction and nonfiction that attempt loosely to "personalize" the experience of war and thus make it possible to experience vicariously the region and psychology of war, Vietnam is unique among other American wars for the volume and variety of subjective accounts it has generated.
>
> Rowe 1986, 127

The significance of subjectivity and the complex relation of an individual with his/her historical era will be my focus in this chapter, binding historical documentaries about Vietnam with the sub-genre of the biography. From the Vietnam War, I chose to analyze Errol Morris' *The Fog of War* (2004), Barbara Sonneborn's *Regret to Inform*, and David Zeiger's *Sir! No Sir!* (2005). These are well-known documentaries that have raised critical attention and stirred discussions about the politics of the representation of Vietnam. The different modes of representation adopted in each of them will allow us to observe in greater detail how the narration, the argument, and the ideological implications of a documentary collaborate to create a different version of the same historical event. Then, I will move on to the second thematic, that of the biographical documentary. When focusing on the life of a particular individual, a documentary filmmaker deploys the same creative tools as for any other historical topic. The biographical focus does not constrain them on any particular mode of representation or argument or ideology. There can be several approaches to individuality, as there can be many different explanations about the meaning of human existence in the course of history. My first case study will be George Butler's *Going Upriver: The Long War of John Kerry* (2004), which will allow us to carry on the discussion of the Vietnam War into the biographical genre. Then, an equally political biography, Chris Marker's *The Last Bolshevik*, will provide another example of how a major personality is embedded in an intensely political environment. Finally, Francois Girard's *Thirty-Two Short films about Glenn Gould* will allow us to close off this section with a highly innovative biography of a celebrated musician. Like the case studies of the fiction film, the analyses that follow do not aim at being exhaustive and thorough. They aim, rather, at delineating the confines of the reading of a historical documentary, pointing out the numerous but also limited ways in which the form of a documentary can generate specific historical explanations.

The Vietnam War

The Fog of War (2004)

Errol Morris' documentary featuring Robert McNamara as a sole interviewee on the topic of war is a rare example of mainstream nonfiction filmmaking that combines a controversial subject with box office success and an Oscar victory. McNamara, the former Defense Secretary under both the Kennedy and Johnson administrations, is considered to this day one of the chief culprits of the Vietnam disaster. Morris' decision to put him center stage alone was heavily criticized by several commentators (Resha 2015). Most interactive documentaries, indeed, contain numerous interviews that often seem to present a range of different perspectives and invite pluralism and diversity. In *The Fog of War*, we only have the voices of McNamara and, occasionally, Morris but the latter's contribution does not go unheeded. From the narrational structure to the archival images, the stylized editing and Phillip Glass' soundtrack, the filmmaker demonstrates a considerable creative control that works in tandem with McNamara's authoritative presence.

The organization of the material separates the interview into eleven segments entitled "Lessons," each presenting a principle driven from McNamara's life experiences that span the greater part of the twentieth century. Even though the order of the events is primarily chronological, there are various temporal movements back and forth, depending on the requirements of the argument at hand. As is typical in interactive documentaries, the goal is to bring forward the personal perspective and explore the strengths and weaknesses of memory in the approach of the historical past. The weight of the interview, as expected, falls on the Vietnam War and McNamara's role in America's most traumatic military conflict. Thus, the interview in this case plays a paradoxical role; on the one hand, it constitutes the personal recollections of an individual who was closely involved in a historical event, while, on the other, it is a public testimony of a key historical figure whose decisions were instrumental in the development of the event in question. McNamara is not merely a veteran or a bystander who can tell us about a subjective experience amounting to an infinitesimal fragment of the war; instead, as a Secretary of Defense, he had the power to decide whether the war would go on or not; whether thousands of Americans would continue to live or die. At least, this is how most Americans think of McNamara. And it is precisely this widespread conception of him that Morris seems to strive to unravel. The choice of the interactive mode allows him to interview his subject, while manipulating the images and sounds in ways that either corroborate or contradict the unique testimony. The lack of other interviews does not render the documentary less objective but it allows it to investigate McNamara from the micro and macro perspective that suits the duality of his historical existence. McNamara was not only a high-rank politician but also a soldier in the Second World War, then a husband, a father, a high-profile academic, a successful CEO at Ford Company as well as a person who, after Vietnam, headed the World Bank and its fight against poverty in developing countries. In this light, his actions within his official capacity during the Vietnam War become not self-contained entities but parts of a multifaceted personality soaked in a complicated historical terrain. The use of specific formal and narrative devices (one interview, archival material, episodic structure etc.) is what gives Morris the opportunity to address his idiosyncratic subject and surpass the binaries of the objective/subjective and personal/official that often seem to demarcate other discussions about history.

Moreover, the interactive form easily accommodates the complexity entailed in the Contextualist argument that Morris advocates in his approach to the historical process.[33] In fact, the Contextualist tendency is shared by both the interviewer and the interviewee, amplifying the power of the argument, while also adding fuel to the criticism against Morris as an exonerator of McNamara. Yet, their argument regarding the function and meaning of history is neither unusual nor unique, despite the open wounds related to the Vietnam experience that dictate a more passionate and partial stance. In fact, Morris vocally objects the black and white approach to history when he notes:

> They should see the *world* in complex terms. I prefer the word "complex" to "ambiguous". One of the things that I find particularly frightening about what is going on in the United States today is that we have a government that refuses to see anything in shades of grey. No subtlety, no complexity, just simply black and white, good and evil.
>
> Cited in Ryan 2004; emphasis in the original

Morris' marked distinction between "complexity" and "ambiguity" is precisely the distinction I have drawn before, especially in the previous chapter, between Contextualism and Organicism. While they both favor synthesis and examine clusters of elements, Organicism vaunts a higher level of ambiguity in the effort to integrate the particular elements into abstract processes. Here, Morris deliberately emphasizes the value of particularity and focuses on the interrelationships between particulars without succumbing to the desire to generalize. In other words, he does not try to get either to the top or bottom of things but expose their horizontal cosmology. By contextualizing McNamara's human existence and embedding him into a dense historical framework that already begins with the First World War, he points to all those historical forces at play that may or may not have shaped his actions during Vietnam. I say, "may or may not" because Morris' answers are not definitive. He does not claim to disclose any hidden truth with final validity. On the contrary, the very phrase "The fog of war" in the title foregrounds McNamara's final claim that war is too complex a phenomenon for the human mind to factor in all the variables and make rational decisions based on them. The argument about the limits of human reason does not necessarily deflect the political responsibility for the war, as the final decision rests with the President. McNamara does not deny the accountability of government officials but he does underline the role of hierarchy in the decision-making process. In a question that addresses head-on the problem of agency, we have the following exchange:

> Morris: To what extent did you feel that you were the author of stuff, or that you were an instrument of things outside of your control?
> McNamara: Well, I don't think I felt either. I just felt that I was serving at the request of the President, who had been elected by the American people. And it was my responsibility to try to help him to carry out the office as he believed was in the interest of our people.

This response highlights the interconnectedness of all players involved (the President, the American people, the Defense Secretary) according to the democratic principles of the American society. It does not relieve anyone of their responsibility, including the American public whose vote determined the Presidency at least on five counts during the period 1955–75. Notice also how McNamara does not consider the Presidency as a general category of power but he differentiates between the characteristics of Kennedy and Johnson when he argues that the former would have handled things differently.

The blatantly contextual argument in *The Fog of War* takes shape by pointing out several facets of the historical reality, while, at the same time, laying bare the lack of autonomous agency in the historical field. On the one hand, McNamara reiterates his emblematic identity as a man of numbers, rational calculation and mathematical precision seeking to maximize efficiency, while, on the other, he is someone who has deeply contemplated on the inescapable and formidable power of chance in political decisions. In his version of the Cuban missile crisis, the nuclear war was averted by sheer luck, as the slightest mistake in the interpretation of Khrushchev's messages could have led things to a point of no return. That was not the achievement of rational individuals but the result of fortunate coincidences. Acknowledging the influence of contingency in such an unselfish manner is a concession that powerful rational individuals like McNamara do not often make. It makes them look weak and not in control of things. Thus, the gesture from McNamara's part should not be interpreted as a means to deflect responsibility but as a contextual way of understanding and accounting for the historical process. Similarly, the sensitive topic of the casualties of war is represented by Morris through a relentless juxtaposition of photographs of dead bodies with numbers and graphs measuring the death toll in the battlefield. At one point, an accelerating montage alternates between the photographic material and its graphic representation in the charts in an effort to capture the invisible thread that connects the particulars and their abstractions. The argument is that war is about both; about the blood of innocent people and the numbers that determine the progression of the war and the respective political decisions. Finally, there is another side to the Contextualist argument in the film related to McNamara's view on the value of hindsight and the importance of counterfactual thinking in history. As he notes:

> Historians don't really like to deal with counterfactuals, with what might have been. They want to talk about history. "And how the hell do you know, McNamara, what might have been? Who knows?" Well, I know certain things.

The consideration of counterfactual paths in history can only be accepted and appreciated from a Contextualist point of view, as all other world hypotheses are premised on very fixed ideas about how the world works. As I noted in the case of *Inglourious Basterds* in the previous chapter, a Mechanistic or an Organicist approach could not give credence to the possibility that things could have been done otherwise. In their framework, neither luck nor human agents could defy the governing principles or laws of our universe and change the essence of history. Not believing in an essence of any kind is what both Morris and McNamara's voices seem to agree on.

This argumentative concurrence between the subject of the documentary and its filmmaker has been interpreted at the ideological level with a high level of suspicion. As a formal vehicle, the interactive mode may accommodate a wide range of ideological positions, the sort of which is often subject to debate. As I noted earlier, *The Fog of War* was rejected as Conservative from a section of Liberal commentators, for whom McNamara remains to this day the architect of a cruel and unjust war. In the case of Morris, his Liberal politics seemed at odds with the latter's role in the Vietnam War, despite the fact that McNamara was the choice of two Democratic Presidents and, of course, he was an avowed Liberal himself. The problem with ideological and moral positions, in general, and the case of Vietnam, in particular, is that they are often hetero-defined by shifting external circumstances that demand equally shifting interpretative frameworks. McNamara knows this and confesses the following:

> LeMay said, "If we'd lost the war, we'd all have been prosecuted as war criminals." And I think he's right. He, and I'd say I, were behaving as war criminals. LeMay recognized that what he was doing would be thought immoral if his side had lost. But what makes it immoral if you lose and not immoral if you win?

This relativistic attitude toward morality should not be viewed as a blow to Liberal values but only as a challenge to abstract idealism. McNamara and *The Fog of War*, in my view, remain firmly attached to the principles of Liberalism and the idea of progress in human history. Free will and rational thinking may be contextualized and approached with skepticism but they are not abandoned; in fact, the very idea of "taking lessons from history" testifies to the reaffirming of these values and the hope for a better future.

In conclusion, the particularities of the representation of Vietnam through McNamara and Morris' lens at the level of narration, argument and ideology will become even further elucidated with the comparison to other notable documentaries on the same subject. The limitations of the interactive mode become palpable, as we juxtapose its historical image to the one produced by Sonneborn's performative and Zeiger's expositional documentaries.

Regret to Inform (1998)

Regret to Inform is a documentary about the experiences of women who lost their husbands in the Vietnam War. It was one of the first attempts to shed light on this more personal side of a military conflict, helping war widows to exchange stories and organize into support groups. Sonneborn decided to make this film in order to explore her own experience as a widow of an American soldier who died in Vietnam, in a country so far away from her own and for reasons she could not fully understand. Thus, an intimate quest for resolution and trauma management is what led her to, first, search for other widows in the United States and, then, venture on a journey to the place where her husband had been killed more than two decades before. The film came out on the thirtieth anniversary of his death and earned Sonneborn and her cause remarkable recognition. It was nominated for an Academy Award for best documentary, and it won several others, including the Best Director and Best Cinematography awards at the 1999 Sundance Film Festival. Quite expectedly, if we place *Regret to Inform* next to *The Fog of War,* we will get the impression that we are watching two entirely different wars. Let us investigate how and why such discrepancy arises in the two images of Vietnam.

The use of the performative mode to approach the historical subject of the war always already excludes any official or political perspective on the matter. Sonneborn is triggered by a deeply personal tragedy and not by any desire to discover "the truth" about Vietnam. As she confesses from the beginning in her voice-over commentary, she wanted to meet all these women and travel to this far-away land because she could not come to terms with her husband's demise. Twenty years after she got the standard government telegram, beginning with the words "We regret to inform you," she would still be haunted by a death that made little sense to her. The entire documentary thus is premised on her inner search for meaning for her loss. Like most performative films, however, the autobiographical impulse of the filmmaker is merely a trigger to discover a wider range of experiences that extent to both sides of the war, including testimonies from Vietnamese women who lived through the destruction and devastation not only of their families but also their entire country. Therefore, the film is made up from three main constructional elements; Sonneborn's travel to Khe Sahn, the area where her husband was killed; testimonies from American and Vietnamese widows who share their personal grief; and archival images of the war mostly featuring soldiers in combat. These three interrelated "plotlines" share the common conviction that the Vietnam War was a brutal and unnecessary evil. The lack of necessity, of course, is not explicated in any concrete historical or political terms but only through the general idea that the Americans had no reason to fight against a people who did not pose a direct threat to the United States. In fact, *Regret to Inform* paints such an ambivalent and vague portrait of the war itself that an uninformed viewer can easily be misled to think that it was a war between the Americans and the Vietnamese alone. At one point, Sonneborn even explains in the commentary that the Vietnamese were calling it the American War, nurturing even further this misguided impression. There is no hint of a civil war, of communism, of deep political and religious divisions in the area and, of course, of the millions of Vietnamese soldiers in South Vietnam who fought and died "on the American side." It is clearly presented as an American-Vietnamese War, with the Vietnamese people united in one front. If one scrutinizes the testimonies of the Vietnamese women, one can find words such as "Saigon police" or "Saigon Administration" that evidently contradict this "us versus them" rhetoric but they are utterly overshadowed by the widespread approach to the Vietnamese women as representative of one nation in unison. Such blatant historical oversight is not, however, so crucial for a performative documentary, which by definition is much less concerned about "what happened in the past" and much more about "how the past is remembered." As I noted in the previous section, the performative mode is a recent development in documentary production, which seeks to shift the emphasis from the objective knowledge about the past to the subjective experience of it, a privilege that was previously bestowed only on the fiction film. In this light, *Regret to Inform* should be appreciated for the ways it delves into the memories of these women and digs up images, emotions, and thoughts that allow us to ponder upon the significance of Vietnam for those whose lives where forever shuttered. We are not dealing here with numbers, graphs, or maps of the operations nor with high-rank decisions about strategies and defensives. We are listening to those whose family was lost, whose house was burnt, whose husband was tortured to death, and to those who had to carry on with the scars of the war and its aftermath. In this account, every individual becomes a meaningful entity who plays a role in a historical process and relates to the wider political and military conditions in ways that they could or could not control. The performative mode, as Nichols explained above, is a distinctive mold that allows the expression of a "social subjectivity," connecting the personal to the political and the individual to the collective in ways that transform one another (Nichols 1994, 96). This notion of social subjectivity becomes palpable in many of the testimonies, especially those of the American widows who describe the feelings and ideas of their husbands when they enlisted. In all cases, the soldiers made conscious decisions to serve their country motivated by a patriotic spirit that would soon be crashed by the harsh reality of the battlefield and the lack of understanding of the necessity of the war. Similarly, a Vietcong woman who describes her involvement in the military operations becomes emblematic of this transitional state between a personal choice and a social or political mandate.

The performative mode in Sonneborn's film expresses a Formist argument of history, as I previously noted. It is a personal account of a dimension of the

Vietnam War, in which every individual is singled out for his or her unique existence. The diverse voices and sides taken on this traumatic experience are not meant to coalesce into a few reigning speaking positions (the widow, the fighter, the victim etc.) but are supposed to remain dispersed into their own particularity. Every woman appearing on the screen and sharing her pain for what she lost in the war is not destined to become an emblem of sorts nor disintegrate into a larger form of identity, such as the American, the Vietnamese, or even the human as a transcendental category. Sonneborn is careful to point out the unique characteristic of Vietnam as an unjust war, without generalizing about the idea of war as a universal evil. Patriotism and dying for one's country is still discussed as an honorable act provided only that the war is truly justified. In fact, the distinction between the Second World War and Vietnam is made at various points in the film, as a clear marker between a war worth fighting and a dishonorable war. The emphasis on the particularity of the historical event is also evident in Sonneborn's almost obsessive attachment to the place where her husband was killed. For years, she could not come to terms with his death unless she went to the very place where his life was brutally ended. The search for the specific site and the visit of Khe Sahn illustrates her need to ground her emotions into something physical, something tangible, which would render his death meaningful. The value of specificity and materiality is also part of the need to build memorials for all those who sacrificed their lives for this greater cause. In its closing moments, the documentary dwells on the names inscribed on the Veterans Memorial in Washington and on a similar wall in Vietnam. The images testify to the desire to respect the individuality of the millions of soldiers as well as to provide a specific and concrete sign of their existence for the future generations. As a whole, *Regret to Inform* strives to create a memorial for those who engaged in battle in Vietnam and their families who suffered just as much whether they were close or far away. The portrait of those involved in Vietnam bears the analytical and dispersive character of Formism, painting its actors with intense and unique colors, without any intention to discover either the provisionity of historical knowledge (Contextualism), or the workings of abstract processes (Organicism), or the application of any governing laws of history (Mechanism).

At the level of ideological implication, I believe that *Regret to Inform* can be interpreted as a Liberal attempt to understand the significance of Vietnam for the lives of those who were directly impacted from the military combat. Sonneborn approaches the war not as a transcendental evil but as a particular military conflict that was morally wrong. As a result, her goal is not to attack the status quo and its institutional grounds but to criticize specific political decisions that spread death and destruction to innocent people. She argues that American soldiers fought a war they did not believe in and they engaged in atrocities well beyond their military duties. At the same time, Vietnamese women and children were doomed to suffer whether they experienced a violent death or survived. To these old wounds, the film strives to bring some sense of closure. By embracing the idea of reconciliation, Sonneborn stands next to a former Vietcong fighter and together they perform a healing ritual that honors their dead. The message of their unison is one of hope; hope that the widows of Vietnam will find some peace in their lives and that their suffering will teach future generations a lesson. The closing epigraph saying that these deaths "will mean what you make them" indicates that *Regret to Inform* is geared towards the future as much as it is about the past. It hopes to contribute to a better understanding of the personal experience of war, so that individual lives will begin to matter in the future.

Sir! No Sir! (2005)

David Zeiger's documentary about Vietnam seeks to unearth a very different side from those discussed above. Unlike McNamara's official take and Sonneborn's personalized perspective, *Sir! No Sir!* deploys the traditional expository mode to reveal a hidden story of the Vietnam War, namely the anti-war movement headed by soldiers within the American military ranks. As the voice-over narrator tells us in the opening moments, "in the decades of debate to follow the end of the war some stories have yet to be heard." This revelatory spirit that counters the official historical portrait of Vietnam immediately ensured the film a place on the activists' agenda, which, at the time, sought to expose the immoral premises of the American involvement in Iraq.

In fact, as Zeiger confesses, "What prompted me to make the film was September 11, and the War on Terror's segue into the Iraq War. I saw that this had suddenly become a story that would have current resonance, something that would immediately connect with what's going on today" (cited in Stein 2005). To this end, Zeiger chronicles the so-called G.I. Movement, which arose from a few isolated malcontents in the mid-1960s to tens of thousands of veterans in the early 1970s. The timing of this film should also be viewed in conjunction with my next case study, *Going Upriver*, which had come out a year before. Like *Sir! No Sir!*, *Going Upriver* returns to the Vietnam war and highlights John Kerry's leadership in the anti-war movement in a similar expository fashion. These two documentaries share many similarities as well as startling differences. Their examination at the level of narration, argument, and ideology will hopefully bring out the diverse mechanisms available for representing the historical past in the documentary tradition.

Zeiger's preference for the expository mode for this topic should not come as a surprise. Even though one could expect a more experimental and reflexive form for an unconventional story like this, the expository mode can accomplish Zeiger's primary goal to spread the story of the G.I. Movement as solid historical knowledge. The voice-over commentary ensures that the film puts forward a specific, clear and coherent argument about the tumultuous power struggles taking place in the United States during the Vietnam War. The obscurity of the soldiers' active engagement in the anti-war protests requires that a voice exposes all the necessary details, makes all the meaningful connections and lays out a clear-cut cause-and-effect logic. Thus, the interviews, the archival material and the images are subordinated to the commentary and serve as illustrations for its overarching argument. *Sir! No Sir!* as its title suggests, wishes to promote the right of soldiers to disobey military orders when they consider them to be morally wrong. The G.I. Movement in the 1960s and early 1970s questioned the purpose of the American activity in Vietnam and unveiled military atrocities that blatantly violated the Geneva Conventions. The difficulty of opposing the governmental policy, deserting the army, and being court-marshaled becomes palpable through the stories of those individuals who faced up to the task with a high personal toll. Examples include Greg Payton, an African-American, imprisoned at Long Binh Jail for refusing to fight; Dr. Howard Levy, jailed for three years for refusing to train Special Forces troops; Navy nurse Susan Schnall, jailed for dropping leaflets from an airplane onto the Presidio army base, and Donald Duncan, a member of the Green Berets who resigned after a year in Vietnam. This inclusive sample aims at illustrating the gender and racial diversity of the participants in the movement and the wide social base of the group. It is another piece of the puzzle, alongside the story of the underground presses and Jane Fonda's FTA performance, that attests to the existence of a strong resistance to the Vietnam War within the armed forces, which was subsequently suppressed for challenging the official American narrative. *Sir! No Sir!* adopts the formal devices of the expository documentary because it aims to persuade us about a hidden truth. This truth may have been concealed so far but Zeiger's research brought it to light and now it stands whole and unequivocal before our eyes. Such is the underlying assumption of every expository documentary, regardless of its theme. Cast in this particular narrative mold, the history of the G.I. Movement is explained as a concrete and self-evident historical development with a beginning (a few malcontents), a middle (a revolutionary peak), and an ending (a purposeful suppression of the revolution). Zeiger provides clear-cut answers to complex historical processes and builds a heroic profile for his participants. Like all expository documentaries, *Sir! No Sir!* leaves very little room for skepticism and ambivalence regarding the veracity of its historical evidence as well as the substance of its argument.

Specifically, its argument, viewed through the prism of White's taxonomy, is of the Organicist kind. Again, like most expository documentaries, Zeiger's film promotes a historical argument that favors synthesis and integration. The very idea that what happened during Vietnam is a blueprint for what is happening in Iraq indicates that history is viewed as series of recurrent phenomena governed by certain rules. Thus, the actions of those defiant individuals should not be interpreted as unique historical instances, as in Formism, but rather as organic elements of larger processes that do not begin or end with the Vietnam War. The larger categories that hover over the testimonies and the archival footage in the film pertain to the notions of the nation, race and the role of the State in a democratic society. For example, almost all the interviewees argue that they love their country and that they would not hesitate to sacrifice for it as long as the fight was worth it. Patriotism and military service are not questioned as ideals but for their specificity within the Vietnam context. Thus, the fault is with the official government and the State apparatuses, such as the police, the judicial system, and the military. The defiance of these formidable forces from the part of individual soldiers, whether before, during, or after their military duties, is considered as an act of revolt that seeks not to abandon the democratic principles but to reinstate them in their rightful place. The ideals of justice, national pride, and sacrifice take on a universal currency that is inherent in human nature and, therefore, the soldiers are in a position to decide for themselves whether the cause of the Vietnam War is honorable or not. Gone is the Contextualist view of history and the relativism of war practices that we witnessed in McNamara and Morris' account. State power in *Sir! No Sir!* takes on the form of pure evil; first, it slaughters thousands of young Americans and millions of Vietnamese; then it fights, beats, and incarcerates all those who oppose the war; and finally, it makes sure that the latter's struggle for a better world is forever erased from public memory. The world in Zeiger's documentary is starkly black and white. And it is a world that is not tied to the specificity of Vietnam but, rather, it resonates with the balance of power and the derelict status of democracy in the contemporary world.

Evidently, this highly organic argument about the American society from the 1960s onwards bears characteristic ideological implications of the Anarchist kind. The social critique voiced in *Sir! No Sir!* bears the structural traits of the Anarchist thinking, as that was developed in White's application of Mannheim's forms of utopian mentality. My predilection for the Anarchist and not the Radical or the Liberal ideology to interpret the film's position requires some explanation. The Radical is a term often attributed to works related to political activism that bring forward cases of social injustice related to class, race, and gender.[34] This is not the sense, however, that we find in White's category of a Radical historical perspective. In the latter, political change is viewed as a fundamental goal that will establish a new form of society, while the idea of constitutional democracy will be rejected as a bourgeois construction. In this frame of action, the vision for a better world is oriented toward the future and the Utopian condition is believed to be imminent. This very precise and programmatic vision of a new political system based on a mechanistic analysis of the historical process is not something to be sustained in films like *Sir! No Sir!* On the other hand, mainstream Liberalism is not an option either. The opposition against the compromises that Liberal ideology entails becomes flagrantly exposed when we look at Zeiger's exclusion of John Kerry from the history of the G.I. Movement. As I noted previously, *Sir! No Sir!* was screened a year after *Going Upriver*, which portrays Kerry's leading presence in the movement. Zeiger, however, chose to erase him completely from the picture. When confronted about this decision, he said the following:

> Because so many people wanted us to put him in [laughs]. That was part of it. Frankly, we didn't have him in mainly because we didn't want that to become what the film was about. The film made about his military service during the campaign, *Going Upriver*, has a lot of footage about his involvement with Vietnam Veterans Against the War, which is also in our film. Ironically, that film was made to help Kerry's campaign, but if anything, it hurt it. It didn't win over anyone that was against him to begin with, but people who supported Kerry because of his anti-war stance during Vietnam saw how startlingly far he's gone in his ultimate betrayal of the stand he took in the 1960s. We thought anything like that would be distraction for this film.

> Cited in Stein 2005

This response is highly informative of the film's ideological implications and it is worth a detailed consideration. First of all, it underlines, jokingly or not, a resistance toward anything mainstream, anything that many people may want or expect. Thus, comprehensiveness and historical accuracy come second to the need to be different or unconventional. Apart from this unconscious intellectual elitism, however, Kerry's absence was avowedly instrumental for the film's emphasis on collective action and coffeehouse counter-culture. Kerry's individual action, his personal initiative, and his mainstream looks and demeanor could not fit in well with the image of the movement that Zeiger wanted to project. Above all, Kerry is considered a traitor; he betrayed all the principles he stood for in the 1960s and he settled for a conventional political career, albeit a Liberal one. In just a few sentences, Zeiger corroborates the reading of the film at the formal, argumentative, and ideological level, a reading that was possible even without this public statement. *Sir! No Sir!* is an expository documentary that constructs the illusion of objectivity and true historical knowledge with the help of a voice-over commentary that pretends to disclose a hidden truth for the first time and from a unique perspective. As in most expository documentaries, the historical argument is Organicist, emphasizing clusters of phenomena and foregrounding the power of a movement and not of individual heroes. Finally, its Anarchist political take is easily inferred by the abstract pleas to the power of the community and humanism as well as by its nostalgia for an innocent past. In the closing moments of the documentary, Jane Fonda and other interviewees think back to those days and admire their strength and their idealistic resolve. The prospects for the world they envisioned, however, become postponed to an indefinite future.

Biographies

Going Upriver: The Long War of John Kerry (2004)

George Butler's biographical portrait of US Senator John Kerry was screened at the time of the 2004 presidential election, when Kerry ran against George W. Bush and the Vietnam War became part of the public debate about the military record of both candidates. *Going Upriver* was characterized by some reviewers as "a pro-Kerry agitprop film," while others emphasized the fine nuances of its portrayal and the balanced approach to the role of the individual vis-à-vis the historical context (Musser 2007). Its formal classification within Nichols' modes of representation is not as clear-cut, as in the previous examples, but I would like to argue that we should categorize Butler's film as an expository documentary. Its key difference from the standard expository tradition is the lack of a continuous voice-over commentary that binds the images together and offers an argument in an explicit and outspoken fashion. Instead, *Going Upriver* comprises numerous interviews with Kerry's friends and family, while it shows rare footage of Kerry's activities, which were shot by Butler during their decades-long friendship. As a professional photographer, Butler had been documenting Kerry's political career for years, collecting material that amounts to an observational recording of the latter's life. Neither the interviews, however, nor the observational material are handled in a way that would allow us to characterize the film as an interactive or an observational documentary, respectively. The interviews contain no interaction on the part of the filmmaker, while the photographs and the footage are at no point highlighted for the immediacy of the recording. On the contrary, the voices of the interviewees blend together into a commentary of sorts that guides the viewer into the life and personality of John Kerry with a degree of authority that emulates the voice-of-God type of commentary of the expository mode. At the opening of the film we hear someone say, "You can't understand John unless you understand what Vietnam is to him and to his life, it is absolutely essential to understanding him," then someone else adds, "It's one form of patriotism to go, which he did, then if you see what is happening is wrong, you also have a patriotic duty to speak out about it," while another one explains, "John Kerry's odyssey is the odyssey of my generation, that was launched by John Kennedy and that great sense of public service, military service and idealism. He went through the Vietnam War and he came out of it with lessons learnt." The sources of these sound bites are not identified by the film, while their words accompany a compilation of past images from Vietnam and a more recent clip of Kerry on a chopper gazing over some rice fields. The shots have no temporal or spatial continuity but they all come together thanks to the causality established between Kerry and his Vietnam experience by the soundtrack. This type of image-sound combination persists throughout the documentary building a very meticulous and tight exposition, despite the absence of one continuous commentary. Thus, the testimonies of the interviewees surpass the limits of the scenes that contain their actual physical presence and become superimposed over expository images that aim to corroborate their recounting. In spite of the multiplicity of voices, the complete harmony and concurrence among the opinions that are expressed and the images that appear with them result in a highly unified portrait of John Kerry that bears all the historical explanations that we have related to the expository mode and its penchant for Organicist arguments. Unlike Zeiger's expository film, however, Butler opts for a Liberal approach to the historical role of his protagonist and his destiny.

Having classified *Going Upriver* as an expository documentary, despite its formal peculiarities, we can begin to explore the various historical explanations that the film supports through its textual and extratextual characteristics. Starting with the level of narration, an expository biography like this raises no question as to whether John Kerry is a historical figure that we can really get to know. Like all traditional approaches, it starts with his young age and it gradually builds a biographical profile characterized by unambiguous consistency. His siblings explain how he was always "the leader of the pack" and how his "derring-do was inherent to him as a kid," making sure that we explain his later actions based on virtues and strengths that were there with him all along. Similarly, the film lines up a series of influences he had from his surroundings; his mother, his father, his activist upbringing, his studies at Yale, and ultimately Vietnam. As the opening voice, mentioned above, had made clear, Vietnam is the key to Kerry's personality. Thus, we witness a linear and straightforward chronology in the reconstruction of his life combined with an equally straightforward cause-and-effect linkage between the significant historical and political events of the era. For example, we learn that Kerry was recruited in the war because the army needed bright young men to lead in the operations and he enlisted out of patriotic duty because he believed the myths of the Cold War. Yet, when he went and saw the injustice first-hand, he felt that the same patriotic duty urged him to oppose the war and defend the innocent lives that were being wasted for a nonsensical cause. This type of recounting of Kerry's life continues after his return to Vietnam, explaining his involvement with the Vietnam Veterans Against the War. The voices that recount these events and explain Kerry's motivations leave absolutely no gap in the story that the documentary wishes to tell. The tight plot construction, the unity of the argument, and the precise correspondence of images and words construct a solid human portrait; Kerry is a charismatic and bright individual who fights for his country, who fights against injustice, who learns from his mistakes, and is always guided by rational judgment. The expository form creates the impression of seamlessness and communicativeness, so that our response to the question "who is John Kerry?" becomes definitive.

Despite the biographical focus on Kerry, however, *Going Upriver* does not host a Formist argument. In other words, it does not aim at construing Kerry as an exceptional human being who carved a unique path in the roads of history. Instead, like most expository documentaries, it is more amenable to an Organicist view of Kerry's trajectory in America's past and present. The Organicist perspective stems from Butler's predilection to constantly embed Kerry's presence into a wider political and ideological frame. Kerry is not a visionary; he is not a loner; he is the emblem of a whole generation. In this light, his personal actions and goals matter for us to the extent that they shed light on to a turbulent period of American history, which redefined American idealism. Kerry put his talents, his bravery, his looks, and his hard work to a higher purpose; to stand for justice and freedom, two values he considered predominantly American. *Going Upriver* intertwines Kerry's life with Vietnam not because it seeks to contextualize him but because it seeks to integrate his deeds into a higher totality. Unlike a Contextualist historian, who would flatten Kerry's existence into a series of interrelated historical agencies, Butler chooses Kerry as a personality who embodies the quintessence of American values. As a son, as a student, as a soldier, as a protestor, and as a politician, Kerry stands as an ideal representative of the American people. His biography is not meant to highlight his unique existence but put forward, instead, all the ways that Kerry is living proof that the American spirit is still alive.

Admittedly, the underlying philosophical argument of the documentary is fully in line with Kerry's presidential campaign and the timing of its screening. Which brings us to the level of ideological implication that can be detected in the film. In contrast to other documentaries that tend to hide their ideological commitments, Butler's friendship with Kerry and the latter's presidential bid as a Democratic candidate delimit the ideological readings of the film to the Liberal perspective. Even if we never had any extratextual hints, however, the form and content of *Going Upriver* project a very openly Liberal perspective on the meaning of politics, justice, and social change. In this regard, its distance from Zeiger's Anarchist vision is abysmal. Whereas *Sir! No Sir!* told a collective story of insubordination as a part of a counter-cultural movement that rejected the established authorities, Butler chose to tell us the story of John Kerry as a successful example of enacting change through the constructive critique and the rational refutation of the government's actions. Kerry's political views are not aphoristic or radical, as his respect for the established political order remains unwavering. This becomes firmly substantiated during the segment dedicated to the anti-war demonstrations in Washington in April 1971. The testimonies and the images from those historic days, including the hearing before the Senate Committee on Foreign Relations, attest to the fact that Kerry got the demonstrators' message across thanks to his "polite protestor demeanor," his maturity, his lack of "disheveled looks" and, above all, his willingness to reason with the enemy. Unlike the majority of the protestors who could not temper their emotions and could not connect with ordinary Americans, as the interviewees claim, Kerry could relate to the establishment and make the public truly listen to him. This is why his speech got an "electric response" and turned him into "instant celebrity." The ideological opposition between *Sir! No Sir!* and *Going Upriver*, which is a typical opposition between Anarchism and Liberalism, is not only tangible when we compare the two documentaries or when we look at Zeiger's contemporary antipathy to Kerry's conventionalism;[35] the battle between a radical resistance of established power structures and a more measured critique and renegotiation strategy was probably present among the demonstrators at the time. According to the veterans interviewed in Butler's film, the resentment towards Kerry's mainstream appearance and his Liberal approach to the resolution of the crisis was there all along. In this light, Zeiger's criticism comes across as disingenuous; Kerry did not change in the process nor did he give up his ideals. The programmatic disagreements between an Anarchist vision, shared by a significant part of the anti-war protestors, and a more Liberal one, resonating with the majority of the American people, were probably felt throughout those tumultuous times. At any rate, what both films seem to share is the expository form and its reassuring voice that it tells us the truth and nothing but the truth about the historical the past. Such fixed certainty is undoubtedly not what we expect to find in the two reflexive biographical portraits that follow.

The Last Bolshevik (1992)

Chris Marker's biographical documentary about the Russian filmmaker, Alexander Ivanovich Medvedkin, is an intriguing example of how a person's life can be explored for all the ways it relates to powerful historical events surrounding them.[36] Unlike Butler's expository treatment of John Kerry's relation to the Vietnam War, however, Marker crafts a highly reflexive account of Medvedkin's inextricable ties to the history of the Soviet Union in the twentieth century. The choice of the reflexive mode generates an entirely different approach to biography, as it probes us to reconsider our established ideas on subjectivity and representation. This demanding task is even further complicated by the fact that Medvedkin's career and several parts of Soviet history are not so widely known. Whereas the expository mode would have ensured a more customary introduction to Medvedkin's trajectory in Soviet cinema and politics, Marker decides to plunge us into an unknown territory, which we have to figure and refigure all at once. Yet, it is an understandable move, if we take into consideration

Marker's personal involvement in the film's subject matter not only thanks to his long friendship with Medvedkin but also in relation to his long-standing commitment to communist ideology. In this light, *The Last Bolshevik* often feels like Marker's attempt to come to grips with his own past that includes both his friend Medvedkin and the ideas that formed him as a political filmmaker of the Left. Such an ideological interpretation, however, will have to wait. We need to start with the form of the film and discuss how the narrative options hold a specific range of historical explanations.

The Last Bolshevik features an opening sequence that condenses several of the formal characteristics that recur throughout the film. First, we read an epigraph by George Steiner: "It is not the past that rules us. It is the images of the past." These two sentences already indicate Marker's preoccupation with the visual image and its formative powers over our engagement with the past. The next image is that of Medvedkin addressing directly the camera and speaking in Russian. His image is soon dominated by a voice-over commentary that does not belong to Marker but it acts as if it did. This commentary begins by giving us some basic biographical information, such as Medvedkin's full name and date of birth. Then it rushes to establish a connection between Medvedkin and history with the following words: "He was five and Lenin wrote *What is to be Done?* Seventeen, and he knew. Twenty; the Civil War. Thirty-six; the Moscow trials. Forty-one; World War Two. Fifty-three; Stalin's death. And when he dies in 1989, it is on the crest of Perestroika." After these factual statements, the voice becomes personal; it addresses Medvedkin as a friend, confessing that now is the time for a belated communication. The image freezes on Medvedkin and zooms in on a gesture he makes with his hands. Marker, via his proxy, explains that now he is ready to write to him, without holding anything back. He is ready to tell him everything, even though he won't ever be able to listen. This brief introductory sequence sets the rules of the game; *The Last Bolshevik* will focus on Medvedkin as a historical figure, who is simultaneously connected both to a wider historical reality (the Soviet Union) and a very specific individual (Marker). Marker's authorial intervention in the project is firmly established and amply justified not only because of their personal relation but also because of his own distinct aesthetic, philosophical, and ideological preferences. We know that this is going to be a reflexive documentary, which will bear the traces of Marker's authorial signature and it will craft a highly mediated portrait of a complex personality.

Indeed, the film proceeds to the task with an episodic structure that contains two large segments entitled "The kingdom of shadows" and "The shadows of a kingdom," while each segment is further dissected into three "letters." The division into all these small parts follows a roughly chronological order, moving from Medvedkin's early age to his death and from the Russian revolution to Perestroika, but, in my view, it primarily expresses Marker's own interpretation of them. Medvedkin remained a solid communist till the very end of his life, despite the gradual disenchantment of his fellow citizens with the communist regime. Marker, however, signals a break in the biography between the kingdom and its shadows around the mid to the late 1930s. He closes the first part with a close-up from Medvedkin's famous film *Happiness* (1935), tracing the terror on the actor's face and employing it synecdochically for the face of the Russian people who had begun to experience the terror of Stalinism. Then, the second part opens with Medvedkin's *New Moscow* (1938), which was banned after its first screening. From then on, *The Last Bolshevik*, through archival footage and interviews with a wide array of personalities (relatives, friends, scholars), begins to document a gradual descent into totalitarianism that ended all prospects for happiness. As Ilona Hongisto eloquently puts it, "In the kingdom of shadows, cinema is equipped with methods that enable the production of happiness in the Soviet state; in the shadows of a kingdom it produces appearances that simply maintain the status quo of the kingdom" (Hongisto 2015, 54).

The reflexivity of the form in the documentary takes on many shapes; the personal tone of the commentary and its self-conscious treatment of the subject matter, the discordance between the visual material and its aural accompaniment, the manipulation of the images with freeze-frames, colors or superimpositions, the repetitions, the direct address at the camera, and the constant mixture of factual with fictional elements. All these expressive strategies reiterate the initial premise, namely that images are our only access to a vanishing past and their inherent malleability blocks us from ever having a single true and definitive version of it. Unlike an expository biography, *The Last Bolshevik* presents Medvedkin as an enigma; on the one hand, he was a sensitive and kind idealist who fought for his country and for a better world. On the other hand, the reality of Stalinist communism was relentless. Marker documents the poverty, the purges, the censorship and, ultimately, the suffocating fear that the Communist Party instilled in the population. The question that Marker does not seem to resolve is how Medvedkin chose to comply with that reality until the end. In this audiovisual posthumous letter to Medvedkin, Marker prefers to refrain from a conclusive judgment on his friend's personality.[37] The formal reflexivity allows him to attribute to his subject a high level of complexity and maintain a tenuous causality between Medvedkin and Soviet history, a causality that can be visited over and over again. Thus, the narrative structure of the reflexive mode invites us to ponder upon the role of the individual and his/her historical conditions as an open-ended affair, triggering multiple, and often conflicting, observations and interpretations.

Once again, complexity should not be confounded with ambiguity. The reflexive mode and its skepticism about the status of truth and objective knowledge tend to generate arguments of the Contextualist kind. Like McNamara and the Vietnam War in Morris' documentary, the historical argument in *The Last Bolshevik* is synthetic and dispersive; it traces a considerable amount of historical elements but refuses to integrate them in larger historical clusters. With communism as a topic and Medvedkin as a filmmaker, Marker could have easily veered toward Organicist views about human nature and happiness with a transcendental overtone. Yet, he keeps pointing to the immanent character of individuality and ideology, rejecting their hierarchical positioning. As Hongisto observes, "*The Last Bolshevik* proposes a non-hierarchical 'flat ontology' between Medvedkin and cinematic characters, between cinematic fables and the history of the twentieth century. This allows the documentary to rewrite the memories of Alexander Medvedkin and his era in film" (Hongisto 2015, 54). Marker explores the triangle "Cinema-Medvedkin-Russian history," moving from one point to another without ever being able to rise to a greater truth. Medvedkin's biography is scattered with movie fragments, newsreels, political figures, fellow-filmmakers, friends and relatives, each giving away a piece of the puzzle and, yet, knowing that many of them will never appear. Not because they are hidden or difficult to discover but because the very idea of reaching the essence of a person or a historical moment is not pertinent. Like Maximilian Schell's *Marlene*, *The Last Bolshevik* builds a meticulous biography of Medvedkin and situates him in a very specific historical context, acknowledging the limitations of the enterprise as well as the power of invention that it entails. The reflexive mode is particularly suited for Contextualist thinking because it foregrounds the affinities of fact and fiction, and it does not pretend to present one final truth about history.

Finally, we have to investigate the ideological implications of Marker's reflexive approach to Medvedkin's life and the belief about human nature and society that it fosters. As I noted in my introductory comments above, Marker's interpretation of Medvedkin's personality bears significantly the marks of the "beholder's share." This may be true for all biographies, or all historical accounts for that matter, but the level of subjectivity here is explicitly higher. The friendship between the two men, the common ideological ground as well as Marker's distinct authorial style, all render the documentary exceptionally personal. In fact, if Marker had wished to come forward and appear in front of the camera, *The Last Bolshevik* could have easily switched to the performative mode. Even as it stands, however, his oblique confession in the opening sequence delimits, from the onset, the ideological readings of this biography. The film is Marker's letter to his friend, with which he wishes to confront him with some bitter comments and an undeniable reality, namely that his life's vision was a total failure. Marker never brought himself to have such a face-off while Medvedkin was still alive. Commentators who studied closely their meetings and their exchanges via letters or interviews noted the following:

> Their relationship serves at times as a synecdoche for the larger relationship between the naïve, gullible European Left and the tired, cruel Soviet behemoth, with each side aghast at recognizing its own reflection in the other, but refusing to see the other—and therefore itself—for what it actually is. Their friendship survived the Soviet invasion of Czechoslovakia in 1968 only, perhaps, because they never discussed it.
>
> Bird et al. 2011, 67

In *The Last Bolshevik,* Marker gets to have the final word and his biographical portrait of Medvedkin and his historical era can no longer embrace the optimism and determination of the Radical ideology. Quite the contrary. The film is haunted by death; the death of a friend, of a dream, of a country. Of everything that was lost, Marker seeks to salvage the innocence and the purity of Medvedkin's soul, trying, in good faith, to get hold of something intangible. Thus, the constant return to *Happiness* as an image of Medvedkin's inherent contradictions. Of the four types of ideological implication that we borrowed from White, *The Last Bolshevik* clearly falls in the category of Anarchism. Marker openly mourns the failure of the revolution and revisits the past with nostalgia and melancholia.[38] His utopian vision is suspended; on the one hand, he knows that "the gesture of revolution is always inscribed with failure" (ibid.), while, on the other, he could not support either the Liberal or the Conservative position. I believe that Anarchism is once again the most suitable ideological category for a Left-wing ideology that still clings to the idea of social transformation and political change but, confronted with the failures of Communism, it postpones revolutionary action to an indefinite future.

Thirty-Two Short Films About Glenn Gould (1993)

This final case study will be dedicated to a biography that takes our focus away from war and politics and directs it to music. François Girard's *Thirty-Two Short Films About Glenn Gould* is a reflexive documentary about the famous pianist Glenn Gould, flaunting an idiosyncratic formal structure that pushes the limits of cinematic representation. The life of Glenn Gould had all the ingredients for a spectacular and dramatic biography, whether one chose to mold it as a classical drama or as an expository documentary. As Dennis Bingham aptly puts it,

> Just as Gould's exacting, uncompromising personality makes him, in his very lack of conventionality, a conventional subject for a biopic, his struggles with the expectations of the musical establishment and the high excitement he inspired in the early years of his career might have made for a dramatic biopic.
>
> Bingham 2010, 138–9

And yet, Francois Girard opted for a highly reflexive form, which challenges all the established formal conventions and defies an easy categorization, even when it comes to its indexing as a fiction film or documentary.[39] Besides, it is what its title says it is, namely thirty-two different films on the same subject. As a narrative ensemble, however, I believe that it can fit into the category of the reflexive mode, which is spacious and diverse enough, as I previously argued. Like all reflexive documentaries, it is a film that probes the binary distinction between fiction and nonfiction, while it tests an extremely wide range of representational practices to approximate Gould's complex personality. The obvious parallel between the film form and Gould's life regards his famous recording of Johann Sebastian Bach's *The Goldberg Variations*. Like Gould's favorite work, the film presents a similar number of variations of a biographical portrait. Apart from these two shaping principles, however, i.e., Gould's complexity and the theme of the variation, Girard's documentary is governed by a more substantial desire to test the limits of our representational logic and to shake our assumptions about what constitutes a human individual. I will discuss the former as part of the film's explanation by mode of representation and the latter as part of its underlying historical argument.

The film bookends the short films on Glenn Gould with two symmetrical sequences. In the opening, a figure slowly traverses a frozen landscape until it reaches the camera. It is Glenn Gould played by the Canadian actor Colm Feore accompanied by an aria from the *Goldberg Variations* in the soundtrack. In the closing moments, we see Gould replay the scene in reverse; he walks away from the camera until he disappears in the horizon. These two scenes contain twenty-nine segments, which communicate aspects of Gould's life in very different representational formats that consistently seek to undermine our standard expectations. These segments can be distinguished largely within four categories:

1. Diegetic scenes (Lake Simcoe, Hamburg, The L.A. Concert, Truck Stop etc.),
2. Abstract sequences (Variation in C Minor, CD318, Gould Meets McLaren, Diary of a Day, Pills etc.),
3. Interviews (Bruno Monsaingeon, Yehudi Menuhin, Crossed Paths etc.)
4. Scenes with Gould alone (Gould meets Gould: text by Gould, Personal Ad, The Idea of North etc.).

Girard evenly switches from one type to another, gradually acquainting us with his peculiar constructional logic. One of the fascinating aspects of his approach is the way he deconstructs the most conventional of these types, namely the diegetic scenes and the interviews. Apart from Lake Simcoe, which introduces us to Gould in his childhood in a fairly traditional manner, the others represent secondary incidents in his life that would normally go unnoticed in the eyes of a biographer. For example, The L.A. Concert takes us behind the scenes of this famous last concert and shows us the moments before Gould entered the stage. Instead of focusing on the actual performance, the film dwells on the minutiae that took place right before, including a brief conversation with a stagehand who asks for his autograph. It is through the note on this autograph that we learn about Gould's unexpected decision to end his stage career right then and there. The shocking revelation draws its distancing effect not only from the nature of the event that it entails but primarily from the narrational strategies of the film. In this diegetic episode, as in all others, Girard tries to defy the norms of classical construction on all axes, i.e., causality, time, and space. We do not have a rational agent with a clear-cut logic in his actions, and we do not get to see the spatial (the stage) and the temporal (the performance) frame that we expect to see. The film denies us both the motivation of this pivotal decision and the access to this historic event in his life. Similarly, the device of the interview is explored in many different ways in several segments. Sometimes, friends, relatives, and colleagues talk about their experiences with Gould in self-contained episodes, while in others, as in "Crossed Paths," their testimonies are playfully juxtaposed with rhythmic editing. Moreover, the idea of getting to know a person through the interview is openly parodied in "Gould Meets Gould: text by Glenn Gould, Questions with No answers" and "The idea of North."

In addition to laying bare the devices of the dramatization and the interview, Girard explores the range of expressivity of abstract imagery. By treating the cinematic image not as a window onto reality but as a graphic surface, he is able to approach in yet another unconventional and self-reflexive manner the existence of his biographical subject. The chords of Gould's piano, his pills, or his X-rays represent Gould metonymically, breaking the rules of realistic representation that relies on the centrality of the human figure and the photographic capturing of the external world. Unlike most fictions and documentaries, *Thirty-Two Short Films About Glenn Gould* does not pretend to represent the life of a historical figure as it really was. Instead, it tries out all the possible forms of a cinematic image in order to break the illusion of immediacy in realistic representation. Thus, the film continuously reminds us that the real Glenn Gould is not to be seen. Pretending to bring him back to life for the sake of a biographical portrait is not within the filmmaker's intentions. On the contrary, he will tell us about this musical genius with every means available, while underlining at every step of the way the distance that separates us from the real Gould.

The skepticism toward the very essence of biography is the fundamental principle of all reflexive documentaries, as we previously saw in the cases of *Marlene* and *The Last Bolshevik*. Consequently, their historical argument is of the Contextualist kind. *Thirty-Two Short Films About Glenn Gould* addresses two key questions: "How do we get to know a person?" and "What does a person consist of?" The reflexivity of the form challenges the possibility of objective knowledge and essential truth about the individual, while it probes us to reconsider the essence of human existence. The visual incoherence of Girard's biographical portrait is philosophically coherent from a Contextualist point of view on both these counts. The film does not seek Gould's essence, nor does it integrate his individuality within a greater category of any kind. It synthesizes an enormous number of elements related to his life but it does not elevate them to a higher level. In this regard, I disagree with Bingham's claim that "Girard's tribute promises transcendence" (144). The fragments of his life do not add up to anything other than themselves, despite Gould's disavowal of immanent philosophies in a telephone interview in Hotel Mawa. There, he says, "I find all the here-and-now philosophies quite repellent, lax if you will," refusing to negotiate the possibility of a hereafter. Regardless of Gould's personal view, however, the biography that gradually builds up from the thirty-one segments[40] does not seem to point toward any greater truth regarding his existence. The relentless specificity on the little things in his life, the details of his eccentricities, the everyday routines, and his peculiar habits keep restraining Gould to a here-and-now, without any chance of escape. His music may have been traveling to other planets but Gould's life, as portrayed in the film, disintegrates into a multitude of earthly experiences. And this brings us to the second question regarding Girard's approach to individuality. Like all biographies, *Thirty-Two Short Films About Glenn Gould* needed to decide how Gould would be related to his historical and artistic environment, selecting a range of elements that would define his personality. His musical talent, of course, was clearly inescapable but Girard does not limit his subject only to one area. In fact, the documentary offers a very dense account of Gould's personality, shedding light on lesser-known facets and multiple dimensions. As Gould himself argues at one point, "The most illuminating disclosures usually derived from areas only indirectly related to the interviewee's line of work." Thus, Gould is placed within a context with numerous agents; his concerts, his recordings, his interviews, his solitary meals, his radio documentaries, his contacts with colleagues and employees, his medication, his piano, his compositions all the way down to papers that were discovered after his death. As I noted above, these elements are not connected to each other with any cause-and-effect logic nor do they integrate into any deeper or higher explanation about Gould. Instead, they invite us to consider how a music genius like him is simultaneously defined by his unique talent as much as he is defined by his everyday habits, his casual encounters, and the pills he incessantly consumes.

Finally, there is the question of the ideological implications that we can trace in *Thirty-Two Short Films About Glenn Gould*. The lack of a political theme and the focus on a personality that was not related to wider historical events renders the task more difficult than in the previous case studies. The cues for its ideological reading are fewer and more implicit but we can still identify elements in the text as well as in Gould's extratextual presence, which could point towards an ideological direction. First of all, we could begin by excluding the Radical and the Conservative variety. Gould's ideas and views on society and power structures would not be characterized by either of these visions. As a musical prodigy, Gould challenged the dominant hierarchies and rebelled against the musical establishment in many ways, especially by his decision to stop his live performances at such an early stage in his career. Yet, his personal revolution and his unconventional methods did not develop into a particularly activist stance; instead, he chose a life of solitude dedicating his time to studio recordings, writing, and radio documentaries. His penchant for innovation, his embrace of technology, and his success at the stock market illustrate a very paradoxical ideological orientation that does not fit easily in our fixed categories. Apart from Gould's own ideology, there is the film itself that eschews Radicalism and Conservatism by means of its highly reflexive form. From Anarchism and Liberalism, I would argue that Girard's biography is more likely to be characterized by a Liberal vision that celebrates the value of the individual, the power of free will, and the optimism for a better world.

A concluding note

Historical documentaries, like historical fiction films, attempt to communicate knowledge about the historical past through a rich variety of forms, arguments, and ideological positions. Nichols' five modes of representation allowed us to categorize a large number of historical documentaries and explore the complicated ways in which form, argument, and ideology collaborate within this particular genre of filmmaking. Compared to the fiction films, Nichols' taxonomy of the documentary was less formally stringent, giving us the opportunity to discuss the possibility of multiple options whether at the level of argument or ideology. Yet, the more open relations between the various historical explanations do not cancel out the central thesis of this project, namely that the historical documentary, as a subgenre of the historical film, attempts to explain the past by representing it. This representation entails a series of formal choices, which in turn facilitate the expression of certain arguments and ideological positions. Thus, any attempt to understand the representation of history in a documentary needs to begin by identifying the narrative strategies that the filmmaker deploys. As soon as we classify a historical documentary within one of the five modes, then the range of combinations that I presented in Table 6.1 guides us toward the more likely arguments and ideological implications that we should expect to encounter. Even though documentaries tend to mix formal categories more easily than fiction films, the schema that I developed proved to be fairly effective in the analysis of the films in the sample. And there precisely lies the value of the method that I have been trying to develop in this second part of the book, i.e., a consistent method for analyzing historical representations. Historical films, whether fiction or nonfiction, tend to adhere to formal, argumentative and ideological patterns that persist in the course of time. A good knowledge of film form and an in-depth consideration of the philosophical and ideological dimensions of historical thinking can ensure an informed and coherent reading of historical works on the screen.

Notes

1   The issue of professional commitment and moral obligation will be further discussed in the conclusion.

2   Nichols quotes White's definition of the "historical work" twice, once in the main text and once in the footnote section. Moreover, he laments the subordination of the documentary to what he calls the "dominant discourses of sobriety," and specifically the subordination of historical documentary to history (1991, 9). However, elevating the documentary to a dominant discourse in the twentieth century is not set as an explicit goal of his in this book.

3   As Nichols concedes already before introducing the modes, "Elements of narrative, as a particular form of discourse, and aspects of realism, as a particular representational style, inform documentary logic and the economy of the text routinely. More precisely, each mode deploys the resources of narrative and realism differently, making from common ingredients different types of text with distinctive ethical issues, textual structures, and viewer expectations" (1991, 34).

4   As I explained in chapter 4, I will be deploying Nichols' five modes of representation as he first formulated them in his publications (1991; 1994).

5   I will focus on the standard documentary format and not the compound form of the TV mini-series, which has the potential of mixing diverse modes within its extended length.

6   Pepper classifies the four world-hypotheses along two axes: the synthetic/analytic and the integrative/dispersive. Specifically, Formism and Mechanism are analytical (they give primary importance to individual elements), while Organicism and Contextualism are synthetic (they use contexts and totalities as their basic level of analysis). On the other axis, Formism and Contextualism are dispersive (they let analysis or synthesis be as it is), while Organicism and Mechanism are integrative (they integrate synthesis and analysis into a systematic cosmos). The reason I feel compelled to emphasize these dimensions in the discussion of the documentary, unlike the case of fiction, has to do with the complexity and hybridity of the nonfiction films at the level of narration.

7   I maintain Nichols' terminology, as he opts for the term "mode of representation" instead of "mode of narration," which I employed in the chapter on historical fiction. However, the historical explanations of each documentary mode, as I approach them here, derive particularly from its compositional elements.

8   Rosenstone offers an interesting reading of this documentary (2006, 77–80).

9   Dziga Vertov's famous phrase "life caught unawares" became a synonym for documentary filmmaking, even though Vertov's style was very far from the observational kind.

10 Nichols also considers it a possibility (2010, 177–9).

11 As Danto explains, history is the result of the distance that separates us from the past and the ability to explain it drawing on knowledge that we acquire post facto (Danto 2007).

12 See chapter 3.

13 For a discussion of *The War Room* and its constructed nature see Thanouli (2013a) and J. Parry-Giles and T. Parry-Giles (1999).

14 I would like to note once again that the combinations of narrative, argument, and ideology that I investigate here concern only the films with historical subjects. Other combinations may be possible for other films with nonhistorical plots.

15 See chapter 5.

16 As Mannheim, notes, "As a fifth claimant to a place among modern currents of thought we should mention fascism, which first emerged in our own epoch. Fascism has its own conception of the relations of theory and practice. It is, on the whole, activistic and irrational. It couples itself, by preference, with the irrationalist philosophies and political theories of the most modern period" (Mannheim 1979, 119).

17 Microhistory is a recent trend in academic historiography described by Sigurður Gylfi Magnússon as follows: "Focusing on certain cases, persons and circumstances, microhistory allows an intensive historical study of the subject, giving a completely different picture of the past from investigations about nations, states, or social groupings, stretching over decades, centuries, or whatever longue durée" (2013, 5).

18 For a detailed description of the particularities of memory and history and their complicated relation, see Lowenthal (1985, 193–238).

19 The same purpose is served in written microhistory. As Carlo Ginzburg observes, "Microhistory has provided an opportunity to subvert pre-existing hierarchies thanks to the intrinsic relevance—demonstrated a posteriori—of the object under scrutiny" (2012, 115).

20 The duration of the documentary varies, as it made different releases in different countries. Lanzmann also released four feature-length films using the outtakes from the original work.

21 For a discussion about the incompatibility of Marxism and memory, see Enzo Traverso (2016).

22 *Shoah* has been interpreted in many conflicting ways. Indicatively, see Chaouat (2016, 160) and LaCapra (1994; 1997).

23 For the concept of "subject" and "speaking positions," see Elsaesser (1996).

24 For a brief account of the film's mixed reception, see Bruzzi (2006, 230–8).

25 In Nichols' account, the reflexive mode is an uneven category that includes assorted types of reflexivity both stylistic and political, even though the weight falls on the former. As he puts it, "What provides the litmus test for political reflexivity is the specific form of the representation, the extent to which it does not reinforce existing

categories of consciousness, structures of feeling, ways of seeing; the degree to which it rejects a narrative sense of closure and completeness" (Nichols 1991, 68).

26 As Ian Aitken notes in *The Concise Routledge Encyclopedia of the Documentary Film*, "[...] the reflexive documentary, and the related 'performative' documentary, has always (and probably always will) remained a minority genre, perhaps because of the extent to which reflexivity inevitably disrupts the coherent diegesis of the film" (2013, 11).

27 Indicatively see Lucy Fischer (2000) and Linda Hutcheon (1989) on *Marlene*, Robert Rosenstone (1995) on *Far from Poland*, and Dennis Bingham (2010) on *Thirty-Two Short films about Glenn Gould*.

28 The problem is not entirely eschewed there either, causing the art-cinema mode to be more inclusive and uneven than the classical. See Thanouli (2009b).

29 An interesting point is raised when we think about the historical argument of the reflexive mode in relation to the work of Dziga Vertov. Nichols considers Vertov as the father of the reflexive documentary and *The Man of the Movie Camera* (1929) as one of the first examples of the reflexive mode (Nichols 1991). Yet, *The Man of the Movie Camera* is not a historical documentary and it does not fall under our scope here. Vertov's historical newsreels and the *Three Songs of Lenin* (1934), however, do qualify as historical nonfiction and do beg the question of classification. On the one hand, we could regard them as the equivalent of the historical-materialist mode in the nonfiction genre, aligning him with Eisenstein and tracing Mechanistic arguments of history in his work. On the other hand, Vertov's objection to the concept of typage and his penchant for the specifics of reality separate him from the Mechanistic views, which, as Pepper notes, are "tempted to throw 'facts' out into unreal" (Pepper 1970, 145). Whether a Mechanistic argument of history and a true Radicalism can be expressed within Nichols' existing modes is a question that I have not been able to answer.

30 The problem of Radicalism in documentary has been insightfully discussed by Jane Gaines in a series of articles (Gaines 1999; 2007; 2015). She identifies the problematic questions regarding political activism and documentary form and she explores the idea of "political mimesis" and realism as a potential vehicle for social change.

31 There have been objections about Nichols' loose use of the term "performance," especially since the term became heavily theorized in the writings of J.L. Austin and Judith Butler. See Bruzzi (2006, 185–7).

32 In *Blurred Boundaries*, Nichols embraces Hayden White's terminology more extensively and correlates, for the first time, a mode of representation with White's types of historical explanation by formal argument. Specifically, he writes, "Performative documentary moves toward those forms of historical explanation described by Hayden White as formist and contextualist but in a far more vividly dialectical fashion" (Nichols 1994, 103).

33 For a philosophical reading of Morris' entire oeuvre, see Plantinga (2009).

34 See note 30.

35 See case study on *Sir! No Sir!*

36 The idea is akin to the one we discussed in *Cinema Combat: Hollywood Goes to War,* where the history of the film genre follows and interacts closely with the major historical events of the twentieth century. On a similar note, both Godard and Tarantino, discussed in chapters 1 and 5 respectively, explored the parallel and intertwined lives of cinema and history, arguing for their complex affinities.

37 As the authors of the catalogue entitled *Vision and Communism* note, "In *The Last Bolshevik* (1993) Marker steps lightly over Medvedkin's Stalinism, though he does feature the shot from *Youth in Bloom* in which small children dressed as border guards lead cartoonish enemies of the people at gunpoint through the streets. He does not mention that Medvedkin was secretary of the Party organization at Mosfilm in the worst years of Stalin's rule" (Bird et al. 2011, 65).

38 For an argument about Marker's melancholy in *The Last Bolshevik* and *Le fond de l'air est rouge* (1977), see Traverso (2016).

39 As Noel Carroll explains, "indexing" is a production and distribution practice that determines whether a film will be tagged as fiction or documentary (Carroll 1996d). In the case of *Thirty-Two Short Films About Glenn Gould,* the indexing is unclear as it often appears in both the category of the fiction film and the documentary. Indicatively, it won several Genie Awards in Canada in the motion picture category, while Amazon and iTunes list it as a documentary. For more on indexing, see the conclusion.

40 The total number of short films including the opening and closing sequences is thirty-one. The discrepancy with the title of the film has been interpreted by some commentators as symbolic; in other words, Girard tells us that a piece is missing, hinting at the puzzle-like nature of Gould's personality. See Rosadiuk (2006).

Conclusion: Filmic History in the Twentieth Century – a Successful Performance of Failure

Automatically produced indexical images and historiography: these two regimes of the indexical trace, two masteries of time and pastness, two experiences of knowledge, two kinds of spectacle, both of which achieved contemporaneous and long-lasting cultural success, as well as controversy.

Rosen 2001, 143

Cinema and written history, as Philip Rosen has aptly put it, have had so much to share as well as contend for throughout the twentieth century. Viewed as two modalities of the real, films and history books have had equal stakes in representing the world, whether in its present or past form, producing and disseminating knowledge about it, while also taking criticism for their respective failures and shortcomings. In this book, I chose to focus on historical films as representations of the past, as they are caught in the crossfire of the battle between historiography and cinema, between reality and fiction, between truth and error. This in-between status of filmic history that clings equally to evidence and documents, on the one hand, but also to imagination and fabrication, on the other, has perennially troubled historians, especially those who viewed themselves as the sole custodians of historical truth. It took the better part of a century for scholars to engage with films depicting the past in a way that acknowledges and appreciates their historical contribution. But even then, the clear demarcation of historiography from historiophoty would persist. As a reaction to this long-standing opposition, I put forward a heretical hypothesis that would reverse the rationale of the prevailing approaches, emphasizing not what differentiates professional history from historical films but what truly unites them. Specifically, I suggested that every historical film, whether fiction or nonfiction, is a magnified miniature of a historical book.[1] The metaphor of the magnified miniature captures two principal elements of filmic representations of the past, namely their condensed nature and their distorting effects. Most commentators are likely to be discouraged by the films' abbreviated form and their overtly fictional ingredients, always finding them inferior to written versions of the past. Instead, I wanted to dwell on the magnifying effects of this miniature; the power of revealing details and mechanisms that tend to go unnoticed in artifacts of a regular size. In this light, I would like to revisit all those sides of history which we were able to discern with the aid of the magnifying glass held by cinematic works.

One of the prominent but highly contested elements of historying in any type, shape, or form is the issue of narration. In historical studies, the discussion around narrativity is an extremely lengthy one but the vast majority of practicing historians still adhere to the idea of narrative being a natural and transparent vehicle of reality (Munslow 2006, 180–3). According to this line of thought, historians discover the story of the events and they simply preserve it in written form for generations to come. It took Hayden White's enormous effort to demur against this widespread mentality, which, above all, seeks to safeguard the notion of objectivity, pure knowledge, and truth. *Metahistory* and the proposition of historical writing as a "poetic act," was considered revolutionary at the time but it failed profoundly at changing the dominant views regarding the historical profession and its purportedly unique privilege over the reality of the past.[2] The idea of emplotment, which White strived to reveal in order to prove the process of fabrication and the power of imagination in any work of history, however, becomes abundantly clear when it comes to the cinema. Historical films, unlike their written counterparts, cannot hide the creative efforts of their makers. In fact, the distorting effects of their constructional elements jeopardize any documentary value or historical validity they may contain. When we compare the poetics of history, as developed by White, with the poetics of filmic history, as I formulated them in the two previous chapters, we realize that the magnifying power of cinematic narration allows us to understand better how the same processes obtain in the written work. The characters as historical agents, the plotlines as trajectories of human action, the spatial and the temporal choices as tangible creative mechanisms, the stylistic flourishes as subjective manipulations, the concepts of causality and unity as parts of a narrative logic, and, finally, realism as a technical convention are some of those characteristics of filmic history that can help us look at written history anew and help us retrace the same operations in the written texts, no matter how well they hide them under footnotes, lists of data, graphs,[3] and the weight of their voluminous content. In other words, filmic histories make White's undertaking considerably easier; by magnifying the operations of the historical narrative process and recasting them in a mode that could easily be construed as ironic, historical films liberate the forces of imagination, while, at the same time, unleash our skepticism regarding our ability to fulfill Ranke's dream to represent the past *"wie es eigentlich gewesen."*

Apart from narration, historical films also allow us to grasp better the entire process of historical representation and its complex relation to reference. In other words, they not only facilitate White's poetics but also Frank Ankersmit's arguments regarding the problem of representation in historiography. As a Whitean disciple, Ankersmit delved deeper into the philosophical implications of historical writing, focusing on the relation of narrative with fundamental concepts such as meaning, truth and reference (Ankersmit 1983; 1994; 2012). His approach to representation is particularly relevant when we compare written and filmic accounts of the past. Specifically, Ankersmit seeks to illustrate how historical writing performs a double operation: on the one hand, it describes the past, while, on the other, it represents "aspects" of it.[4] The descriptive function refers to external reality and it can be verified if its statements contain propositional truths or not. For instance, "Napoleon died on May 5, 1821 on the island of Saint Helena" is a descriptive statement, which can be confirmed as true or false. The representational side of historical discourse, however, does not simply refer to the past in the common sense of reference, i.e., by picking things out uniquely, but, rather, it attributes aspects to it. For instance, when one depicts Napoleon's personality or explains his behavior in a certain way, we cannot, just as easily, confirm whether this particular representation is true or not. Representations give us aspects of the past reality and not a direct reference to it. As a result, Ankersmit explains the representational process as a "three-place operator," which works as follows: a *representation* (1), offers us the *"presented"* or *"aspect"* (2) of a *represented reality* (3) (Ankersmit 2012, 73; emphasis in the original). What is important, as he insists, is that we distinguish between (2) and (3), so that we do not mistake representation for reference. Notice how in Ankersmit's definition, the "reality of the past" as an ontological existence is not included in any of the three places; instead, historical representation never leaves the realm of representation and it remains self-referential and recursive.[5] And notice now, how this challenging and controversial approach to historical representation in written form becomes self-evident when we deal with cinematic historical fictions.[6] Jean Louis-Comolli's famous article "A Body Too Much" captures precisely this three-place operation in the case of the cinema. As Comolli explains, when we watch historical figures in fiction dramas, we encounter additional difficulty in considering the historical representation as plausible and truthful because the body of the actor always stands out as fake. He employs the example of Louis XVI played by Pierre Renoir in *La Marseillaise* (1938) to illustrate the trouble we encounter when we are supposed to believe that Renoir is Louis XVI. The representation of historical characters is burdened by the tension between what appears on the screen (the actor's body) and the represented personality (Louis XVI) who is familiar to the audience from other representations or other sources. Even though any actor portraying an imaginary character still needs to metamorphose the physical appearance into a role, for historical personages the barrier is significantly higher. As Comolli notes, "Pierre Renoir, it is clear, faces a far more taxing bargain. We really do know that he is not Louis XVI and never quite will be. Something undecidable floats around him, a blur in the image, a duplication: there is a ghost in his body" (Comolli 1978, 47). It is precisely this "blur" or "ghostly presence," however, which can help us grasp the complex process of representation as a "three-place operator," as Ankersmit described it above.[7] This "body too much" creates enough discrepancy between what appears on film (*the presented*) and what it represents (a version of Louis XVI) that we begin to take notice of representation's dual dimension. Whereas in most history books, we need to struggle to conceive the "presented" and the "represented reality" separately, in historical fiction films this nuanced distinction becomes exaggerated and overstressed. Historical films, in a way, resemble the caricatures[8] that Ankersmit frequently employs as examples for illustrating how the grossly exaggerated nature of a "presented" may nonetheless represent accurately the portrayed object (Ankersmit 2012, 71–98). Of course, any discussion of the sketch or the caricature as a realistic representation takes us back to the debate of the digital and realism, which we presented in chapter two as part of the problem of medium specificity. There, we drew a parallel between analog cinema/written history, on the one hand, and digital cinema/filmic history, on the other, in an effort to capitalize on the conceptual power of the analog/digital binary as metaphor. This metaphor invited us to think of written and filmic history in terms of their materiality, their forms and practices, their ontological status, and their trends in realism. After meticulous scrutiny, we argued that representation is always a code that seeks to simulate presence where only absence exists. The presence can be filled with celluloid, words, or pixels but, in all cases, what we have is the simulation of presence. The operation of simulation is obvious in the case of the digital, just as the process of fabrication and invention are obvious in the case of filmic history. However, instead of condemning the digital or history on film as ontologically "less real," we emphasized how these new categories allow us to grasp better and to identify with more insight all those representational processes under way in earlier modes, such as analog film or written history.

What this investigation also brought to the surface is the constant struggle of most representations to come across as plausible, truthful, and realistic. Realism has had a long pedigree in the history of cinema and even longer, admittedly, in the history of historiography, as White's analysis plainly demonstrated in *Metahistory*. Realism viewed as a corruptible set of conventions that relates to socially and culturally determined notions of verisimilitude and truth always points outwards, i.e., toward all those extra-textual forces that shape Foucault's "regimes of truth."[9] When we leave the realm of historical representation, whether on paper or on film, we need to address all those institutional parameters that determine the production and dissemination of truth in a given society. In that domain, too, filmic history functions as a magnified miniature that allows us to observe all those non-discursive parameters that regulate the workings of historical knowledge and power. As I argued in chapter 3, the historical work always needs to be embedded in its institutional framework, while it also needs to be examined with the help of the "historicized" concepts of art, science, and philosophy whose meanings and practices shift through the ages. There, what Foucault's work allowed us to realize is that any discussion of the historical discourse is bound to be related to non-discursive practices that form a formidable ensemble of forces. Here, I would like to introduce another Foucauldian concept that describes this ensemble, and is none other than the "apparatus" (dispositif). In his latest writings, Foucault offered a tentative definition of the apparatus, as follows:

> What I'm trying to pick out with this term is, firstly, a thoroughly heterogenous ensemble consisting of discourses, institutions, architectural forms, regulatory decisions, laws, administrative measures, scientific statements, philosophical, moral and philanthropic propositions—in short, the said as much as the unsaid. Such are the elements of the apparatus. The apparatus itself is the system of relations that can be established between these elements.
>
> Foucault 1980, 194

The apparatus is a useful addition to the Foucauldian vocabulary, as it organizes Foucault's thoughts around the discursive, the non-discursive, and the power/knowledge binary,[10] which are all essential to any discussion about history.[11] Evidently, written history as discipline and filmic history as popular entertainment constitute two distinct but often interconnected apparatuses,[12] which respond to certain needs. As Foucault notes about any apparatus, it is a "formation which has as its major function at a given historical moment that of responding to an *urgent need*" (195; emphasis in the original). In this light, the emergence of academic history in the nineteenth century and cinematic history in the twentieth indicate a shifting of needs, which were going to be met by different mechanisms. Remember how we discussed the institutional changes in chapter 3 in terms of what Lukacs described as the "devolution" of historical academicism and the "evolution" of the historical appetite in popular culture (Lukacs 2011). The crisis in the historical profession and the boom of historical films throughout the twentieth century are developments pointing to broader epistemic changes, which will be addressed further on. What interests me here is to underline the descriptive strength of the magnified miniature metaphor not only at the textual/discursive level but also the non-discursive. As an apparatus, filmic history relies on an ensemble of forces that resemble and often imbricate those of professional history. The main differentiating factor, however, is that the non-discursive mechanisms of filmic history play out their powers in the open. In other words, the majority of the forces that regulate the production and dissemination of historical moving images enter the public sphere and the public eye in ways which were never possible for academic history. The role of authorship, erudition, archival work, production values, distribution, exhibition, reception, ideology, and subjectivity— to name some key parameters—have become standard topics in newspapers, journals, TV programs, and academic scholarship, with each outlet constantly exploring, debating and criticizing historical films not only for their representations but also for the conditions of their production and circulation as well as their effects. We take it for granted that we will discuss—and possibly disagree—about whether Oliver Stone is a historian or not, or if a production company has vested interests in the making of this or that historical epic, or if a historical drama promotes this or that ideology, or if viewers are hailed as national subjects or as consumers. The same scrutiny, however, is not feasible for the apparatus of academic history. The personal preferences and inclinations of the historian, the practical limitations of the archives, the access to historical sources, the inconsistencies of the historical method, the pressures of the faculty, the ideological orientations of each department, the constraints of the university presses, or the national identity-building of the readership are all part of an apparatus that determines the power/knowledge of historical thought. This means that the knowledge contained in a historical book draws its power from a very specific epistemic context that renders this knowledge intelligible and authoritative. And yet, none of the forces in this context are prone to wide skepticism or come openly into question by the academic community or the public. It is once again, the magnifying glass of cinematic history, which allows us to observe, despite its warped viewpoint, the complexity of an apparatus that deals with history and the multiplicity of agencies at work in the effort to produce knowledge and power through historical representation. Whereas the apparatus of academic history reinforces its legitimacy and its privilege to historical truth by downplaying and even eliminating the traces of its non-discursive practices, its cinematic counterpart thrives on controversy and public power struggles. Take *Schindler's List* or *JFK*, for example. There have been long and laborious debates about Spielberg and Stone's personal stakes in these historical portraits, about their relations to official documents and sources as well as their extraordinary effects on people's perception of the Holocaust and the Kennedy assassination respectively. Their textual and extratextual features have been scrutinized and have been taken apart in an effort to unravel the forces that shaped not only their narratives but also the second life these works took on well after their screenings. Evidently, the apparatus of filmic history factors in as a measure of success not only the plausibility and the truthfulness of the representations but also the possible incongruities and disagreements that may result from the overall enterprise of cinematic historying. This added self-consciousness of the cinematic apparatus does not really expose the entirety of its processes but it does invest on the problematization of historical knowledge and our access to the historical past. Above all, it requires us to reconsider the mechanisms that regulate what passes as truth in our current age and retrace our thinking when it comes to the role of fiction in our relation to external reality. In plain words, it probes us to ask ourselves again: How does the distinction between fiction and reality function in contemporary society? Can fiction claim a legitimate role as a mediator of truth or is it still considered as a synonym for falseness? How does each apparatus of history, i.e., academic and filmic history, negotiate the presence of fiction in their accounts of the past?

In the case of the cinematic apparatus of history, the distinction fiction/ nonfiction works on several levels. As I noted in chapter four, a filmmaker who aspires to do history in images faces two major generic options, namely to create a historical fiction film or a historical documentary. Each choice entails a distinct production and distribution system, a diverse range of narrative modes, a separate exhibition circuit and, possibly, an entirely different audience. When tagging a film as fiction or documentary, the industry, with the filmmaker's consent, seeks to craft a specific contract within the apparatus, which regulates all phases of production, distribution, exhibition, and consumption. In each of these phases, different rules, regulations, and expectations apply, building a strong institutional barrier between fiction films and documentaries. When it comes to their contents and the interpretative schemata deployed by the viewers, Noël Carroll aptly describes the power of "indexing" a film in one category or the other:

> Indexing a film as a fiction or nonfiction tells us what the film claims to refer to, i.e., the actual world or segments of possible worlds; and indexing tells us the kind of responses and expectations it is legitimate for us to bring to the film. In short, insofar as indexing fixes the attempted reference of a given film, indexing is constitutive of whether the given film is an instance of fiction or nonfiction, which amounts to whether it is to be construed as fiction or nonfiction.
>
> Carroll 1996d, 238

Carroll's distinction between the reference to the "actual world," on the one hand, and "possible worlds" on the other clearly echoes Aristotle's famous distinction between history and poetry.[13] It is a distinction, however, that becomes remarkably tenuous when dealing with the subcategories of the historical fiction film and the historical documentary. In these cases, the already complex and often contested process of reference and representation blatantly illustrates that separating fiction from nonfiction both at the level of narrative and the level of audience expectations is so vexing that it often becomes irrelevant. Even though the distinction fiction/nonfiction remains highly operative at the non-discursive level, regulating and separating fiction filmmaking from documentary practices, when we are left with the historical films themselves, our task to discern fiction from nonfiction becomes a problem. Filmic history, whether in the genre of fiction or documentary, is a breed that resists the established categories and divisions, both from the side of cinema and from the side of professional history. For if historical documentaries were able to successfully portray the historical past, as Carroll's indexing would suggest, then trained historians would not hesitate to include documentarians in their ranks. Evidently, this is hardly the case. Along the same lines, if a historical fiction, like *Schindler's List*, were only referencing "possible worlds" and not the actual past, then its ties to Oskar Schindler, Amon Göth, the concentration camps, and the Holocaust would be entirely fake. This is hardly the case either. What both historical fictions and documentaries have in common is that they direct our attention to the binary fiction/nonfiction in an unprecedentedly self-conscious manner, playing out in the open the ambiguities and discrepancies entailed in any attempt to approach reality, past or present. They are both confronted with the same paradox, namely that fiction always stands in the way of reference and vice versa. This is why in this book on historical representation in the cinema I felt compelled to address both cinematic traditions and pay attention to their formal particularities. For any discussion on historiophoty is bound to be incomplete, unless it includes both fictions and documentaries, as two distinct genres sharing, nonetheless, the same underlying epistemological concerns.

When we turn to the apparatus of written history, however, the distinction between fiction and nonfiction is definitive and absolute.[14] Academic history, as a distinct discipline that developed in the nineteenth century, is premised on the idea of objectively knowing what *really* happened. In his analysis of the historical profession, Alun Munslow distinguishes between three threads of historical thought: the Reconstructionist, the Constructionist and the Deconstructionist (Munslow 2001; 2006). The first two kinds include the vast majority of practicing historians who are dedicated to the principles of empiricism[15] and are guided by the ambition to discover *the truth* about the past. According to their rationale, the past once existed as an integral entity and the historian is able to recover it through the laborious and objective study of evidence. In Geoffrey Elton's words:

> For the historian the reality—yes, the truth—of the past exists in materials of various kinds, produced by that past at the time that it occurred and left behind by its testimony. Historical evidence is not created by the historian, and little of it was deliberately created for him; it is simply that deposit of past happenings that still exist to be looked at.
>
> Elton 1991, 52

Despite various conceptual differences,[16] Reconstructionist and Constructionist historians share the fundamental belief in the unequivocal ontological status of the past—it really did exist—as well as their unwavering trust in the historian's ability to retrieve it. As Munslow observes, "The distinction between history and fiction resides in the professionalism of the historian as much as in the constraint to recount what actually happened rather than invent it" (Munslow 2001, 43). In fact, the apparatus of history can only function to the extent that this abstract pact between professionalism and objectivity is in place. The edifice of academic scholarship can only produce power/knowledge, in Foucault's terms, only if history is viewed as entirely separated from fiction. Unlike all forms of filmic history, which take fiction and nonfiction as coexisting elements in various degrees, academic history postulates history and fiction as mutually exclusive.

A breach of this pact was committed by those historians and philosophers of history who, increasingly since the 1960s, questioned all the fundamental tenets of professional historiography, forming a third pole of historical thought called Deconstructionist. Roland Barthes, Hayden White, and Michel Foucault, whose writings figured prominently in this study, are clearly cases of Deconstructionist thinking, constantly pointing out the limitations of empiricist epistemology and challenging the clear-cut divisions between history and literature (White and Barthes) or truth and fiction (Foucault). As we have seen so far, these scholars focused on concepts such as narrative, discourse, and truth to indicate the opacity of language, the deadlocks of the correspondence theory of truth, and the power of invention in historical writing. When Foucault admits, "I'm well aware I have not written anything but fictions, which is not to say they have nothing to do with the truth," he blatantly entertains the skepticism toward the core values of academic historiography (cited in Flynn 2005, 45). The absolute separation of history and fiction within academia is viewed by Keith Jenkins, another prominent deconstructionist, as ideologically complicit. The stubborn adherence of professional historians to empiricism[17] allows the apparatus and its hidden ideological mechanisms to self-perpetuate. As he puts it:

> For the past, if it is to help ensure the reproduction of the status quo within acceptable limits (within those famous "liberal tolerances") cannot be totally open so as to allow innumerable inheritances, abnormal genealogies, interminable idiosyncratic figurings and refigurings and "lessons" to suit all and every occasion— this is far too risky.
>
> Jenkins 2003, 17–18

Even though deconstructionists view the rigidity of the academic discipline from different ideological perspectives and they envision different futures for the role of historical thinking in our society, they all agree that nineteenth-century historiography promised the world an impossible task. Of them all, nobody stresses the idea of failure more than Jenkins in his book *Refiguring History* (2003) from which I extracted the passage above.[18] "Failure" is an important notion that Jenkins emphasizes when it comes to the representation of the past from an idealist perspective. He does not view failure as disillusionment nor as a reason to abandon historical activity. Rather, he invites the "old discipline" to "gratefully accept and celebrate" the inevitable failures of historical representation instead of trying to overcome them (3). His mission statement is the following:

> To try to work the discourse of history in the direction of radical, open-ended democracy that grasps the impossibility of enacting a total historical/historicizing closure of the past whilst recognizing that its refigured ways of figuring things out 'will never have been good enough' – and that this is the most desirable thing.
>
> Jenkins 2003, 5

What the "refigured ways of figuring things out" implies is that historical writing is a type of discourse that cannot be grounded on the traditional opposition between fact and fiction, and that its purposes can never be settled once and for all. Historians are bound to produce failed representations of the past whose failure is not something to be denied but valorized (25). In this light, failure, which is written into the very idea of history, becomes a quality that we should seek to explore with an open mind and creativity. History as failed representation may ask us to relinquish our standard expectations, nurtured by the apparatus of academic history, but it would never ask us to stop making meaning out of the past. History as failed representation simply factors in the limitations of representation into the equation of our metaphysical and cognitive pursuits in an effort to metamorphose them into creative possibilities instead of crippling handicaps.

This novel approach to historical thinking is also hinted at by Ankersmit in his discussion of the affinities between history and psychoanalysis. Ankersmit observes that most professional historians collect evidence in order to reveal a historical reality lying hidden somewhere and awaiting discovery. However, the past is neither ontologically constituted like that nor is it epistemologically accessed that way. It is something that one can explore in the manner that a psychoanalyst seeks to explore the human mind.[19] As he explains:

> Both the psychoanalyst and the historian try to project a pattern *onto* the traces and do not search for something *behind* the traces. In both cases, the activity of interpretations is understood strictly nominalistically: there is nothing in historical reality or in the mind of the neurotic that corresponds with the content of interpretations.
>
> Ankersmit 1994, 173; emphasis in the original

From this perspective, history and psychoanalysis generate a repertory of interpretations using sources and testimonies as stones of a mosaic, with which one can compose a variety of patterns. The ensuing fluidity of the interpretations cancels out the possibility of discovering one true essence of the past (or the psyche) but welcomes openness and creativity. In addition, Ankersmit embraces another common element in these two practices, namely the role and significance of what Freud calls the "*Fehlleistung*," i.e., the slip in speech, memory or action. In Ankermit's words, "It is apparent randomness, the slips of the tongue, the *Fehlleistungen* of the past, the rare moments when the past 'let itself go,' where we discover what is really of importance for us" (174; emphasis in the original). *Fehlleistung*, or parapraxis, as is more commonly called in English, is an intriguing concept that emphasizes once again the importance of failure. It describes all those moments when a person fails to perform as expected, revealing nonetheless crucial information about themselves. In the case of history, according to Ankersmit, professional researchers should seek to learn not only from what the evidence overtly states but also from what it often inadvertently discloses in moments of lapse or breakdown. This second, more focused, application of failure in the historical method equally undermines the primacy of realistic representation, introducing a different logic and a fresh way of looking at the fragments of the past.

For all their insights and their persistent criticism of Reconstructionist and Constructionist historiography, however, the works of Jenkins and Ankersmit remain impressively ineffective for the standard practitioners of historical writing to this date. The questioning of the mechanisms of the apparatus of academic history is carried out only with great difficulty within the discipline. Historical representation on paper is still considered à priori as a trustworthy, truthful and accurate account of things past. Filmic representations, however, were right from the start viewed as creative mediations. When cinema emerged at the end of the nineteenth century, its technology may have been related to various practices, such as war, optics, or medicine,[20] but it was art that made the highest bid. The fact that audience and scholars alike approached the moving images, from the onset, more as paintings than microscopes—much to Jean-Luc Godard's chagrin, as we saw in chapter one—set up expectations that were related to art rather than science. The two key questions that have preoccupied film scholars to this date pertain to the status of cinema as art and its relation to physical reality. No matter how scholars have answered these questions through the passage of time, cinema's ontological status would never be viewed as akin to that of science. Even theorists like Siegfried Kracauer and André Bazin, who primarily promoted cinema as a modality of the real, would never expunge the role of fiction and invention from the cinematic discourse. As a result, the ideas and arguments that developed vis-à-vis the possibilities of representation on film, both for the genre of fiction and nonfiction, would dwell on a complex approach toward the role of imagination that could not easily maintain a solid and absolute separation of fact from fiction. In fact, the degree of scrutiny and the length of the discussions regarding the ontology of cinema throughout the twentieth century indicate that film scholars had to work from the start with an unprecedented degree of self-knowingness. Whereas thinkers on written discourse may continue, even today, to take the relation between words and the world as direct and unproblematic, film theorists were—luckily, I may say—not treated to such a luxury. Even though images, just like words, have consistently sought to represent reality, their ways of doing so were not viewed just as natural and straightforward. If we would like to take advantage of the heuristic strength of White's four tropes, discussed in chapter three, we could argue that representation in the cinema is always already ironic, openly repurposing the means of metaphor, metonymy, and synecdoche in order to approximate the real world. In cinema, distinctions such as truth/falseness and reality/illusion were systematically explored both stylistically and thematically in cinematic theory and practice from the very beginning, despite the prevalence of narrative realism, which crystallized in the classical Hollywood cinema from 1917 onwards.[21] The advent of digital technology made all these initial characteristics even more prominent. As we saw in chapter two, the passage from analog celluloid to digital pixels may have initially caused serious concerns regarding the loss of the real but the careful investigation of the technical, formal, and semiological properties of these modalities revealed substantial continuities. The digital did not cause us to lose reality but it helped us, instead, realize even further our multifariously mediated access to it. As a whole, the "ironic status" of the cinematic image, whether analog or digital, is precisely what renders it exceptionally hospitable to philosophical concepts and arguments. Its visual and aural parameters allow it to play in a metaphorical, metonymic or synecdochic manner even with the most opaque philosophical ideas. Here, it is worth quoting at length Thomas Elsaesser who summarizes below the ways in which cinema has been theorized through key philosophical issues:

> Film theory over the last 50 years has answered them with a long list of metaphors: reality as God had intended to reveal it (Bazin), a natural language without a language system (Metz), the very logic of our subjectivity (Baudry, Heath via Lacan-Althusser), the tragic destiny of gendered identity (Mulvey), the nature of human consciousness (Michelson), the unsymbolizable real (Žižek), the figural (Lyotard), the body, the senses, touch and skin, the death drive, affect, attraction, time, the brain, the perceptual modeling of our hard-wired cognitivist schemata and so on.
>
> Elsaesser 2008b, 239

What is conspicuously absent from this fairly comprehensive list is indeed the relation of cinema with historiography. Kracauer, in *History: The Last Things before the Last*, was the first one to systematically explore the affinities of the cinematic medium with the historical practice, but he is hardly remembered for it. Yet even there, as we saw in great detail in chapter one, Kracauer's argument did not relate historical representation on film with history on paper; in fact, he categorically rejected the idea of the historical fiction film. To him it was a failure. What this book has sought to do, chapter after chapter, is to look closely at this failure and see what it can show us. The magnified miniature, the metaphor I have opted for, emphasizes precisely the failure, the distortion, the discrepancies between the representation and the real world. The filmic representation of history is a particular type of representation that magnifies not only the properties of the medium but also those of its content, giving us the opportunity to observe up-close the mechanisms of cinema and history at the same time. Thus, if Kracauer had wanted to understand the photographic images better, then he should have, perhaps, taken the historical film a lot more seriously. He should have looked beyond failure, noticing all those elements that failures successfully expose. Indeed, the failures of historical films bring forward the very process of historical thinking and historical storytelling, perfectly exemplifying what Godard wanted to show with *Histoire(s) du Cinéma*. As I noted in chapter 1, Godard was the first to envision an audiovisual historiography, which would capitalize on the possibility of error and the mixture of fact and fiction. The double inscription of his film's title aimed at capturing something that ordinary language fails to do, namely allowing fact and fiction to coexist in the same space. Against Godard's better judgment, however, it is not only films like his own, which are capable of resurrecting the past and performing the Orphean myth. It is every film that portrays a historical situation and tells a story about the past in its own failed way. Admittedly, historical cinema is not the only artifact that can be interpreted as an instance of the myth of Orpheus and Eurydice. Roland Barthes has employed it extensively in his discussion of literature (Barthes 1970). It is the one, however, which performs Orpheus' failure most spectacularly. And in the course of this celebrated and spectacular failure, history on film, thanks to—and not despite of—its magnifying distortions, gives us the opportunity to observe closely all those processes at work in any historical activity and, particularly, the professional historical writing.

Filmmakers and their collaborators were the first to realize how much they had in common with trained historians, as David Eldridge underlines in his study[22] (2006, 197). For the viewers and theorists of historical films, however, the shortcomings of the cinematic accounts have had blinding effects, instead. Misguided by the ideological mechanisms of the apparatus of academic history and its sanctioned privilege to historical truth, commentators were bound to judge history on film according to the criteria and the standards of empirical epistemology. In this light, the prominence of fiction and narration in filmic representation amounted to a profoundly flawed and distorting characteristic of the cinematic medium. This is why the weight of the debate on historical cinema fell on issues of medium specificity. Compared to the moving images, words were unequivocally considered more reliable vehicles for historical thinking. Of course, deconstructionist thinkers changed all that. The contributions of Foucault, White, Barthes, Ankersmit, and Jenkins, to name only those who were presented in some detail here,[23] questioned the mechanisms of language as a natural representation of the world around us, and by extension, as the innocent and transparent instrument for historians. By pointing out the failure of historical writing to meet the aspired empirical and positivist standards of the discipline, they allowed us to discern how the failures of history on film relate to those on paper.

Apart from the general notion of failure in Jenkins' sense, i.e., the failure to represent the past according to the correspondence theory of truth, historical films also allow us to observe Ankersmit's more nuanced take on the historical method, namely the importance of "parapraxis" for understanding the past. For this unusual representational and interpretative technique, we are indebted to Elsaesser's latest work on the representation of terror and trauma (Elsaesser 2008a; 2013). While studying the films of the New German Cinema in the 1960s and 1970s, Elsaesser noticed that a whole generation of German filmmakers had a tough question to face regarding the treatment of Jews in their stories. As he notes:

> So the question to be put to the directors of the New German Cinema would therefore have to be: how to show what is not there, especially if its not-being-there is not missed? In other words, how can the cinema show this missing as missing, how can it "perform" this double missing, and come to terms with it? The issue becomes one of representation itself.
>
> Elsaesser 2008a, 108

This exceptional predicament in the representation of Jews is explicated by Elsaesser with the help of Freud's *Fehlleistung* used as the basis of a complicated argument on representation that extends to the Holocaust, other traumatic events, history, and ultimately reality. But let us unpack this a little.

Like Ankersmit, Elsaesser, first, notices how the Freudian slip is a concept that underlines the value of error and the power of breaking expectations. When a person has a momentary lapse in speech or in action, it affects both their performance as well as our assumptions about it. From this initial significance he moves on to the etymology of the German word *Fehlleistung*, seeking to unearth further meaning. Thus, he breaks it into its two components, namely "*Fehl*" meaning failure and "*Leistung*" meaning performance, arguing that we can translate it either as a "failed performance" or as a "performance of failure." The former amounts to what he calls "the politics of parapraxis," entailing the public events or occasions, such as official speeches and anniversaries, when public figures fail to perform as expected. This failure is not attributed to mere chance or incompetence but also points to unresolved and deeply conflicted aspects of history and identity. The latter is what concerns the films themselves and it is called "the poetics of parapraxis," which tries to resolve the problem of the unrepresentability of the Holocaust. Failed performances are, in fact, precisely those moments that a historian who follows Ankersmit's advice would find most fascinating. They reveal the fissures in the official narratives of the past and the impossibility of ever fully coming to terms with it. The performances of failure, on the other hand, interest historians, film scholars, and the audience alike, as they watch the films' failed attempts to handle traumatic events with the desired sense of finality and closure. Clearly, the weight of Elsaesser's work falls on the poetics of parapraxis and so is my own here. Thus, I would like to explicate it further and see how it may help us relate this specific case of representation to the wider issue of historical representation.

In Elsaesser's account, parapraxis is presented as a double-sided and self-divided concept, which plays around certain key antitheses, such as active/passive, language/embodiment, intention/contingency, past/present, and other/self, and opens us to multiple interpretations at varying historical junctures. A parapractic film chooses to tackle the impossibility of representation and the excess of information or emotion in ways that resist closure, symmetry, or balance, bringing forward poetic elements that suggest miscommunications, reversals, causal gaps, unanticipated consequences and deferred action. The notion of failure ingrained in *Fehlleistung* is often instantiated through the suspension of the normal codes or conventions of representation or the deployment of figurative tropes, such as *catachresis* or *zeugma*, to indicate a double purpose (Elsaesser 2013, 104–6). At this level of generality, parapraxis is constituted as a very specific representational technique, which surfaces in rather rare moments and is often at odds with other narrative elements, such as classical realism or melodrama. Elsaesser, however, is tempted to take this idea a step—or even several steps—further when he argues:

> [...], the term's usefulness and viability in historical contexts other than the Holocaust and Germany's "mastering the past" may clarify the question with which I began, namely whether there is something inherently parapractic in the cinema itself that finds in traumatic situations the objective correlative of its own functioning as a recording and a reproduction apparatus, when capturing the unique moment and replaying it forever: two modalities out of sync with each other, and yet the recto and verso of cinema.
>
> Elsaesser 2013, 110

The key, of course, in this passage is the phrase "inherently parapractic in the cinema," which transforms parapraxis from a representational device to an aspect that permeates the entire practice of the cinematic medium. I am careful to say "practice" and not "essence" or "nature," avoiding the pitfalls of the word "inherently" and taking into account that Elsaesser would be the last one to cling to ideas of medium specificity.[24] Also, this entire book would have been written in vain, if we were to return to the idea that cinema has its own unique way of dealing with history. What Elsaesser's work on parapraxis, both at the specific and the philosophically broader sense,[25] shows, however, is that historical cinema, unlike written history, has a way of openly confronting and exploiting the failure of representation. Historical films become "successful performances of failure" not only because they trigger unintended consequences or deal with the problem of too much/too little information, as Elsaesser would argue, but also because they fulfill Freud's initial requirement of the Freudian slip, namely its interpersonal dimension. In other words, a Freudian slip is only considered as such, if the failure is perceived by somebody else, generating a sense of awkwardness or incongruity. As Elsaesser explains, "*parapraxis* as an interpersonal phenomenon thus becomes an enabler of dialogue, even in a potentially antagonistic situation, and even in the face of disavowal, while allowing for contingency and chance: all, however, in the mode of 'failure' and 'performance'" (ibid.). Historical films can be considered parapractic in their entirety, or inherently parapractic if you may, precisely because they are bound to fail and everybody is going take notice. Every image, every dialogue, every character, every action is going to be measured against our expectations to see "things as they *really* were" and they are always going to be found wanting. Even when the filmmakers have put their most painstaking efforts to "get things right," the result will always be viewed with suspicion, knowing that it is merely a reconstruction, which cannot possibly amount to the things of the past. This added self-knowingness of the cinematic medium is what shapes the expectations of all creators and spectators alike, pushing them to anticipate from historical films not their "success" but their "successful performance of failure."

Throughout the twentieth century and well into the twenty-first, historical films have been consistently "performing failure," gradually shifting our notions regarding the form of the historical work, the definition of historical truth, and the value of historical imagination. We have come a very long way from the wholesale rejection of the historical fiction film to our present moment, when traditional historians not only acknowledge the contribution of cinematic historying but are even willing to hand over the baton to filmmakers for preserving the past. Notice the reaction of a classic historian, Andrew Roberts, to Nolan's *Dunkirk*, which became an instant hit with audience and critics, too. As a Reconstructionist professional, he clearly investigates the film for its precision to technical details of this major historical event as well as its depiction of the balance of power among the counties that were involved. In his evaluation, of course, he assumes that he *really* knows all the correct details and his own account of the event is not only truthful but also complete. There cannot have been anything that he missed out, anything that may have remained unknown to historians, and anything that may be explained otherwise. In a nutshell, Roberts' commentary on Nolan's filmic representation is the embodiment of the principles of the nineteenth century academic historiography, as we have explicated them so far. What changes, however, is this. After playing Everett's Game[26] and lamenting the various historical inaccuracies of the film, he writes the following:

> It is a shame that Nolan is now propagating them—especially since this might be the only contact that millions of people will ever have with the Dunkirk story for years, perhaps even a generation. At a time when schools simply do not teach the histories of anything so patriotism-inducing as Dunkirk, it was incumbent on Nolan to get this right. [...] So despite my annoyance at how many little details are off here—for example, Tom Hardy firing 75 seconds' worth of ammunition when he would really have only had 14.7, or choppy weather when the Channel was really like a mill pond—I must confess that such problems are only for military history pedants like me. What Nolan has gotten right is the superb spirit of the British people in overcoming hatred, resentment, and fury with calmness, courage, and good humor.
>
> Roberts 2017

This passage is interesting on several counts. First of all, Roberts celebrates *Dunkirk* as a "successful failure." Not as a "successful performance of failure" but as a plain "successful failure." What is the difference? The difference is that

Roberts still clings to the Reconstructionist ideal, according to which a written historical account is a success, i.e., a complete and truthful rendering of the historical past. The film, weighed against this ideal, cannot but be a "failure," albeit a successful one, to the extent that it captures the general spirit of the situation. What is more interesting, however, is that Roberts finds the strength to overcome his disappointment at cinema's failure and resign to the fact that filmic history has undertaken a task previously reserved only to him and his fellow -historians. In fact, he does not hesitate to acknowledge the superiority of the historical film in the contemporary age, given the power/knowledge it is capable of producing over an entire generation of people. At the same time, however, he claims the right to his self-importance. He implies that "military pedants" like him may continue to be relevant in their pursuit of accuracy and precision, but the very degrading of "traditional historians" to "pedants" indicates a considerable shift of power in the handling of historical truth and meaning.

This small example is indicative of the greater changes in the "regime of truth" in our current age, which we have been addressing all along in this book at various stages. Foucault's approach to truth, history, and knowledge helped us, in chapters 2, 3, and 4, to position the problem of historiophoty within a very broad framework of epistemic changes and it allowed us to compare it to academic historiography without the prejudices of traditional epistemology. Our repositioning of filmic history as a "successful performance of failure" points to a new phase of historiography in the twentieth century, which forms a complicated relation to its predecessor, i.e., the professional history of the previous century. Filmic history does not reject the formal, argumentative, and ideological devices of written historical works, as we saw in great detail in chapters 5 and 6. All the historical explanations that White had traced in written histories can be found in the audiovisual works as well. In fact, they can be found a lot more easily, as films tend to exaggerate, condense, and often oversimplify their representational techniques, recasting in an ironic mode all those mechanisms that previously remained latent. This ironic distance of historiophoty in relation to the modernist principles of academic historiography, however, indicates a distinct epistemic logic. Whereas written history presents formal, argumentative and ideological explanations in the effort to definitively tell us "the truth" about the past, the filmic history puts forward the same explanations in the effort to give us "a truth" about the past. And this is why fiction is not a problem for the cinema. For the successful performance of failure, the role of imagination is not incompatible with that of truth.

At the same time, however, filmic history should not be viewed as a return to the mythmaking of oral traditions or the pre-modern historical romances, which fused fact and fiction indiscriminately. History on film works, as we have seen, in close dialogue with the achievements and the principles of professional historiography, which provide a point of constant reference and comparison as well as a point of critique. The wealth of historical knowledge as well as the historical theories that developed throughout the nineteenth century are not lost; they are merely reworked—or retrofitted, as Elsaesser would put it—to serve a new logic. No historical reality is thus abandoned nor our incessant need to make meaning out of the past is jeopardized. We are simply more aware of the limits of our representational capacity and more skeptical as to the universality of ideals, such as truth. The clear dichotomies between truth and error, as well as between history and myth, on which the entire tradition of academic history is premised, give way to a historical mode that allows history's three key dimensions, the scientific, the artistic, and the philosophical, to play out their vices and virtues in the open. The broader implications of filmic history's new logic are hard to determine and they certainly exceed the scope of this book. For instance, will the impact of cinematic representations gradually marginalize the practice of academic history? If historians continue to be regarded merely as pedants, then university funding as well as history teaching in education may continue its downward spiraling and come to a grinding halt. Or even if historians do carry on, will they be forced to reconsider the ways they conduct and present their research? Already, debates have sparkled regarding the differences between analog and digital archives, mirroring those that troubled film theorists when the digital technology entered the filmmaking process (Dougherty and Nawrotzki 2013).

At any rate, the developments in historiophoty and historiography in the years to come will have a central place in the wider political and philosophical debates regarding the meaning of truth, knowledge, power, and subjectivity in our Western societies. Just as history developed in the nineteenth century as the cornerstone of the Modern Age and its epistemic principles, to remember Foucault once again, history in images is bound to play an equally decisive—and possibly divisive—role in the twenty-first, shaping our ways of being in and knowing about our world. It is unfortunate that Foucault is no longer around to develop more insights regarding our contemporary age,[27] or add more sides to his "polyhedron of intelligibility."[28] Evidently, he would be most fit to explore the idea of "post-truth," another term that has become popular nowadays. At any rate, I cannot help finding it rather ironic that historical representation in the cinema has reached such an apogee of power, shaping so powerfully our relation with the past. From a marginal and disrespectable genre in Kracauer's eyes, historical fictions and documentaries have become prevailing and invaluable vehicles for historical thinking.[29] This is attested by the critical appraise and their tremendous popularity with a vast and ever-expanding audience. Hopefully, what my book will achieve is to show that these historical representations are invaluable for our historiographical and philosophical explorations. By performing failure so successfully, history on film confronts us with the difficulty of matching our words and images to the historical past, bringing out the forces of imagination and fabrication entailed in this process. In other words, historical films are not only important artifacts that make-up our contemporary mythologies. This was Warren Susman's suggestion with which I opened this book. He reminded us of Vico's appreciation of language, mythologies, and antiquities as valuable sources of historical knowledge. What I suggest, instead, is that historical films should be studied and respected for all the ways they prove to us Vico's other famous idea,[30] namely that the true is something we make.

Notes

1 The metaphor of the "magnified miniature" was inspired by another metaphor, namely the metaphor of the digital that I discussed extensively in chapter 2.

2 As Alun Munslow notes, "Despite the Whitean Revolution, most historians continue to neglect the concept and functioning of discourse—the telling of the story. This could be regarded as surprising given that the content of the past cannot tell itself" (Munslow 2010, 151; emphasis in the original).

3 Jack Hexter meticulously illustrates how the presentation of data in graphs or footnotes contributes to the rhetoric of historical writing (Hexter 1971a).

4 For a nuanced definition of the term "aspect," see Ankermit (2012, 68–73).

5 To restore a certain connection with external reality, Ankersmit introduces the term "aboutness" instead of "reference" (2012, 79–81).

6 The same argument can be easily extended to historical documentaries.

7 In fact, Ankersmit employs a similar phrasing when he describes the process of representation as follows, "Each representation, then, carries its own represented or aspect along with itself-much in the way we are accompanied by our shadow on a sunny day—and each of these represented is indissolubly linked to one, and only one, particular representation corresponding to it" (2012, 72).

8   As Ankersmit notes, "Think of caricatures. In caricatures, aspects of a person's physical appearance are grossly exaggerated according to the representational insight that the caricaturist wishes to convey. And even though demonstrable distortions arise at the level of truth, the caricature, or the distorted portrait, may nevertheless sometimes give us a better image of or a more profound insight into somebody's personality than a photo, or what we would call a good likeness" (2012, 98).

9   See end of chapter 2 and chapter 3.

10 For the dynamic relation of knowledge and power and their connection to the concept of truth, see Foucault (1991a). For secondary literature on Foucault's binary concept of power/knowledge, see Rouse (2005) and Mills (2003, 67–79).

11 Foucault did not particularly discuss history as an apparatus in the way that he specifically discussed prisons, hospitals, or juridical systems as State apparatuses but the application of the term to the discipline of history is possible even without Giorgio Agamben extension of the term in *What is an Apparatus?* (Agamben 2009, 14).

12 My approach to filmic history as an apparatus is distinct from the well-known apparatus theory in film studies developed in the 1970s. A strictly Foucauldian application of the term "apparatus" is incompatible with the Freudian or the Marxist framework that governed the deployment of the term in film theory. See the "Apparatus Theory (Baudry)" entry in *The Routledge Encyclopedia of Film Theory* edited by Branigan & Buckland (2013, 14–20).

13 In Aristotle's words: "From what we have said it will be seen that the poet's function is to describe, not the thing that happened, but a kind of thing that might happen, i.e. what is possible as being probable or necessary. The distinction between historian and poet is not in the one writing prose and the other verse-you might put the work of Herodotus into verse, and it would still be a species of history; it consists really in this, that the one describes the thing that has been, and the other a kind of thing that might be. Hence poetry is something more philosophic and of graver import than history, since its statements are of the nature rather of universals, whereas those of history are singulars" (cited in Kelley 1991, 62).

14 It has not always been the case. See a brief overview of the history of historiography in chapter three.

15 The six principles of empiricism mentioned in Munslow's account are the following: first, the past (like the present) is real and "truth" corresponds to that reality through the mechanism of referentiality and inference—the discovery of facts in the evidence. Second, for Reconstructionists, facts normally precede interpretation, although Constructionists argue that inductive reasoning cannot operate independently of the deduction of generalized explanations. Third, there is a clear division between fact and value. Fourth, history and fiction are not the same. Fifth, there is a division between the knower and that which is known. Sixth, truth is not perspectival (Munslow 2001, 38).

16 In fact, the key difference between Reconstructionists and Constructionists is the latter's deployment of concepts and models of explanations, such as race, gender, class to describe and explain historical reality. Whereas the former are pure Formists, in Hayden White's terms, who purportedly describe historical events in their uniqueness, the latter tend to be of the Organicist or even the Mechanistic kind, employing general models of explanations to approximate historical reality.

17 As he puts it, "Most professional historians remain stubbornly 'modernist'; that is, they remain intent on producing substantiated, empirically detailed and well-researched accounts in the name of accuracy and balanced, meticulous scholarship" (Jenkins 2003, 15).

18 Another important attempt to deconstruct the historical profession and to reevaluate the notion of "fallacy" in the historians' accounts is found in Peter Charles Hoffer's works (2004; 2008).

19 Ankersmit supports the affinities between psychoanalysis and history employing the arguments of Duby and Lardreau in *Geschichte und Geschichtswissenschaft* (1982).

20 The study of early cinema, combined with the advent of digital technology over the last few decades, led to the approach of film history as media archaeology, indicating several paths that the technology of cinematic production and projection could have but did not take. See Elsaesser (2008b).

21 For classical cinema, see Bordwell et al. (1985). For early cinema, see Elsaesser (1990).

22 See chapters 3 and 4.

23 For a more comprehensive account for the deconstructionist approach, see Munslow (2001; 2006).

24 See chapter 2.

25 It would not be the first time that an insight on the representation of the Holocaust finds wider applicability in the representation of history as a whole. As Robert Rosenstone has noted, "The problem of representing the Holocaust can also be seen as the core problem of history. Can we really represent the past, factually or fictionally, as it was, or do we always present only some version of the way it possibly was or may have been?" (Rosenstone 2006, 135). Even though not all past events are traumatic, it is the traumatic ones which accentuate the key problem of representation, namely to make presence out of absence.

26 See chapter 3.

27 Admittedly, there is a long and rich bibliography on the era of postmodernity, which forms a complicated relation with that of modernity. I have deliberately avoided this term so far, since it often disintegrates in its own fragmented, dispersed and superfluous application to various incongruent phenomena. The Deconstructionist thinkers, such as Ankersmit, Jenkins, and White, which I have discussed extensively, are all related to the ideas of postmodernity, despite the era's tense and irresolvable

contradictions. It is interesting and, I would even say bold, on Robert Rosenstone's behalf to publish his latest book with the title *Adventures of a Postmodern Historian: Living and Writing the Past*, ignoring the backlash against the term "postmodern" over the last couple of decades (Rosenstone 2016).

28 See chapter 3.

29 What is also ironic is that from the perspective of this book, historical cinema becomes inextricably linked to the ideas of postmodernity. This contradicts the dominant approaches that have explored the cinematic medium as a quintessentially modernist artifact. For an overview of these approaches, see Donald (2010).

30 I am referring to Vico's "verum-factum" principle. For a detailed discussion of this concept, see Berlin (1980) and Morrison (1978).

Bibliography

Agamben, Giorgio (2009), *"What is an Apparatus?" and other Essays*, trans. D. Kishik and S. Pedatella, Stanford: Stanford University Press.

Aitken, Ian (2013), *The Concise Routledge Encyclopedia of the Documentary Film*, London: Routledge.

Altman, Rick (1999a), "A semantic/syntactic approach to film genre," in L. Braudy and M. Cohen (eds.), *Film Theory and Criticism: Introductory Readings*, New York: Oxford University Press, 630–41.

Altman, Rick (1999b), *Film/Genre*, London: British Film Institute.

Ankersmit, Frank Rudolf (1983), *Narrative Logic: A Semantic Analysis of the Historian's Language*, Den Haag: Nijhoff.

Ankersmit, Frank Rudolf (1994), *History and Tropology: The Rise and Fall of Metaphor*, Berkeley: University of California Press.

Ankersmit, Frank Rudolf (2012), *Meaning, Truth and Reference in Historical Representation*, Ithaca: Cornell University Press.

Aumont, Jacques (1999), *Amnésies: Fictions du Cinéma d'aprés Jean-Luc Godard*, Paris: Éditions P.O.L.

Barnouw, Dagmar (1994), *Critical Realism: History, Photography, and the Work of Siegfried Kracauer*, Baltimore: John Hopkins University Press.

Barta, Tony (ed.) (1998), *Screening the Past: Film and the Representation of History*, Westport: Greenwood Publishing Group.

Barthes, Roland (1970), *Writing Degree Zero*, trans. A. Lavers and C. Smith, Boston: Beacon Press.

Barthes, Roland (1981a), *Camera Lucida: Reflections on Photography*, trans. R. Howard, New York: Hill and Wang.

Barthes, Roland (1981b), "The Discourse of History," *Comparative Criticism*, 3(1): 7–20.

Barthes, Roland (1986), "The Reality Effect," in Roland Barthes, *The Rustle of Language*, trans. R. Howard, Berkeley: University of California Press, 141–8.

Barthes, Roland (1987), *Michelet*, trans. R. Howard, Berkeley: University of California Press.

Basinger, Jeanine (2003), *The World War II Combat Film: Anatomy of a Genre*, Connecticut: Wesleyan University Press.

Beattie, Keith (2004), *Documentary Screens: Nonfiction Film and Television*, Hampshire: Palgrave Macmillan.

Becker, Carl Lotus (1932), "Everyman His Own Historian," *The American Historical Review*, 37(2): 221–36.

Beckett, Samuel (2010), *The Unnamable*, London: Faber & Faber.

Bentley, Michael (ed.) (2006), *Companion to Historiography*, London: Routledge.

Berkhofer, Robert (1997), "The Challenge of Poetics to (Normal) Historical Practice," in K. Jenkins (ed.), *The Postmodern History Reader*, London: Routledge, 139–57.

Berlin, Isaiah (1960), "History and Theory: The Concept of Scientific History," *History and Theory*, 1(1): 1–31.

Berlin, Isaiah (1980), *Vico and Herder: Two Studies in the History of Ideas*, London: Chatto & Windus.

Bingham, Dennis (2010), *Whose Lives are They Anyway? The Biopic as Contemporary Film Genre*, New Brunswick: Rutgers University Press.

Bird, Robert, Christopher Heuer, Tumelo Mosaka, Stephanie Smith, and Matthew Jackson (eds.) (2011), *Vision and Communism: Viktor Koretsky and Dissident Public Visual Culture*, New York: New Press.

Bolter, Jay David and Richard Grusin (1999), *Remediation: Understanding New Media*, Cambridge: MIT Press.

Bordwell, David (1985), *Narration in the Fiction Film*, Madison: University of Wisconsin Press.

Bordwell, David (1989a), *Making Meaning: Inference and Rhetoric in the Interpretation of Cinema*, Cambridge: Harvard University Press.

Bordwell, David (1989b), "Historical Poetics of Cinema," in Barton Palmer (ed.), *The Cinematic Text: Methods and Approaches*, New York: AMS Press, 369–98.

Bordwell, David (1997), *On the History of Film Style*, Cambridge: Harvard University Press.

Bordwell, David (2006), *The Way Hollywood Tells It: Story and Style in Modern Movies*, Berkeley: University of California Press.

Bordwell, David (2017), "Dunkirk Part 2: The Art Film as Event Movie," David Bordwell's website on cinema. Available at: www.davidbordwell.net/blog/2017/08/09/dunkirk-part-2-the-art-film-as-event-movie/ (accessed October 12, 2017).

Bordwell, David, Janet Staiger, and Kristin Thompson (1985), *The Classical Hollywood Cinema: Film Style and Mode of Production to 1960*, New York: Routledge.

Branigan, Edward (1992), *Narrative Comprehension and Film*, London: Routledge.

Branigan, Edward and Warren Buckland (eds.) (2013), *The Routledge Encyclopedia of Film Theory*, Abingdon: Routledge.

Bruzzi, Stella (2006), *New Documentary: A Critical Introduction*, Abingdon: Routledge.

Burgoyne, Robert (1990), "The Cinematic Narrator: The Logic and Pragmatics of Impersonal Narration," *Journal of Film and Television*, 17(1): 3–16.

Burgoyne, Robert (1991), *Bertolucci's 1900: A Narrative and Historical Analysis*, Detroit: Wayne State University Press.

Burgoyne, Robert (2008), *The Hollywood Historical Film*, Malden: Wiley-Blackwell.

Burgoyne, Robert (ed.) (1997), *Film Nation: Hollywood Looks at U.S. History*, Minneapolis: University of Minnesota Press.

Burgoyne, Robert (ed.) (2011), *The Epic Film in World Culture*, New York: Routledge.

Burnetts, Charles (2016), "Of Basterds and the Greatest Generation: The Limits of Sentimentalism and the Post-classical War Film," *Journal of Film and Video*, 68(2): 3–13.

Carr, Edward Hallett (1987), *What is History?* London: Penguin Books.

Carroll, Noël (1996a), "Medium Specificity Arguments and the Self-consciously Invented Arts: Film, Video, and Photography," in N. Carroll (ed.), *Theorizing the Moving Image*, Cambridge: Cambridge University Press, pp. 3–24.

Carroll, Noël (1996b), "The Specificity of Media in the Arts," in N. Carroll (ed.), *Theorizing the Moving Image*, Cambridge: Cambridge University Press, 25–36.

Carroll, Noël (1996c), "Concerning Uniqueness Claims for Photographic and Cinematographic Representation," in N. Carroll (ed.), *Theorizing the Moving Image*, Cambridge: Cambridge University Press, 37–48.

Carroll, Noël (1996d), "From Real to Reel: Entangled in Non-fiction Film," in N. Carroll (ed.), *Theorizing the Moving Image*, Cambridge: Cambridge University Press, 224–52.

Chaouat, Bruno (2016), *Is Theory Good for the Jews? French Thought and the Challenge of the New Antisemitism*, Liverpool: Liverpool University Press.

Chatman, Seymour (1990), *Coming to Terms: The Rhetoric of Narrative in Fiction and Film*, Ithaca: Cornell University Press.

Collingwood, Robin George (1994), "Lectures on the Philosophy of History," in J. van der Dussen (ed.), *The Idea of History*, Oxford: Oxford University Press, 359–425.

Comolli, Jean-Louis (1978), "Historical Fiction: A Body Too Much," *Screen*, 19(2): 41–53.

Danto, Arthur (2007), *Narration and Knowledge*, New York: Columbia University Press.

Darghis, Manohla (2015), "At the Cannes Film Festival, Some Gems Midway Through," *The New York Times*. Available at: www.nytimes.com/2015/05/21/movies/at-the-cannes-film-festival-some-gems-midway-through.html?ref=movies (accessed September 12, 2017).

Davis, Natalie Zemon (1987), "Any Resemblance to Persons Living or Dead: Film and the Challenge of Authenticity," *The Yale Review*, 76(4): 457–82.

Davis, Natalie Zemon (2000), *Slaves on Screen*, Cambridge: Harvard University Press.

Delage, Christian (2013), *Caught on Camera: Film in the Courtroom from the Nuremberg Trials to the Trials of the Khmer Rouge*, Philadelphia, PA: University of Pennsylvania Press.

Dewey, John (1938), *Logic: The Theory of Inquiry*, New York: Henry Holt and Company.

Dick, Bernard (1985), *The Star-spangled Screen: The American World War II Film*, Kentucky: University Press of Kentucky.

Doherty, Thomas (1993), *Projections of War: Hollywood, American Culture and World War II*, New York: Columbia University Press.

Donadio, Rachel (2015), "In 'Son of Saul', Laszlo Nemes expands the language of Holocaust films," *The New York Times*. Available at: www.nytimes.com/2015/12/15/

movies/in-son-of-saul-laszlo-nemes-expands-the-language-of-holocaust-films.html (accessed September 12, 2017).

Donald, James (2010), "Cinema, Modernism, and Modernity," in Peter Brooker, Andrzej Gasiorek, Deborah Longworth, and Andrew Thacker (eds.), *The Oxford Handbook of Modernisms*, Oxford: Oxford University Press, 503–20.

Dougherty, Jack and Kristen Nawrotzki (eds.) (2013), *Writing History in the Digital Age*, Ann Arbor: University of Michigan Press.

Dray, William (2006), "Philosophy and Historiography," in M. Bentley (ed.), *Companion to Historiography*, London: Routledge, 746–64.

Duby, George and Guy Lardreau (1982), *Geschichte und Geschichtswissenschaft: Dialoge*, Frankfurt: Suhrkamp Verlag AG.

Edidin, Peter (2005), "Confounding Machines: How the Future Looked," *The New York Times*. Available at: www.nytimes.com/2005/08/28/weekinreview/confounding-machines-how-the-future-looked.html?mcubz=1 (accessed August 26, 2017).

Eisenstein, Sergei (2014), *Film Form: Essays in Film Theory*, trans. and ed. Jay Leyda, New York: Harcourt.

Eldridge, David (2006), *Hollywood's History Films*, London: I.B. Tauris.

Elsaesser, Thomas (1972), "Between Style and Ideology," *Monogram* (3): 4–12.

Elsaesser, Thomas (ed.) (1990), *Early Cinema: Space, Frame, Narrative*, London: BFI Publishing.

Elsaesser, Thomas (1996), "Subject Positions, Speaking Positions: From Holocaust, Our Hitler, and Heimat to Shoah and Schindler's List," in V. Sobchack (ed.), *The Persistence of History: Cinema, Television and the Modern Event*, New York: Routledge, 145–83.

Elsaesser, Thomas (1998a), "Louis Lumière—The Cinema's First Virtualist," in T. Elsaesser and K. Hoffmann (eds.), *Cinema Futures: Cain, Abel or Cable? The Screen Arts in the Digital Age*, Amsterdam: Amsterdam University Press, pp. 45–62.

Elsaesser Thomas (1998b), "Digital Cinema: Delivery, Event, Time," in T. Elsaesser and K. Hoffmann (eds.), *Cinema Futures: Cain, Abel or Cable? The Screen Arts in the Digital Age*. Amsterdam: Amsterdam University Press, 201–22.

Elsaesser, Thomas (2001), "Postmodernism as Mourning Work," *Screen*, 42(2): 193–201.

Elsaesser, Thomas (2008a), "Absence as Presence, Presence as Parapraxis: On Some Problems of Representing 'Jews' in the New German Cinema," *Framework: The Journal of Cinema and Media*, 49(1): 106–20.

Elsaesser, Thomas (2008b), "Afterword—Digital Cinema and the Apparatus: Archaeologies, Epistemologies, Ontologies," in B. Bennett, M. Furstenau, and A. Mackenzie (eds.), *Cinema and Technology: Cultures, Theories, Practices*, Basingstoke: Palgrave Macmillan, 226–40.

Elsaesser, Thomas (2013), *German Cinema—Terror and Trauma: Cultural Memory since 1945*, London: Routledge.

Elsaesser, Thomas (2014), "Siegfried Kracauer's affinities," *NECSUS: European Journal of Media Studies*, 3(1): 5–20.

Elsaesser, Thomas (2016), *Film History as Media Archaeology: Tracking Digital Cinema*, Amsterdam: Amsterdam University Press.

Elton, Geoffrey (1991), *Return to Essentials: Some Reflections on the Present State of Historical Study*, Cambridge: Cambridge University Press.

Falzon, Christopher (2013), 'Making history,' in Christopher Falzon, Timothy O'Leary and Jane Sawicki (eds.), *A Companion to Foucault*, Wiley-Blackwell, 282–96.

Falzon, Christopher, Timothy O'Leary, and Jane Sawicki (eds.) (2013), *A Companion to Foucault*, Oxford: Blackwell.

Ferguson, Niall (2011), *Virtual History: Alternatives and Counterfactuals*, London: Penguin Books.

Ferguson, Niall (2017), "The meaning of Dunkirk," *The Boston Globe*. Available at: www.bostonglobe.com/opinion/2017/07/24/the-meaning-dunkirk/PFNucgZaCxdjxAd5OCLnFM/story.html (accessed September 12, 2017).

Ferro, Marc (1983), "Film as an Agent, Product and Source of History," *Journal of Contemporary History*, 18(3): 357–64.

Ferro, Marc (1987), "Does a Filmic Writing of History Exist?" *Film and History: An Interdisciplinary Journal of Film and Television Studies*, 17(4): 81–9.

Ferro, Marc (1998), *Cinema and History*, Detroit: Wayne State University Press.

Fischer, Lucy (2000), "Marlene: Modernity, Mortality, and the Biopic", *Biography*, 23(1): 193–211.

Flynn, Thomas (2005), "Foucault's Mapping of History", in G. Gutting (ed.), *The Cambridge Companion to Foucault*, New York: Cambridge University Press, 29–48.

Foucault, Michel (1980), "The Confession of the Flesh", in C. Gordon (ed.), *Power/ Knowledge: Selected Interviews and Other Writings, 1972–1977, by Michel Foucault*, New York: Pantheon Books, 194–228.

Foucault, Michel (1990), "The Return of Morality", in L. Kritzman (ed.), *Politics, Philosophy, Culture: Interviews and Other Writings, 1977–1984*, New York: Routledge, 242–54.

Foucault, Michel (1991a), "Truth and Power", in P. Rabinow (ed.), *The Foucault Reader*, London: Penguin Books, 51–75.

Foucault, Michel (1991b), "Nietzsche, Genealogy, History", in P. Rabinow (ed.), *The Foucault Reader*, London: Penguin Books, 76–100.

Foucault, Michel (1994), *The Order of Things: An Archaeology of the Human Sciences*, New York: Vintage Books.

Foucault, Michel (2002), *The Archaeology of Knowledge*, London: Routledge.

Friedländer, Saul (1992), *Probing the Limits of Representation: Nazism and the "Final Solution"*, Cambridge: Harvard University Press.

Fuchs, Eckhardt and Benedikt Stuchtey (eds.) (2002), *Across Cultural Borders: Historiography in Global Perspective*, Maryland: Rowman & Littlefield.

Furley, David John and Alexander Nehamas (eds.) (2015), *Aristotle's "Rhetoric": Philosophical Essays*, Princeton: Princeton University Press.

Gaines, M. Jane (1999), "Political Mimesis", in J. M. Gaines and M. Renov (eds.), *Collecting Visible Evidence, Volume 6*. Minneapolis: University of Minnesota Press, 84–102.

Gaines, M. Jane (2007), "Documentary Radicality", *Revue Canadienne d'études Cinématographiques/Canadian Journal of Film Studies*, 16(1): 5–24.

Gaines, M. Jane (2015). "Second Thoughts on 'The Production of Outrage: the Iraq War and the Radical Documentary Tradition,'" in A. Juhasz and A. Lebow (eds.), *A Companion to Contemporary Documentary Film*, Malden: Wiley-Blackwell, 410–30.

Ganjavie, Amir (2016), "The Reality of Death: An Interview with László Nemes about 'Son of Saul,'" *MUBI*. Available at: https://mubi.com/notebook/posts/an-interview-with-laszlo-nemes (accessed October 12, 2017).

Gaudreault, André and Philippe Marion (2012), *The Kinematic Turn: Film in the Digital Era and its Ten Problems*, Montréal: Caboose.

Ginzburg, Carlo (2012), "Our Words, and Theirs: A Reflection on the Historian's Craft, Today", in S. Fellman and M. Rahikainen (eds.), *Historical Knowledge: In Quest of Theory, Method and Evidence*, Newcastle-upon-Tyne: Cambridge Scholars Publishing, 97–119.

Grindon, Leger (1994), *Shadows on the Past: Studies in the Historical Fiction Film*, Philadelphia: Temple University Press.

Gutting, Garry (ed.) (2005), *The Cambridge Companion to Foucault*, New York: Cambridge University Press.

Guynn, William (2006), *Writing History in Film*, New York: Routledge.

Hansen, Miriam (2012), *Cinema and Experience: Siegfried Kracauer, Walter Benjamin and Theodor W. Adorno*, Berkeley: University of California Press.

Hexter, Jack (1971a), "The Rhetoric of History", in J.H. Hexter (ed.), *Doing History*, Bloomington: Indiana University Press, 15–76.

Hexter, Jack (1971b), *The History Primer*, New York: Basic Books.

Hoffer, Peter Charles (2004), *Past Imperfect: Facts, Fictions, Fraud American History from Bancroft and Parkman to Ambrose, Bellesiles, Ellis, and Goodwin*, New York: Public Affairs.

Hoffer, Peter Charles (2008), *The Historian's Paradox: The Study of History in Our Time*, New York: New York University Press.

Hongisto, Ilona (2015), *Soul of the Documentary: Framing, Expression, Ethics*, Amsterdam: Amsterdam University Press.

Howell, Amanda (2013), "Vietnam War", in I. Aitken (ed.), *Encyclopedia of the Documentary Film, 3-Volume Set*, Abingdon, New York: Routledge.

Hughes-Warrington, Marnie (2007), *History Goes to the Movies: Studying History on Film*, Abingdon: Routledge.

Hutcheon, Linda (1989), *The Politics of Postmodernism*, London: Routledge.

Ieven, Bram (2013), "Memories of Modernism: Jacques Rancière, Chris Marker and the Reels of Modernism", in P. Bowman (ed.), *Rancière and Film*, Edinburgh: Edinburgh University Press, 83–98.

Godard, Jean-Luc and Youssef Ishaghpour (2005), *Cinema: The Archaeology of Film and the Memory of a Century*, Oxford: Berg.

Jakobson, Roman (1971), *Selected Writings vol. 2: Word and Language*, Hague: Mouton.

Jay, Martin (1986), *Permanent Exiles: Essays on the Intellectual Migration from Germany to America*, New York: Columbia University Press.

Jenkins, Keith (1995), *On "What is History?": From Carr and Elton to Rorty and White*, London: Routledge.

Jenkins, Keith (2003), *Refiguring History: New Thoughts on an Old Discipline*, London: Routledge.

Jenkins, Keith and Alun Munslow (eds.) (2004), *The Nature of History Reader*, London: Routledge.

Jones, Peter (1998), "The First Post-modern Historian", *The Telegraph*. Available at: www.telegraph.co.uk/culture/4713780/The-first-post-modern-historian.html (accessed August 1, 2017).

Kaes, Anton (1992), *From Hitler to Heimat: The Return of History as Film*, London: Harvard University Press.

Keeton, Patricia and Peter Scheckner (2013), *American War Cinema and Media Since Vietnam: Politics, Ideology, and Class*, New York: Palgrave Macmillan.

Kelley, Donald (1991), *Versions of History: from Antiquity to Enlightenment*, London: Yale University Press.

Kerner, Aaron (2011), *Film and the Holocaust: New Perspectives on Dramas, Documentaries and Experimental Films*, London: Continuum.

Kittler, Friedrich (1989), "Fiktion und Simulation", in J. Baudrillard (ed.), *Philosophien der neuen Technologie*, Berlin: Merve Publishers, 57–80.

Kittler, Friedrich (2010), *Optical Media*, Cambridge: Polity Press.

Koch, Gertrud (2000), *Siegfried Kracauer*, trans. J. Gaines, Princeton: Princeton University Press.

Kodat, Catherine Gunther (2000), "Saving Private Property: Steven Spielberg's American Dream Works", *Representations*, 71(1): 77–105.

Kracauer, Siegfried (1947), *From Caligari to Hitler: A Psychological History of the German Film*, Princeton: Princeton University Press.

Kracauer, Siegfried (1960). *Theory of Film: The Redemption of Physical Reality*, New York: Oxford University Press.

Kracauer, Siegfried (1969), *History: The Last Things Before the Last*, completed by Paul Oskar Kristeller, New York: Oxford University Press.

LaCapra, Dominick (1994), *Representing the Holocaust: History, Theory, and Trauma*, Ithaca: Cornell University Press.

LaCapra, Dominick (1997), "Lanzmann's 'Shoah': 'Here There Is No Why,'" *Critical Inquiry*, 23(2): 231–69.

Langer, L. Lawrence (2006), *Using and Abusing the Holocaust*, Bloomington: Indiana University Press.

Lefebvre, Martin and Marc Furstenau (2002), "Digital Editing and Montage: The Vanishing Celluloid and Beyond, *Cinémas*, 13(1–2): 69–107.

Loshitzky, Yosefa (ed.) (1997), *Spielberg's Holocaust: Critical Perspectives on Schindler's List*, Bloomington: Indiana University Press.

Lowenthal, David (1985), *The Past is a Foreign Country*, New York: Cambridge University Press.

Lukacs, John (1985), *Historical Consciousness: The Remembered Past*, New York: Schocken Books.

Lukacs, John (2011), *The Future of History*, New Haven: Yale University Press.

MacCabe, Colin (1999), "Bayonets in Paradise", *Sight & Sound*, 9(2): 10–14.

Macnab, Geoffrey (1999), "Soldier Stories", *Sight & Sound*, 9(2): 14.

Mannheim, Karl (1979), *Ideology and Utopia: An Introduction to the Sociology of Knowledge*, London: Routledge.

Manovich, Lev (2001), *The Language of New Media*, Cambridge: MIT Press.

Magilow, Daniel and Lisa Silverman (2015), *Holocaust Representations in History: An Introduction*, New York: Bloomsbury.

Magnússon, Sigurdur Gylfi and István Szijártó (2013), *What is Microhistory? Theory and Practice*, London: Routledge.

Mattheisen, Donald (1992). "Filming U.S. History During the 1920s: The Chronicles of America Photoplays", *The Historian*, 54(4): 630–3.

McNeill, William Hardy (1986), *Mythistory and Other Essays*, Chicago: University of Chicago Press.

Medvedkin, Aleksandr (2016), *The Alexander Medvedkin Reader*, Chicago: University of Chicago Press.

Megill, Allan (1987), "The Reception of Foucault by Historians", *Journal of the History of Ideas*, 48(1): 117–34.

Mills, Sara (2003), *Michel Foucault*, London: Routledge.

Moss, Mark (2008), *Toward the Visualization of History: The Past as Image*, Lanham: Lexington Books.

Morris, Nigel (2007), *The Cinema of Steven Spielberg: Empire of Light*. London: Wallflower Press.

Morrison, James (1978), "Vico's Principle of Verum is Factum and the Problem of Historicism", *Journal of the History of Ideas*, 39(4): 579–95.

Mottram, James (2002), *The Making of Memento*, London: Faber and Faber.

Munslow, Alun (2001), *Deconstructing History*, Abingdon: Routledge.

Munslow, Alun (2006), *The Routledge Companion to Historical Studies*, New York: Taylor & Francis.

Munslow, Alun (2010), *The Future of History*, Basingstoke: Palgrave Macmillan.

Munslow, Alun (2015), "Genre and History/Historying", *Rethinking History*, 19(2): 158–76.

Munz, Peter (2006), "The Historical Narrative", in M. Bentley (ed.), *Companion to Historiography*, London: Routledge, 833–52.

Musser, Charles (2007), "Film Truth in the Age of George W. Bush", *Framework: The Journal of Cinema and Media*, 48(2): 9–35.

Namier, Lewis Bernstein (1952), *Avenues of History*, London: Hamish Hamilton.

Neale, Steve (1995), "Questions of Genre", in B.K. Grant (ed.), *Film Genre Reader II*, Austin: University of Texas Press, 157–83.

Nemes, László (2016), "László Nemes on Son of Saul: 'These people have no past, only the present'." *The Guardian*. Available at: www.theguardian.com/film/video/2016/apr/19/laszlo-nemes-on-son-of-saul-these-people-have-no-past-only-the-present (accessed October 12, 2017).

Nichols, Bill (1991), *Representing Reality: Issues and Concepts in Documentary*, Bloomington: Indiana University Press.

Nichols, Bill (1994), *Blurred Boundaries: Questions of Meaning in Contemporary Culture*, Bloomington: Indiana University Press.

Nichols, Bill (2010), *Introduction to Documentary*, Bloomington: Indiana University Press.

Novick, Peter (1988), *That Noble Dream: The "Objectivity Question" and the American Historical Profession*, New York: Cambridge University Press.

O'Brien. Matthew (2012), "A Full Fact-Check of Niall Ferguson's Very Bad Argument Against Obama", *The Atlantic*. Available at: www.theatlantic.com/business/archive/2012/08/a-full-fact-check-of-niall-fergusons-very-bad-argument-against-obama/261306/ (accessed November 7, 2017).

O'Connor, John (1990), *Image as Artifact: The Historical Analysis of Film and Television*, Malabar: R.E. Krieger Pub. Co.

Parry-Giles, Shawn and Trevor Parry-Giles (1999), "Meta-Imaging, The War Room, and The Hyperreality of U.S. Politics", *Journal of Communication*, 49(1): 28–45.

Peirce, S. Charles (1991), "Peirce on Signs: Writings on Semiotic by Charles Sanders Peirce", in Hoopes, James (ed.), Chapel Hill: University of North Carolina Press.

Pepper, C. Stephen (1970), *World Hypotheses: A Study in Evidence*. Berkeley: University of California Press.

Peretz, Eyal (2010), "What is a Cinema of Jewish Vengeance? Tarantino's Inglourious Basterds", *The Yearbook of Comparative Literature*, 56: 64–74.

Pihlainen, Kalle (2015), "Realist Histories? When Form Clashes with Function", *Rethinking History*, 19(2): 177–92.

Plantinga, Carl (1996), "Moving Pictures and the Rhetoric of Nonfiction Flm: Two Approaches", in D. Bordwell and N. Carroll (eds.), *Post-Theory: Reconstructing Film Studies*, Madison: University of Wisconsin Press, 307–24.

Plantinga, Carl (2009), "The Philosophy of Errol Morris—Ten Lessons", in W. Rothman (ed.), *Three Documentary Filmmakers: Errol Morris, Ross McElwee, Jean Rouch*, Albany: SUNY Press, 43–59.

Plato (1925), *Phaedrus*, in H.N. Fowler (trans. and ed.), *Plato in Twelve Volumes, Vol. 9*. Cambridge: Harvard University Press.

Pramaggiore, Maria (2013), "History as Palimpsest", in Robert Rosenstone and Constantin Parvulescu (eds.), *A Companion to the Historical Film*, London: Blackwell, 30–52.

Propp, Vladimir (2010), *Morphology of the Folktale, vol. 9*, Austin: University of Texas Press.

Rancière, Jacques (2006), *Film Fables*, Oxford: Berg.

Ray, Robert (1985), *A Certain Tendency of the Hollywood Cinema, 1930–1980*, Princeton: Princeton University Press.

Renov, Michael (1993), *Theorizing Documentary*, New York: Routledge.

Renov, Michael (2004), *The Subject of Documentary*, Minneapolis: University of Minnesota Press.

Resha, David (2015), *The Cinema of Errol Morris*, Middletown: Wesleyan University Press.

Roberts, Andrew (2017), "Dunkirk Undone", *The Commentary*. Available at: www.commentarymagazine.com/articles/dunkirk-undone/ (accessed August 28, 2017).

Rodowick, David (1987), "The Last Things Before the Last: Kracauer and History", *New German Critique*, 41: 109–39.

Rogne, Erlend and Hayden White (2009), "The Aim of Interpretation is to Create Perplexity in the Face of the Real: Hayden White Conversation with Erlend Rogne", *History and Theory*, 48(1): 63–75.

Rollins, Peter and John O'Connor (2008), *Why We Fought: America's Wars in Film and History*, Lexington: University Press of Kentucky.

Rosadiuk, Adam (2006), "Thirty Two Short Films About Glenn Gould", in J. White (ed.), *The Cinema of Canada*, London: Wallflower Press, 163–71.

Rosen, Philip (2001), *Change Mummified: Cinema, Historicity, Theory*, Minneapolis: University of Minnesota Press.

Rosenstone, Robert (1995), *Visions of the Past: The Challenge of Film to Our Idea of History*, Boston: Harvard University Press.

Rosenstone, Robert (2006), *History on Film/Film on History*, Harlow: Pearson Education.

Rosenstone, Robert (2013), "The History Film as a Mode of Historical Thought", in R. Rosenstone and C. Parvulescu (eds.), *A Companion to the Historical Film*, New York: John Wiley & Sons, 71–87.

Rosenstone, Robert and Constantin Parvulescu (eds.) (2013), *A Companion to the Historical Film*, New York: John Wiley & Sons.

Rosenstone, Robert (2016), *Adventures of a Postmodern Historian: Living and Writing the Past*, New York: Bloomsbury.

Rouse, Joseph (2005), "Power/Knowledge", in G. Gutting (ed.), *The Cambridge Companion to Foucault*, New York: Cambridge University Press, 95–122.

Rowe, John Carlos (1986), "Eye-witness: Documentary Styles in the American Representations of Vietnam", *Cultural Critique*, 3: 126–50.

Ruiz, Bryan Rommel (2011), *American History Goes to the Movies: Hollywood and the American Experience*, New York: Routledge.

Ryan, Tom (2004), "Making History: Errol Morris, Robert McNamara and The Fog of War", *Senses of Cinema*. Available at: http://sensesofcinema.com/2004/politics-and-the-documentary/errol_morris_interview/?gclid=Cj0KCQjwjdLOBRCkARI sAFj5-GC1flEE_-qE6e802R9Z8-QU6pZiQMCq2TTUYn4fzC0KejNGHK8_ Gp4aAv76EALw_wcB (accessed October 12, 2017).

Schatz, Thomas (1998), "World War II and the Hollywood 'War Film,'" in Nick Browne (ed.), *Refiguring American Film Genres: History and Films*, Berkeley: University of California Press, 89–128.

Setka, Stella (2015), "Bastardized History: How Inglourious Basterds Breaks Through American Screen Memory", *Jewish Film & New Media: An International Journal*, 3(2): 141–69.

Shull, Michael and David Wilt (1996), *Hollywood War Films, 1937–1945: An Exhaustive Filmography of American Feature-length Motion Pictures*, Jefferson: McFarland.

Slater, J. Thomas (1991), "Teaching Vietnam: The Politics of Documentary", in M.A. Anderegg (ed.), *Inventing Vietnam: The War in Film and Television*, Philadelphia: Temple University Press, 269–90.

Smyth, Jennifer (2006), *Reconstructing American Historical Cinema: From Cimarron to Citizen Kane*, Lexington: University Press of Kentucky.

Smyth, Jennifer (ed.), (2012), *Hollywood and the American Historical Film*, New York: Palgrave Macmillan.

Solomon, Stanley (1976), *Beyond Formula: American Film Genres*, New York: Harcourt Brace Jovanovich.

Sordeau, Henri (2009), "Quentin Tarantino Talks Inglourious Basterds", *Rotten Tomatoes*. Available at: https://editorial.rottentomatoes.com/article/quentin-tarantino-talks-inglourious-basterds-rt-interview/ (accessed October 12, 2017).

Spielmann, Yvonne (1999), "Aesthetic Features in Digital Imaging: Collage and Morph", *Wide Angle*, 21(1): 131–48.

Stein, Jonathan (2005), "Sir, No Sir! An interview with David Zeiger", *Mother Jones*. Available at: www.motherjones.com/politics/2005/09/sir-no-sir-interview-david-zeiger/ (accessed November 4, 2017).

Stern, Fritz (1973), *The Varieties of History: From Voltaire to the Present*, New York: Vintage Books.

Stubbs, Jonathan (2013), *Historical Film: A Critical Introduction*, New York: Bloomsbury.

Susman, Warren (1985), "Film and History: Artifact and Experience", *Film & History: An Interdisciplinary Journal of Film and Television Studies*, 15(2): 26–36.

Tanke, J. Joseph (2013), "On the Powers of the False: Foucault's Engagements with the Arts", in Christopher Falzon, Timothy O'Leary and Jane Sawicki (eds.), *A Companion to Foucault*. Chichester: Wiley-Blackwell, 122–36.

Taylor, Ella (2007), "The 5,000-pound Maus: On the Anniversary of Kristallnacht, Art Spiegelman Revisits his Legacy", in J. Witek (ed.), *Art Spiegelman: Conversations*, Jackson: University Press of Mississippi, 191–5.

Temple, Michael and James Williams (eds.) (2000), *The Cinema Alone: Essays on the Work of Jean-Luc Godard, 1985–2000*, Amsterdam: Amsterdam University Press.

Thanouli, Eleftheria (2005), "The Thin Red Line and the World War II Hollywood Tradition, *Kinema*, 23(1): 45–60.

Thanouli, Eleftheria (2009a), *Post-Classical Cinema: An International Poetics of Film Narration*, London: Wallflower Press.

Thanouli, Eleftheria (2009b), "'Art Cinema' Narration Today: Breaking Down a Wayward Paradigm", *Scope*, 14: 1–14.

Thanouli, Eleftheria (2012), "Film Style in Old Greek Cinema: The Case of Dinos Dimopoulos", in Y. Tzioumakis and L. Papadimitriou (eds.), *Greek Cinema: Texts, Histories, Identities*. London: Intellect, 221–38.

Thanouli, Eleftheria (2013a), *Wag the Dog: A Study on Film and Reality in the Digital Age*, New York: Bloomsbury.

Thanouli, Eleftheria (2013b), "Narration", in E. Branigan and W. Buckland (eds.), *The Routledge Encyclopedia of Film Theory*, London: Routledge, 330–3.

Thanouli, Eleftheria (2013c), "Diegesis", in E. Branigan and W. Buckland (eds.), *The Routledge Encyclopedia of Film Theory*, London: Routledge, 133–7.

Thanouli, Eleftheria (2015), "A Nazi Hero in Greek Cinema: History and Parapraxis in Kostas Manousakis's *Prodosia*," *Journal of Greek Media & Culture*, 1(1): 63–77.

Thorburn, David and Henry Jenkins (eds.) (2003), *Rethinking Media Change: The Aesthetics of Transition*, Cambridge: MIT Press

Toplin, Robert Brent (2002), *Reel History: In Defense of Hollywood*, Lawrence: University Press of Kansas.

Traverso, Enzo (2016), *Left-Wing Melancholia: Marxism, History, and Memory*. New York: Columbia University Press.

Tortajada, Maria and François Albera (2015), *Cine-Dispositives: Essays in Epistemology Across Media*, Amsterdam: Amsterdam University Press.

Turim, Maureen (1999), "Artisanal Prefigurations of the Digital: Animating Realities, Collage Effects, and Theories of Image Manipulation, *Wide Angle*, 21(1): 51.

Uricchio, William (2003), "Historicizing Media in Transition", in D. Thorburn and H. Jenkins (eds.), *Rethinking Media Change: The Aesthetics of Transition*, Cambridge: MIT Press, 23–38.

Van der Knaap, Ewout (ed.) (2006), *Uncovering the Holocaust: The International Reception of Night and Fog*, London: Wallflower Press.

Vanoye, Francis (2005), *Récit écrit, récit filmique*, Paris: Armand Colin.

White, Hayden (1973), "Foucault Decoded: Notes from Underground", *History and Theory*, 23(1): 23–54.

White, Hayden (1978), *Tropics of Discourse: Essays in Cultural Criticism*, Baltimore: John Hopkins University Press.

White, Hayden (1987), *The Content of the Form: Narrative Discourse and Historical Representation*, Baltimore: John Hopkins University Press.

White, Hayden (1988), "Historiography and Historiophoty", *The American Historical Review*, 93(5): 1193–9.

White, Hayden (1992), "Historical Emplotment and the Problem of Truth", in S. Friedlander (ed.), *Probing the Limits of Representation: Nazism and the "Final Solution"*, Cambridge: Harvard University Press, 37–53.

White, Hayden (2014), *Metahistory: The Historical Imagination in Nineteenth-Century Europe*, Baltimore: John Hopkins University Press.

Whittock, Trevor (1990), *Metaphor and Film*, New York: Cambridge University Press.

Williams, Alan (1984), "Is a Radical Genre Criticism Possible?" *Quarterly Review of Film Studies*, 9(2): 121–5.

Widdis, Emma (2005), *Alexander Medvedkin: The KINOfiles Filmmaker's Companion Vol. 2*, London: I.B. Tauris.

Winkler, Martin (ed.) (2009), *The Fall of the Roman Empire: Film and History*, Malden: Wiley-Blackwell.

Witt, Michael (2013), *Jean-Luc Godard, Cinema Historian*, Bloomington: Indiana University Press.

Ziolkowski, Theodore (2004), *Clio the Romantic Muse: Historicizing the Faculties in Germany*, Ithaca: Cornell University Press.

Index